ONE WISH...

WON BATTLE!

The faithful will be tested…

James N. Rybak

Copyright © 2014 by Pencil Werk Press
All rights reserved. This book or any portion thereof
may not be reproduced or used in any manner whatsoever
without the express written permission of the publisher
except for the use of brief quotations in a book review.

Printed in the United States of America

First Printing, 2010

Second Edition, 2014

Library of Congress Control Number: 2014907123

Published by Pencil Werk Press

ISBN 978-0-9960374-0-2

Pencil Werk Press
P.O. Box 452
Paw Paw, Mi 49079

Email: info@pencilwerkpress.com

Written by: James N. Rybak

Edited by: Fred Henderson

Cover art and design by Dan Monroe

I dedicate this book to my loving parents, family, and friends:

To my dad, Peter, who always told me when I was a kid, "If you get into a fight, make sure the other guy starts it first because if I find out you started it, you will have to answer to me." "Now, Son, there are three places to hit a man: the nose, the eyes, or the groin!

Punch him in one of those places and when he goes down, kick him in the other two until he stops moving!" True words of wisdom! My dad was not a violent man. He was joking.

Dad was a medic/x-ray technician during WWII. Dad also taught me the importance of the family name. He would always say to me when I left the house, "The family name holds honor and respect; remember whose name you have."

To my mom, Hilda, who sent me back to clean the bathroom three times when I was twelve years old because I didn't clean it correctly. Thanks, Mom. Women love guys who know how to clean up after themselves. Mom also taught me that there is nothing greater in life than to serve our Heavenly Father!

To my brother and best friend John, who stood by my side through all of this, and still stands by my side today. I love you, Brau! To my sisters Cindy and Liz, who always were there for me, too, with encouragement, love, support, and hugs when needed. All my love to you!

To my good friend Nellie, who perseveres and never gives up!

-James

Acknowledgments

Web Sites
m-w.com
Dictionary.com
Wikipedia.com

Swordsknivesanddaggers.com
Meditationconcepts.com

Books
Louise L. Hay's *You Can Heal Your Life*

Songs
Josh Groban: "Broken Vow"
Chicago: "Hard to Say I'm Sorry"
Shedaisy: "Rush"
4Him: "Candle in the Rain"
Rebecca St. James: *Here I Am*
Films and Television
What Dreams May Come
The Simpsons
The Wizard of Oz

Contents

Chapter 1	**A Simple Prayer, One Wish…**
Chapter 2	**Class Is Now In Session**
Chapter 3	**A New Start**
Chapter 4	**Phase 1**
Chapter 5	**Lana**
Chapter 6	**Unusual Surprises**
Chapter 7	**Phase 2**
Chapter 8	**Phase 3**
Chapter 9	**Phases 4 and 5**
Chapter 10	**Phase 6**
Chapter 11	**Phase 7**
Chapter 12	**The Journey Home**

Contents (Continued)

Chapter 13   **Home at Last**

Chapter 14   **Life, Loss ... and Wonder**

Chapter 15   **A Prelude...**

Chapter 16   **Here We Go Again...**

Chapter 17   **The Book ... New Experiences**

Chapter 18   **Won Battle!**

Foreword

How do we measure a man's worth?
By his possessions, wealth, or status?
How does God measure a man's worth?
By the conviction of his faith? Or is it the strength of his heart?
What I am about to share with you is a true story.

Chapter 1

A Simple Prayer, One Wish…

As I turned to my left, I saw an angel standing there. He looked at me and said, *"Jim, you have done nothing wrong. God has been waiting for you to come to this area so that He may implement His plan for you. You have a very special place in His heart, and I have been sent here to protect you. No one can harm you!"*

Okay, well, I guess I should probably share with you some of the moments leading up to this time in my life, or I fear the flavor of the moment will be lost. My name is James. Most people call me Jim. I am what you would call a regular guy. I am 40 years old as I write this. Today, the month is July. The year is 2007. Bear with me as I take you back some years in my life. Stop your groaning! I promise it will be entertaining.

The year was 2000. At the age of 33, I had been married for almost nine years. My wife Trish and I had just moved to a small town in Iowa. I had been a priest for nearly the past ten years. I belong to a Christian Organization that is in every country with a membership worldwide of over 10 million. Our doctrine is based on the following bible verse:

Acts 2:42 (NKJV).
And they continued steadfastly in the apostles' doctrine and fellowship, in breaking of bread, and in prayers.

The only goal of my church is to prepare us for Christ's return. We don't advertise. Word of mouth is the main reason we have had so much success, and we don't become politically aligned with anyone. I was born into this faith and have always served with a joyful heart. When they asked for volunteers to establish a new congregation in Iowa, my wife and I jumped at the chance. Oh, I should also point out that most of the ministers in my organization do not get paid. All of us have full-time jobs on top of the ministerial responsibilities.

I will not bore you with all of the details involved with both of our leaving well-paying jobs, and then the struggle that ensued with trying to obtain gainful employment. Let's just say that you would think because we volunteered to help out the Lord that he would make it a little easier for us. NOPE! We did eventually find well-paying jobs.

Anyway, let's jump ahead two years to 2002. The congregation now had fourteen members. I had just held a service that was about free will, and how it is the only true thing that we can offer to the Lord, besides our hearts. What is the definition of free will? Let's see what Merriam-Webster says:

Free Will

**1: voluntary choice or decision <I do this of my own free will>
2: freedom of humans to make choices that are not determined by prior causes or by divine intervention**

I went home that night and prayed a simple prayer by myself: "Dear Lord, I feel I'm stagnating in my faith. I am giving you my free will. I have one wish: I want to be closer to you than any other human has ever been before, and I don't care what it takes! I trust you so much that no matter what happens to me, I know that when I come out the other end, I will be fine!"

Yes, I know, pretty crazy! I would be lying to you if I told you that this was the first time I did this. You see; this would be the third time! Yes, you heard me: the *third* time. Okay. Calm down! The first time I gave up my free will was in 1989. I was 22 years old. Perhaps you're thinking, "Golly, how is it that Jim can remember all of these specific years?" It's very simple. Every time something devastating, crippling, and painful happens in my life; it's very easy for me to remember the pain and the exact time frame. But it's all good!

I was a successful parts counterman for an upscale auto dealership. I went to our midweek church service, which happens every Wednesday night. When I came home that night after service, I told the Lord, "I'm giving you my free will; just wanted to let you know that I love you." When I got to work the next day, the owner called me into his office. As I sat down, my boss walked behind the owner and stood next to him. Very curious...hmm.... The owner said, "I'm letting you go." I looked at him puzzled and asked why. He then said, "Um, some tires and batteries are missing, and you would be wise if you were to get your things and leave." I sat there for a minute. By the way, no one has ever accused me of being wise. (Well, that's not entirely true. There is usually an "ass" attached to the end of the word "wise.")

I looked at the two of them and said, "Last time I checked, I would have to say that I own an Oldsmobile, not a fancy European car like the ones we sell and service here." The owner said, "Just go, Jim." I looked at him and said, "Oh, I get it; this is because I complained to you that my manager was a slobbering drunk when he came to work every day. And he falls asleep at his desk, and I'm tired of covering for him. No problem. I'll leave! I knew I should have asked my manager who it was that he was always going out and getting drunk with. Hey, look. I guess I am wise; it didn't take long for me to figure that out!" (See, wise-ass.)

As I drove home, I started to laugh to myself as I was reminded of my prayer from the night before. I said, "Good one, Lord! I'm on to you!" I kept the faith, and after struggling for about four months, I was employed again. I was even making more money than before. Folks, the Lord will never give you less than what you had when he takes something away from you!

Interestingly enough, one of my closest friends made the comment that during that four- month period, I never complained, got upset, or even got mad that I was being put through it. I looked at him and said, "I have come to find that the Lord hears my prayers, so now I am very careful about what I pray for."

I'm still waiting for the Lord to hear the prayer where I asked Him to make me rich! I tell Him all the time, "Lord, we have been doing the I'm having a hard time making ends meet thing for most of my life. Can we try the I'm stinking rich thing and as you are fully aware, Lord I would be more than happy to split the lottery winnings with you 50/50!" Oh, He doesn't answer your prayer either? Well, now I don't feel so bad so let's keep moving right along.

The second time I gave up my free will was in 1993. I was twenty-six years old. I was just about to get married within the next few weeks; full of life and excitement, just waiting to see what the future held in store.

Hey! I like stirring the pot a little now and then, and I figured things were going great; what a great time to show the Lord how much I trust him! So I gave him my free will.

At the time, I was a warehouse/inventory control clerk for a prosthetics company. I had found a company that would clean and resharpen the surgical instruments that we used for all of our procedures so that they would look brand new. The owner of my company had just closed a big deal with one of our largest clients. He promised our client that he would sell them two sets of "new" surgical instruments. He came to me and said, "Take two of the best used instrument sets we have and have that company that cleans and sharpens our sets for us work their magic." I foolishly asked, "Why?"

You would think that, at that point in my life, I would just stop asking that question. I just couldn't help it. My boss then proceeded to tell me that he was going to send these used instruments to our largest client instead of the "new" ones and that we would keep the "new" ones for ourselves. Yes, I know; what a horrible man ... Jesus is even crying right now.

So what do you think I did? That's right! I ran over to the salesman who was in charge of our largest client and shared this information with him. He stormed into the owner's office and gave him a piece of his mind. He told the owner that he would quit if he didn't give our largest client the new instruments they paid for. Needless to say, the owner said, "Fine, whatever!"

So, I get married. I had an interesting honeymoon. (That will have to be explained in another book.) I came back ready to work because I had a new bride to take care of! On my first day back, the owner called me into his office. Are you ready? Brace yourselves. He said, "I have to let you go." I, of course, being ever curious, asked, "Why?" He proceeded to tell me that some sets of instruments and implants were missing, and seeing that I was on call twenty-four hours a day with full access to the warehouse, he knew that I was at fault. I looked at him and said, "You are aware that I was out of town for the past week, right?" He said, "Oh, this happened before you left. So just to show you that I'm not a bad person, you can still work here for another two weeks while you look for a new job, and then you're fired." "Really?" I asked. I leaned forward in my chair and said, "Let me get this straight. You are accusing me of stealing from you. And you know that's not true. The real reason you're firing me is because I wouldn't let you rip off our largest client. But because I told the salesman about it, you are feeling guilty that you are throwing a newlywed man out in the cold. So to appease your conscience, you're firing me, not today, but in two weeks?" He said, "Yes."

As I quietly went back to my office, I smiled and thanked the Lord that He at least let me enjoy my interesting honeymoon. (Nope, I'm still not going to tell you about it!) I do believe that it took me only two months to find a new job, one that again ended up paying me more. You just got to love the Lord! Oh, I almost forgot to tell you. Our biggest client suffered a heart attack and died not too long after all of this happened, and my ex-boss had to close the company because he relied on our largest client for most of his business.

Okay. So now we are back to my simple prayer from the beginning of the book: "Dear Lord, I feel I'm stagnating in my faith. I am giving you my free will: I have one wish. I want to be closer to you than any other human has ever been before! And I don't care what it takes! I trust you so much that no matter what happens to me, I know that when I come out the other end, I will be fine!" Three days later, my wife, Trish, comes to me and says: "I can't do this anymore. I want a divorce!"

Now, most people asked me if that came as a surprise to me. I would have to say, yes and no. Yes, because no one actually wants to think about divorce. I consider divorce one of the most debilitating things that can happen to a person. Others have told me that it ranks right up there with the death of a parent. No, because we had been having problems for the past year. I told a lot of friends and family that essentially we fell out of love. We became roommates. At the time, I knew that this was going to be one of the hardest things I would ever have to go through. Boy was I wrong! You're just going to have to keep reading to see what I mean.

Two weeks after she asked me for a divorce, I packed up my SUV mostly with clothes, and told her I would be back after we decide how we would split things up. She immediately told me that she wanted to keep the house. I said OK.

As I drove back to Chicago, where I'm originally from, it hit me all of a sudden. I heard that simple prayer playing through my mind. As I relived that moment, tears welled up in my eyes, and I began to cry harder than I thought I possibly could. It's about five and a half-hour drive to Chicago from where I had lived, so being stuck with myself in the SUV for that amount of time; I can tell you, was no fun at all! I moved in with my older sister Ann and her two kids. I should probably tell you at this point that I have an older brother Peter. Then comes Ann, and then comes me. They say middle children are always the best adjusted. Well, you won't think that about me by the time you finish this book. And then there's Ellen. You know; I have to hand it to my parents when they had us: boy, girl, boy, girl. Here's another bit of family trivia.

(Don't worry, there isn't a test later.) All four of us sing in our church choir. Peter sings bass, Ann sings alto, I sing tenor, and Ellen sings soprano. My folks birthed the "Family Von Rybak."

As I made every trip back and forth from my SUV to my room in the basement, I kept asking myself if it were actually happening. Then I tripped over one of the kids' toys and almost broke my neck. I snapped right out of that and thought, yes, this is certainly happening! Once I got things moved in and found myself alone sitting in my little bedroom with all of my earthly possessions, I began to cry. I said to the Lord: "You took my wife, my house, my ministry." Yes, my ministry. My church's standard policy on divorce is an automatic six-month leave of absence so that you are given the time to work out your problems.

Okay, back to my conversation with the Lord: "You took my wife, my house, my ministry, my congregation, my job. You took everything from me. And, yes, you even took my two dogs! Now, I am in no way comparing myself to Job in the Old Testament, Lord, but I have to tell you that my current situation leaves that kind of taste in my mouth." Tears were streaming down my face, and at times when I thought I just couldn't cry any harder, I surprised even myself. I then said, "If you have a bet with Satan like you did in Job's time; He's going to lose! Two months later, I still couldn't find a job but it was that most wonderful time of the year, Christmas! I thanked God for my family, especially my sister Ann because, without her and her family, I would have been living out of a cardboard box. Well, not really. I would probably be forced to live with my parents, but then I would have needed therapy and as you already know, I don't have any money for that! (I'm joking; my parents are great.)

As the New Year came into being, my creditors kept insisting that I pay them! Apparently, if you throw the bill away every month, they continue to send you complimentary copies, tack on some interest, and still expect you to pay them. Yes, I know how crazy that sounds, but, really, it's true. I'm hoping that all of you reading this know that I'm kidding! Can anyone tell me if any of your creditors ever believed you when you told them the truth about your situation or do they just automatically think you're lying? If it weren't for my dad helping me out during this period, I probably would have lost even more than I did. Every now and then when I would ask my dad for a little help, he would say to me, "You know, kid..." Yes, even at my ripe old age of 35 dad still called me kid. So as I was saying, he would say, "You know kid, every time I help you out you're spending your inheritance!" I would look at my Dad and say, "Whoa, Whoa! I have an inheritance?"

Two months later, in February 2003, my brother Peter was married on February 15. He met Linda at a mutual friend's wedding. After less than six months of dating, Peter moved to the west coast and was married shortly after. (I have a saying: "Love is blind and stupid!" I'll explain later.)

As for me, I still had no job, no money, no income to be seen, but yet the bills just kept piling up. I sat at my sister's computer looking for a job on every Web site created by man, having no luck whatsoever. I'm sure you have heard the phrase "every person has a breaking point." This just so happened to be my day. As I sat there, I started to become extremely angry. Anger turned into seething rage. Seething rage turned into quiet rage!

For me reaching the point of quiet rage is a dangerous situation. When I get to this point, I become very silent. I stop thinking that there is any hope. I stop trying to figure a way out of the situation. This is the place in my life where if someone were to draw a line in front of me and tell me if I just step over the line you are officially done, I would step over that line! That's it! I've given up! I've thrown in the towel! I am done!

Just when I thought my one foot was stepping over the line, Tina, a friend of my sister Ann, was over visiting her. She said to me, "Jim I can feel how angry you are and how hopeless you feel." Here's what makes this part interesting. Tina was sitting in the kitchen. I was sitting in the living room. There were two walls between us. So how was it that Tina could feel what I was feeling? Tina is clairvoyant! Wait. Now, before you start getting any crazy ideas, let's see what Merriam-Webster's definition of this word is.

Clair-voy-ant.
French, from **clair = clear + voyant**, present participle of voir to **see**.
: Able to see beyond the range of ordinary perception.
CLAIRVOYANT = CLEAR SEEING

She walked to where I was sitting and stuck her head around the corner very slowly. Maybe she was expecting me to punch her out. She pulled up a chair and sat across from me. She then said in a sweet, quiet voice, "Jim; I know this period of time has been very difficult and trying for you. I can feel how upset and hopeless you think this is. Would you like my help?" I said, "What can you do?" She said, "If there is one thing I know about you, Jim, it would have to be how strong your faith is! I have watched you over the past years, and I have seen just how much you trust God. I would like to share a phrase with you that I don't tell many people." She then said the five magic words that changed my life. "Let go and let God!" She continued, "It is very apparent to me that the Supreme Being has a plan for you. Your problem is that you are not allowing Him to make you into the person He needs you to be. I know you trust Him, Jim. If you would just let go of all of the emotions you are feeling and let God do what He thinks is best for you, you will find that things will work out better than you ever thought." I said, "Can you help me?" She said, "I can ground out all of the negativity in your space and help you to focus better."

At this point, I honestly didn't care what she was talking about or what she was going to do. I just didn't want to feel like this anymore. She said, "Close your eyes and take some deep breaths. With each breath, picture your problems leaving your body as a waterfall rushing down the mountainside." She had her hands stretched out over the top of my head. As I sat there, I could actually feel something happening. She said, "Think of your anger and put it in a barrel. As you take a deep breath, let go of it and watch it go over the waterfalls and leave you."

I did what she asked. She pinpointed every feeling I was having: anger, disappointment, failure, anxiety, hopelessness, and fear. With each breath, I created a mental "barrel" and placed every one of these emotions in it one at a time and then I let go of it and watched it leave the river and go over the waterfalls never to be seen again.

After twenty minutes, she stopped and said, "Do you feel any better?" I said, "I have no idea what you just did, but I feel wonderful." I said, "What did you do to me?" She said, "It's a form of meditation."

She said, "There's a place in Chicago that I used to go to a lot for a healing; I haven't been there for a while, but if you would like to come with me I think it would do you a world of good." With the expression on my face, I'm pretty sure that you wouldn't have to be clairvoyant to know what I was thinking right at that moment. Tina smiled and said, "It's an energy healing. Basically, you sit in a chair, and one of the healers moves their hands back and forth, never touching you. They flush out all of the negative energy in your space and then fill you back up with your own energy, and you heal yourself." I smiled and said; "How much does it cost to go to the merry old land of Oz?" She said, "Five dollars." I said, "I can afford that!"

As I was getting ready to go to bed that night, I prayed, *"Okay, Lord, you heard my conversation with Tina today. You know where she is taking me. You are going to have to give me some sign to let me know that it's okay with you for me to pursue this. You know, as always; I trust you, and whatever you want me to do, I will do."*

As Tina and I drove to the city, she began to tell me about the energy points we have in our bodies. They are called chakras, which is the Sanskrit word for wheel. You have seven major chakras in your body, where energy flows through. If one or more chakra gets plugged up or isn't spinning as fast as it normally should, you may feel that your life is stuck in a rut, and you can't figure out how to move forward. You may be one of those people who are always physically sick. An energy healing helps to unplug the blockage and gets you moving forward again. As Tina continued to talk, I kept reminding the Lord that He still needed to give me some sign, but nothing came.

As we walked into the room where the healings were taking place, I thought to myself, what a dump! None of the furniture matched, the carpet, was stained, and the place was very nasty looking. I quickly said a prayer: *"Dear Lord, I hope we don't have to sit on the floor!"* Tina introduced me to the instructor, Saleena. She looked at me and asked, "Are you here for a healing?" I said, "Yes I am. Be gentle with me; this is my first time." She smiled and said, "We are very busy tonight. I am going to have to ask you to have patience." I sat there for thirty minutes, watching other people while they sat in chairs and had others standing in front of them moving their hands back and forth but never touching them; only occasionally the people standing would ask those in the chairs to take deep breaths. I thought to myself, *What a bunch of nutballs!* And still, no sign from God. As time went by, I just sat there observing. All of a sudden, Saleena walked up to me and said, "I don't normally give healings, but because it's so busy tonight, would you please follow me out into the hall, and I will give you your healing." Still no sign from God!

I followed her out into the hall, but before I left the office, I looked back at Tina as if this were the last time I was going to see her, and I quietly told the Lord, *"Now would be a good time for a sign, and I forgive Tina for bringing me here."*

Saleena told me to sit in the chair with both feet firmly on the ground in front of me. She told me that the first thing she was going to do was to ground me. She asked, "Do you know what that means?" I said, "You're going to send me to the corner to think about what I've done?" She smiled and said, "No, Jim. There is a chakra at the base of your spine. It is called the root chakra or #1 chakra. I am going to make a cord that will connect to your first chakra, and then I will anchor it to the center of the earth." I smiled and said, "Great!" while quietly praying to myself, *"Lord… HELLO…looking for a sign…now would really be a good time!"*

Saleena told me to take a deep breath as she connected the cord. She said, "There are two channels that run up the front of your chest and two channels that run up your back. There are channels that run through your legs and arms." She told me she was going to be running some energy through all of the channels and flush them out. Okay, whatever! She then told me again that the first chakra is called the root chakra. It holds the basic needs for protection, survival, security, safety and self-preservation. She told me that there was some blockage and that she would remove it and get the flow of energy back to where it should be. As I sat there, I felt nothing happening. She said in a quiet voice, "You may or may not feel anything." *Pretty creepy,* I thought. She spent about five or ten minutes moving her hands around. As she was standing beside me; her right hand was in front of me, and her left hand was behind me, near the base of my lower back.

As she moved her hand in an upward direction, she would stop and explain to me which chakra she was working on and what it controlled. The second chakra is located two inches below the navel and is rooted into the spine. It is called the belly chakra. It holds the basic needs for sexuality, sensuality, creativity, open-mindedness, intuition, self-worth, and emotions. The third chakra is called the solar plexus. It is located two inches below the breastbone in the center behind the stomach. It is the center of personal power, self-control, self-acceptance, passion, ego, anger, impulsiveness, and inner strength. Folks. Have you ever had a gut feeling? You say to yourself, if only I would have… The third chakra has a lot to do with honoring yourself.

The fourth is called the heart chakra. It is located behind the breastbone on the spine between the shoulder blades in the back. It is the center for love, forgiveness, compassion, understanding, trust, and empathy. From this chakra, you learn to love yourself and others. As she reached this place in my chest, she told me that she was on my heart chakra. The funny thing was that I could actually feel something happening. She spent a lot of time there. At one point, Saleena looked at me and said, "Are you going through something traumatic in your life right now? Your heart has cracks in it." I looked at her with some amazement as I said, "I'm going through a divorce right now." All she did was smile and say, "That would explain it." *Hmmm,* I thought, *how could she have known there was a problem?*

The fifth is called the throat chakra. It is located in the V of the collarbone, right where your voice box is. It is the center of communication, expression, sound, and dreaming. It is how we express ourselves through creativity of thought, writing, and speech. It is how we communicate with others and our higher self.

The sixth is called the third eye. It is located in the center of your forehead, just above the eyebrows. This is the center for the mind, foresight, clairvoyance (clear seeing), intuition, imagination, interpretation, insight, awareness, and enlightenment. At this point, Saleena had probably spent almost 45 minutes on me. Periodically, she would tell me to take deep breaths and just let go of whatever she pointed out to me. Then she got to the seventh chakra, which is called the crown. It is located on the top of your head. It is the center for enlightenment, inspiration, spirituality, idealism, knowledge, spiritual will, and wisdom.

As she put her hands on top of my head, she paused and then started to laugh. I looked at her and said, "C'mon now; share with the class." She said, "The Supreme Being"—which is how she refers to God—"is very amused with you. You make Him laugh. You have a very close relationship with Him. He enjoys your conversations." I believe at this time; the Hallelujah Chorus should have been playing in my mind because I said to God, "Thanks for the sign!" How else would she have known that about my Heavenly Father and me unless He revealed it to her? It just causes me to love the Lord more when He answers my prayers. I love that Guy!

She then told me to sit still as she gathered up all of my energy. She said, "Wherever you go, you leave your energy. I am now collecting it all." She then said, "During your healing, things were flushed out of your space, which leaves openings. If I don't fill the openings back up with your energy, then other things will creep in and fill them for you."

Saleena told me to take a deep breath and then said, "Here it comes." I sat there for almost ten minutes as she walked around me filling me back up. She said, "This is going to take some time because you have been to a lot of places. Once your energy is back in your space, your own body will know what to do with it, and you will start to heal yourself."

She then said, "Your body is angry at you!" I said, "What?" She said, "It wants ice cream!" She then told me that I am not my body. It is only a shell that holds our soul and spirit. We are our soul and spirit! Sometimes our bodies don't understand what we are doing to them. She said, "You have been working out a lot, haven't you?" I said, "Yes!" She said, "You probably are stuck on a plateau and can't lose any weight, am I right?" I said, "Yes; that's why I can't have any ice cream!" She said, "Talk to your body and explain to it what you are trying to accomplish." I said, "Are you nuts?" She said, "I'll bet you, if you talk to your body and give it some ice cream; you will start to lose weight." I told her, "Okay, I'll try it."

On the way home, I talked to my body. (Yes, I know how crazy this sounds.) I said, *"Okay, body. I'm trying to lose weight so that you and I can feel better. I'm sorry if I've been working you out too hard. I'll tell you what; I'm going to get two different flavors of ice cream. We are going to have a little scoop of each, but only if you promise me that we will start losing weight again!"* Guess what happened? I lost five pounds that week, eating ice cream every night! I kid you not!

As I drove home with Tina on the night of the healing, I shared my experience with her. She said, "I don't know if you know this, but Saleena never gives healings. She must have seen something in your space that intrigued her." I said, "I have no idea what she may have seen. All I know is I asked God for a sign, and He gave me one. I think I would like to learn more about this whole thing." She said, "You are more than welcome to come with me on Tuesdays, if you would like." I told her to count me in.

One month later, in March, I decided to move in with my little sister Ellen and her family because Ann's daughter Nicole had kindly given up her room for me while I'd been staying there. The problem was she had to share a room with her younger brother, Scott. Let me just say that my niece and nephew didn't always get along. My sister Ellen gave me my own room in the basement of their home, which to this day I am still extremely grateful. Ellen's two children were still very young and didn't mind sharing a bedroom.

For the next few weeks, every Tuesday, Tina and I would drive into the city—almost an hour drive, but we didn't mind. We would make the time go by faster just talking with each other. I was intrigued by Tina's gift. Later on, I would come to find just how valuable a friend she was for me. I learned over time that, after every healing, a new space is created for you and you step into it and move forward in your life.

I know this much: all of the negative emotions that used to consume me were gone, and my outlook on life was a positive one.

Tina also turned me on to a self-help book called *You Can Heal Your Life* by Louise L. Hay. The central idea of the book is that, for every physical ailment your body has, there is a psychological problem that you are not dealing with. When we ignore a problem in our life, our own spirit tries to get our attention. When the problem goes unacknowledged for a long period of time, the problem becomes a physical one that the body can't ignore and must start to deal with. Some of the ideas in the book are as follows:

>   Headaches = Judging yourself
>   Sinus infections = Someone close to you is annoying you
>   Feet or knee problems = Fear of moving forward in your life
>   Cold sores = Unspoken anger
>   Twisted ankle = Guilt

Hay's book has a positive affirmation for almost every aliment and sickness you can think of. By acknowledging these problems and saying these affirmations on a daily basis, your body lets go of the negativity and begins to heal itself. I can honestly tell you that I didn't believe that every problem that was listed was actually caused by some psychological problem I may have been going through. What I can tell you is that after reading this book, I learned to love myself. Have you ever stood in front of a mirror and then told yourself that you love the person that you are staring at? It took me weeks before I could actually say these words to myself and mean it. Once I did it, though, my entire outlook on life was filled with hope and courage, and I developed a better attitude!

In April, I was legally divorced. Trish and I remained friends through the whole ordeal.

By May, I still couldn't find any work. No job in sight, no matter how many Web sites I browsed. I was sending out three to five resumes a week. Not one interview. I kept asking if the Lord were testing my patience, my sanity, or my ability to stretch one dollar to see just how far it would get me. I thanked God continually for my family's help. On the up side of things, because I had no job I spent a lot of my time working out and taking long walks. After a few months, I managed to lose eighty pounds. As of today I can proudly tell you that I have kept all of it off. Diet and exercise work! The only problem for me is I have to do it every day, or I will gain everything back. No thanks!

One day Saleena approached me and told me that she thought I would greatly benefit from a reading. I asked, "Really, what's that?" She said, "I will sit across from you and read your space. Your spirit will reveal things to me, and I will share them with you. Each time you acknowledge what your spirit is telling me, you will create a new space for yourself to move into, and your life will grow." As I sat there, I was a little nervous. Saleena picked up on that right away. She told me to relax and that my spirit wouldn't show her anything that would embarrass me. She told me that my spirit had only my best interest in mind. I agreed to the reading.

Saleena told me that my spirit was quite a character. (I'm quite a character, so that wasn't hard to believe.) My spirit uses humor to get its point across to me. She told me about my past lives. Even to this day, I don't honestly believe any of that. She told me that my spirit was running into a wall and then vibrating the way a cartoon character does. She said, "Your spirit is telling me that you feel as if you are getting nowhere in life because you just keep hitting wall after wall." I thought, *"YES, keep going!"* She told me things about my family. She asked, "Are you aware of the fact that you are like the canary in the mine shaft for your family?" I looked at her, puzzled. She then told me that if something new happens in life, my family sends me in to investigate the situation. If I come out of it okay, then they will try it too. I told her that, yes, I already knew that. She described my parents and three siblings to me in detail. Pretty wild!

She spoke of my church and the leadership, and the structure of my beliefs. At one point, she stopped and said nothing for a few minutes. After a while, I asked her if everything was okay. She looked at me and said, "You actually believe." I said, "Yes." She said, "I don't think you understand what I'm saying. You actually believe that if you live your life according to the ways you have been taught by your church that you will get the prize!" I said, "Yes...I guess I don't understand what point you are trying to make about this." She said, "I have never met anyone like you, someone who actually, truly, deep down in their heart believes! I come across a lot of people from all walks of faith, and they think they understand their faiths, but when I look deep down into their spaces, they show me that they really don't understand what their church has been teaching them." I said, "I have no reason to doubt my faith, religion, or church. It is all I have ever known. I have experienced things in my life that confirm to me that I am on the right path."

Suddenly she smiled at me and said, "Your spirit revealed to me that you are a priest and have been for many years, but you are not active right now. Your church is treating you just like your family does; you are the canary in the mineshaft for them, too. They sent you here to gather information for them. You are unique. Do you know that our two worlds, my way of life and your Christian beliefs and way of life, never mix well together? But here you are! The Supreme Being must have a very special plan for you. His Son Jesus wants me to tell you something." I said, "Hang on a minute! You know who Jesus is?" She said, "Yes. Just because I choose to call God the Supreme Being doesn't change the fact that I am aware of his Son. We are both on different paths, hoping to claim the same prize." I asked, "Fine, what does Jesus want to tell me?" She said, "He wants you to know that no matter what happens to you, He will always be there for you. You are never alone, and that He and his Father love you very much!" I sat there stunned for minutes. As tears welled up in my eyes, I pondered over what a complete stranger just told me. Incredible, I thought. Deep down in my heart, I had always wondered if Jesus genuinely cared about me, so often when I prayed, I would just focus on God. I always knew Jesus was standing there listening. As I drove home, I prayed in the car and thanked God and Jesus for letting me know how much they loved me and that I never have to feel alone again. I told Jesus that I would be talking more with Him, and would like to become closer to

Him, too.

Now, here's a short quiz to see if you've been paying attention. If I were officially put on a six-month leave of absence beginning in October, when should I have been reinstated? And the answer is…MAY! May 19, 2003, to be exact! So I had no job, just been working out a lot, lost 80 pounds? Remember?

Here's what I forgot to tell you. Back in February, I met with one of the leaders of my church. In the coming chapters when I refer to the leaders of my church, in a not-so-flattering way, I will not use their office titles like apostle, bishop, or district elder. I will use their first names only because I have an enormous respect for the work of the Lord. The offices or ministries in His work are perfect! But He chooses to use imperfect men, like myself, who are decidedly human, and all of us make mistakes.

As I was saying, in February I met with a leader called Ron, who knew my name but didn't actually know me, since we had never worked together. On a few occasions, we met to discuss my reinstatement. He would tell me that I make him nervous because I wanted so badly to be put back on active duty. In my church, you don't decide to carry a ministry. The leaders approach you and ask if you would be willing to carry a ministry and the responsibilities that go along with it. The need is based on the growth of the congregation. When a brother appears to be too anxious to receive a new or a greater office, it sends a red flag up, and the church leaders think that he may be looking to feed his ego in some way. I don't blame them. But I have never let my ego play a role in the Lord's work. He can replace me at any time if He wants. For me, it has always been a privilege to serve the Lord.

As I spoke to Ron about how I felt, I told him that being a serving priest has always been my greatest joy. The Lord took everything away from me. All I have ever wanted was to serve Him, and now I couldn't even do that anymore. Ron looked me and told me that there wasn't anything he can do until after the six-month leave of absence was over.

In June, I was still on leave. Every time I would bring up my reinstatement with Ron; he would just brush over it, and tell me he was thinking about it. Give him more time, he would say. At one point, I got so angry about it that I demanded he have lunch with me so that we could talk about it. I may as well have had lunch with a wall: walls have no expression either. Ron told me he questioned my actions and asked again why I felt I had to be reinstated. I told him that I didn't have to, but I would like to.

I asked, "Why you would question me, a brother who served faithfully for eight years as a deacon and ten years as a priest, and two of those years as a rector?" The commission of a rector is given to the priest who is now charged with leading a local congregation. In other words, the rector is the head priest. Remember, I was put in charge of the congregation in Iowa, so I was referred to as the rector of that congregation. Ron questioned my actions. I told him he should look at my past if he wanted to judge me. "Ask the other leaders I have served under what their impression of me was." He said, "I have. They tell me if you can't have your way, then screw everyone else." I said, "Really?" But I knew what he was talking about.

In my small congregation, we did not have an organist. Music is a significant part of our church services. We were paying for one of our members to learn how to play the piano, but it would be years before she would be able to play anything for the services. I had asked on numerous occasions if I could pay a professional organist, but each time I got shot down. Well, I just wouldn't take no for an answer, so I never let up.

The excuse they gave me was, "We don't pay any of our other organists in our church. Why would we pay one for your congregation?" To which I would reply, "Every other congregation has two or three members that can play. I have no one!" That's what Ron was referring to.

I finally gave up on the organist when they put me on a leave of absence, and I left the area to move back to Chicago.

Why am I sharing this with you? I just want to point out the fact that on top of having no job, and no ministry, I was having a hard time finding something that would help me define who I was. In life, most people define themselves by their careers, hobbies, families, or the status they hold. I had nothing, and during this time frame, I always felt lost, and that I didn't fit in anywhere.

Chapter 2

Class is now in session…

Over the past couple of weeks, I had come in for many healings and numerous readings from Saleena and even some of her students. One day in June, after a reading, Saleena approached me and said that she was forming a class on how to do basic meditation. She called the class "Meditation 1: The Basics." She asked if I would be interested. The class would get together over a six-week period at 3:00 pm on Sundays for three hours. I walked into the first class. There was a total of six students including myself. Four of my classmates were students still studying for their degrees; the fifth was an older lady; and then there was the plucky me. Saleena had all of us sit in chairs, in a semicircle. She then told us what the meditation basics were.

1. How to ground
2. How to move energy
3. How to control your auras
4. How to stay in your own space and get into the center of your mind

She began by telling us that everyone is clairvoyant from birth. As we grow older, we choose to forget about this innate ability. The class would retrain us to get that ability back. She told us that everything in life has energy. The only time something doesn't have energy is when it is dead. Most people who get sick all the time do not move much energy through their spaces. How often do athletes get sick? Not too often. The reason they stay healthy is that while they are exercising, they are moving energy through their spaces, flushing out all the stress and problems they faced that day. Everything is washed away in the movement of energy all around them. Energy moves through us with ease. When a person feels pain, it is because something is blocking the movement of energy. That is why we call it disease…do you get it? Dis-ease! Energy should be moving through us with ease. I thought to myself, well that makes a lot of sense. She said, "Place your feet firmly on the floor. If you are going to ground yourself, you must have contact with the earth. Even though we are three stories up from the ground, this building is in contact with the earth. The reason we ground first is to create an outlet for us to release from our space." We all closed our eyes and took a few deep breaths. "It is important that you breathe correctly," Saleena reminded us. I thought to myself, *Lady, I've been breathing correctly for thirty-six years without passing out once.* She told us to breathe in through our nose and exhale out of our mouths as if we were blowing a kiss.

She told us just to practice our breathing techniques. "Every time you breathe, you will be moving energy. Breathe slowly and controlled." We practiced breathing for fifteen minutes. Saleena then taught us how to ground ourselves. She told us that once you are grounded, you will feel as if you have more time than you know what to do with. You will never be late again; no one can sneak up on you and scare you, and you will think more clearly.

She told us to take deep breaths and picture a cord just behind our backs. She told us to put some color in the cord. The more color, the better. Mine looked like a rainbow threw up all over it. She then told us to make it four inches in diameter. "Now, picture the center of the earth. It is hot with fire; flames are shooting up from it. Lava is flowing in all directions." She then told us to picture our colorful cord driving through the earth's crust until we saw it embed itself into the solid core of the center of the earth.

Pretty wild. I did just what she asked. She then told us to "clairvoyantly" turn around and give our cord a tug. "Does it feel as if it's attached," she asked? Most of us said yes. She then told us to take a deep breath and guide our cord into our first chakra. I have to tell you that, through this whole process, I didn't feel anything at all, but I went along with it.

She then taught us about earth energy and cosmic energy. Earth energy comes up through your feet. Cosmic energy comes in through the top of your head. As you take deep breaths both of these energies flush through your whole body and go out through your grounding cord. It was the most incredible sensation I have ever felt!

The next Sunday, Saleena taught us how to get into the center of our heads or the center of our minds. As we grounded and took deep breaths, she asked us to focus our attention on the center of our foreheads. She said, "Mentally draw a line around your head just above your ears. Now draw a vertical line that would run across your nose and back around the base of your skull until the line comes back over the top of your head. Now, focus in on the point where the two lines intersect. That is the center of your head."

As we continued to focus our attention, she told us that the center of our head is the place where all clairvoyant abilities come from. She asked us to create a structure that would make us comfortable. Some thought about a beach house, some a summer home. I thought of an alpine ski lodge. I have never been skiing, but I like snow, mountains, and the whole ambiance of that kind of setting. Once we had our structures, she said, "Now furnish them with whatever you want." My lodge had a rustic look, an early American flavor to it. Log timbers stretched across the cathedral ceilings. There was an enormous fireplace with a roaring fire. The entire two-story lodge was filled with overstuffed couches and chairs. The west wall of the lodge had one large window from floor to ceiling and beyond the edge of the property was a majestic lake that had a snow covered mountain sitting just behind it. I would sit in a chair and watch the sun set behind the mountain as I meditated. Ahh, very tranquil.

Saleena then told us that we would know when we were in the center of our heads because we would find ourselves standing in the center of the structure we just created. From there, we will have the ability to see into our own space, as well as our surroundings. This is a safe place for us to come and rest while we meditate.

We then learned about our auras. In short, there are seven layers to our auras. They act just like the earth's ozone layer. Our auras protect us from harmful energies that we may come in contact with. There is a lot more to your aura than just that, but this is enough information for our purposes right now.

We learned how to control the size and shape of our auras. A normal aura is about a quarter inch from the surface of your skin. It is shaped like an egg as it surrounds you. We then learned how to control our auras. We took turns casting them over each other. When someone put his or her aura over me, it was the most uncomfortable thing I had ever felt. Saleena explained that everyone has a space. It is usually three to four feet around you. When we threw our auras, we were invading our classmates' space and vice-versa. That's why it felt uncomfortable. It felt as if I was suffocating. She then told us to be careful with our auras and practice with them.

As the classes progressed, Saleena would ask each of us how our week was, and whether any of us had done anything interesting. One week I eagerly raised my hand to share with the class my experience. I then told my fellow clairvoyants that while I was on the highway driving home a few days earlier, some guy kept riding my bumper. I was going well over the speed limit, and there wasn't anywhere for me to go. After about ten minutes, I had just about enough. So I took some deep breaths and concentrated on the size of my aura. I then threw my aura behind me, right into the driver's face. All of a sudden the guy hit his brakes and dropped back about two car lengths. I was totally amazed that it worked! As I received numerous accolades from my classmates, Saleena looked at me and said, "Jim, how many times do I have to tell you to be nice?" She then started to tell the class that they shouldn't do what I did, but every one of my classmates came to me after class and said that they were going to try it. I just laughed.

One Saturday night as I was lying in bed, I slowly closed my eyes for a few seconds. All of a sudden, I could see two men walking toward me. I opened my eyes quickly and sat up in bed. I looked all over the room, and there was no one there. I laid back down and as soon as I closed my eyes, there they were, standing right in front of me. I sat up in bed with my eyes still closed. As they both stepped closer to me, I saw who it was. Both of these men were my grandfathers. But, they had both died! My dad's father had passed away when I was just a small child. My mom's father had passed away when I was thirteen years old. They walked right up to me, smiled and said nothing. Both of them were carrying a small box. They handed me each of their boxes, waved at me, and walked away. I just sat there for a while, completely stunned. Then all of a sudden a warm feeling came over me. I was a little confused about this whole situation. The one thing that surprised me about this encounter was that I wasn't frightened at all.

The next morning at church, I pulled my sister Ann aside and told her what had happened. My sister Ann has had a gift since she was nine years old. She can see souls who have died. They come to her and ask her to help them. She can see into the future as well as the past. If I were standing in your kitchen right now and called Ann, she could describe everything in your kitchen, all the way down to the little knickknacks sitting on your stove. My family always thought Ann just wanted the attention, but there were just too many things that proved she actually had a gift and wasn't crazy!

As I shared with her the details, she looked at me and told me that she felt that what they gave me was something good. She said, "Our grandfathers are very proud of you!" Later that day before class, I pulled Saleena aside and shared all of this with her. She smiled and said, "Your grandfathers gave you their blessing. That's what was in the boxes." She said, "How wonderful, Jim, that your first experience would be with your own grandfathers." Unbeknownst to me this would be the first of many encounters to come.

The following week at the end of class, Saleena encouraged all of us to practice what we'd learned. Because I had no job, back at home, I had a lot of time to practice. I decided one afternoon, while I was meditating, to go into my heart chakra. Don't ask me why. I just did it. As I took deep breaths, I focused my attention on my heart. All of a sudden, I found myself walking through a tunnel. At the end of the tunnel, I could see a room that looked like an office. All four walls were made of solid oak. There were bookcases filled with books on every wall and off to the side was a very cozy-looking fireplace with a robust fire burning. In the center of the room was a great big, solid oak desk with what looked like an extremely comfortable chair. I sat in the chair and pulled myself up to the desk. As I got closer, I could see that there were a number of books lined up vertically across the desk with their spines facing me.

I sat in wonder as I read the titles: *Dating, Engagement, Wedding, Honeymoon, Family Parties, Laughter* and they kept going all the way to the end book, titled *Divorce*. To my right sitting on the desk surface was what looked like a glass puzzle that was shattered into numerous pieces. I opened the books one by one. Inside each book was what looked like every mental picture I had ever taken with my mind. I slowly started to relive the prior ten years of my life with my wife. As I kept taking deep breaths I could feel tears rolling down my face, and my heart began to ache. I read book after book. Periodically, I would take a puzzle piece and put it where I felt it belonged.

After three weeks of going into my heart chakra, I finally reached the book titled Divorce. As I flipped through the pages, I wept bitterly. At times, I would stop looking at the memories and just cry. When I had finished going through it, I put the book back in its place. There was one piece of the puzzle sitting next to my arm. I stood up and put the last piece in its place. I stared at the puzzle in complete awe. It was shaped like a big heart! As I read these books, I was clairvoyantly putting my broken heart back together again.

When I had finished with everything, I stood up and surveyed everything that was on the desk. I thought about the phrase Tina had told me: "Let go and let God!" I took a big deep breath and let go. All of a sudden a big wind swept across the desk and carried everything toward the fireplace. In almost an instant, the fire consumed everything. It was all gone! I sat back down in the chair and stared in complete shock as new books slowly started to appear on the desk. All the spines were completely blank. I sat back in the chair, put my feet up on the desk and said to myself, *I wonder what my future relationships will bring.*

When I walked into class the following Sunday, Saleena looked at me and said with a smile on her face, "What did you do? You look completely different, Jim!" I shared with her how I'd gone into my heart chakra. She looked at me and said, "I never taught you how to do that. Jim, you keep telling me that you are not clairvoyant. I have no doubt that you truly are!"

By the middle of July, thanks to my sister Ann, I got a job, as a file clerk, making twelve dollars an hour! My sister was working for a mortgage company at the time, and they needed a little summer help. So I said, "What the heck, why not!" If the Lord were testing my humbleness, I think He struck me to the core. I went from being General Manager of Sales and Marketing to a file clerk. Talk about ego. I didn't have one anymore. Being a file clerk was probably the best job I ever had. No stress! No worries about meeting deadlines! No employees to supervise! I just had to worry if the copier had enough paper in it. Pretty sweet!

At the end of July, the church leader Ron wanted to have another meeting with me. So we met at a restaurant one Thursday evening, and he brought another leader with him whose name was Steve. As we sat and talked, Ron kept looking at me funny. I finally asked what the problem was. He said, "There's something different about you. You are not the same person you were a few month ago." I said, "No, I'm not.." I then shared with both of them everything I had learned about meditation and how I was able to face my problems and work through them. At the end of our little meeting, Ron said, " Lets talk again in two months." I said, "Fine."

In September, Saleena formed a second class, called "Meditation 2: How to Control Energy." As I walked into class, there were a lot of familiar faces from the Meditation 1 class. Within the first few classes, we learned how to protect our space. She taught us how to create a rose and place it on the edge of our space. The rose will tell people you come in contact with that this rose represents a clairvoyant boundary line that they are not allowed to cross.

Have you ever sat and talked with someone who was angry or upset about something? As they talked with you, did you start getting angry and upset, too? By the time the person who is upset is done talking with you, they feel better but now you are really ticked off! The person essentially took all of their negative energy and dumped it into your space. What a nice friend!

By placing a rose in front of you, your friend will know clairvoyantly, that they need to keep out of your space. I have tried it on numerous occasions and have found it works quite well. I have sat across from friends who were ranting and raving. As they spoke, spit was flying from their mouths, that's how mad they were. The whole time I would just sit there calmly and listen to them talk and not feel a thing. I still use this tool even today.

Saleena next taught us how to take something negative and destroy it. Only on the rarest occasions would we do this. She taught us how to fill a room with our own energy so we would feel more comfortable.

For instance, during the prior few months, I'd had a few job interviews. I would meditate prior to going to the interview. I would think about the address and then picture the room I would be interviewing in. I would then fill it with my own energy. I can tell you that every time I did that, the interviews went great, and I was never nervous. I was never offered a job, but that's not the point I'm trying to make here. It works!

Do you remember my brother Peter who was married back in February? Over the few months following the wedding, Peter and Linda were not getting along very well. They would have one fight after another. It would get so bad that Linda would call my family and unload her side of the story. It seemed that my brother was always at fault. It seems to me that it takes two to have a fight. Unfortunately, my mother would buy into Linda's stories. Mom would then call me and ask me to call my brother so that I could "straighten him out." There are always two sides to every story. The trick is figuring out who's not telling the complete truth. There was just too much drama between my brother and his wife: I could write another book about that.

I was happy to be officially going on my third interview with the same company. There was a light at the end of the tunnel. I thought I did pretty well on the third interview. Too bad I didn't know how to walk on water. I think that would have clinched it for me. They never called me back! Oh, well, I was still keeping the faith.

Occasionally, I would pray something like this: *Dear Lord, hi, its Jim; remember me? I'm the guy that gave you his free will almost a year ago. Remember, Jim. I still need a little help here. I still can't seem to find any work. Oh, by the way, a job would really be nice about now.* The Lord and I are very close. That's why I felt I could talk to Him like that. No thunderbolts came down and struck me. I know the Lord has a great sense of humor. He made me!

Soon after, I finished the Meditation 2 classes, Saleena asked me if I would be interested in learning how to give other people healings just like the one she gave me. Seeing that I still had a lot of free time on my hands, I said, "Why not!

Healing 101 had a lot of the same people from the other two classes. Saleena went over the steps that one takes while giving a healing. The most interesting thing I found was while you sit and receive a healing, the one who is performing the healing benefits too. As they give you a healing, the same areas in their space are being cleaned out, too. The first thing we were taught was to ask the person if he or she would like a healing. It is out of respect that we ask. We will be entering the recipient's space, and we must have his or her permission first.

First, we would ground the recipient and his auras, then run energy through each layer of his aura and then clean out his channels. Next, we would start with the first chakra, and continue until we reached the crown or seventh chakra. And then, we would return all of his own energy and fill him back up. That sounds pretty easy. *No problem, I thought, I can do that!* Saleena then started talking about our own personal "healing master." I thought, *Um, this wasn't in the brochure!*

Okay, here's the explanation. A healing master is a spirit, a *good* spirit. Healing masters are created by God and paired up with healers like all of us in the class. We are superior to them. They serve us. In exchange, we share our life experiences with them. Boy did mine get more than it bargained for! We could let them tag along with us to work. (That's if I had a job.) We can take them to the store, to a movie, or even to church. This is how it works. There is a spiritual cord that we as the healers plug into the back of our right hands. The energy will flow from the healing master through our hand into the individual that we are giving a healing to. Yes, I know how weird that sounds!

The healing master already knows what color the energy should be for that person. Before the person sits in a chair to await the healing, the master has collected all the information about the recipient. The master even knows how long to spend on each area of the person. At times, the masters will tell us information that we will share with the person getting the healing.

The time came for us to meet our healing master. Saleena told us that the Supreme Being Himself hand made and chose our healing masters based on our needs and personalities. Yes, I already know what you are thinking. God's going to give me one who's crazy!

We all grounded and went into the center of our heads. Saleena invited our healing masters to walk slowly up behind us. One by one each of us waited quietly. She then told them to introduce themselves one at a time to their prospective healer. When it was my turn, I sat ready and eager to meet my healing master. All of a sudden, I heard a quiet voice behind me. All it said was, *Hi, my name is Marty.*

I said, *Hi, my name is Jim; it's nice to meet you.* I opened my eyes and began to look around, but I couldn't see Marty. Saleena said, "Jim, you have to close your eyes and stay in the center of your head. You will not see him with your natural eyes. The only way you will see him is by looking through your third eye clairvoyantly."

I closed my eyes and asked Marty if he would please step closer to me because I couldn't see him. Out of the shadows came a figure. I stared at him as he lifted his arm and waved to me. Are you wondering what Marty looks like? He is about five feet four inches tall. He is balding with just a little brown hair on both sides of his head. He wears small, round, wire-rimmed glasses. His eyes are hazel. He looks like an accountant, with a bow tie. (Sorry to offend any accountants.) He was also wearing a sweater vest. Marty seems to think that he is strikingly handsome. (I put that into humor him. Don't tell him I said that.)

Okay, to this day, I swear Marty had an English accent the day we met. He tells me I'm crazy; that he never had an accent and that I just made that up because I *wanted* him to have an English accent. I asked him, *why would I make up something like that? I know what I heard coming out of your mouth.* Can you see how the two of us get along?

As we talked to each other, my impression of Marty was that he was the kindest, sweetest, most gentle spirit I had ever met. I say that as if I meet spirits every day! I'm sure you get the point. Over time, I have come to find that the Lord did pair us together perfectly. Marty's just as sarcastic as I am. He has the same sense of humor as I have. At times, I have to remind him that he is not my wife and should stop nagging me! Marty and I have become very close friends. I can actually say I love the little goofball.

As Marty and I worked together doing our first healing, on one of my classmates, it took me a little time to get used to the feeling in my hand. Have you ever put your hand on a washing machine when it was on the spin cycle? That's what my hand felt like. My whole hand was vibrating.

As I progressed through the healing, I found that I would spend most of my time on the chakras. I didn't really see anything; it was more about what I felt. In some cases, I knew there was a blockage even before Marty said anything. It was the strangest feeling when there was a blockage. The energy flow from my hand would slow down until the blockage was removed. The flow would then return to the same intensity as before.

Marty would tell me where to focus the energy and for how long. We would move very methodically through all of the chakras. Occasionally, Marty would say something to me, and I would mention it to the person I was healing. As soon as the recipients acknowledged what I was telling them, the energy would increase, and the flow was restored for that chakra.

Week after week, we would all take turns giving our fellow classmates healings. Saleena would instruct us on which technique worked better on each part of the body. After a while, I began to hear and see Marty more clearly. Marty and I worked so well together without me even saying an audible word. I would just say it in my head, and Marty heard me as plain as if I were to have said it out loud. (No, I'm not suffering from a psychotic episode.) When I wasn't in the class, I invited Marty to join me wherever I went. One time, I took him to the grocery store with me. When it came time to carry everything out to the car, he told me he didn't have a physical body. What a lame excuse!

Saleena told us to use our healing masters to help ground our own houses, cars, or anything we wanted. Every now and then, I would ask Marty to ground my car. I actually slept better on nights when I asked Marty to ground my bedroom. Saleena said we could even use our healing masters to save us parking spaces. My sister and her family lived in a condo at the time and trying to find a parking spot near the home was almost impossible. So I gave Marty a try one evening. We were going out to dinner and usually if we came home late in the evening, all of the parking spots would be filled, and one of us would have to park two blocks away. I asked Marty if he would save us a spot close to the home, but I didn't tell my family. He said *No problem*.

When we came home a few hours later, it was almost 10:00 PM. My brother-in-law Fred commented, "It would take a miracle to find a spot at this time." As we pulled around to the front of the condo, right there in plain view was a parking spot. I then shared with my family that not only could Marty move, and clean energy, but this most powerful spirit could save us parking spots too! A barrage of thanks poured out of the mouths of my family. Marty accepted the thanks graciously. After a while, I started giving my family healings. It was a monumental day in the Rybak family when my dad, the world's biggest skeptic, let me give him an energy healing. He still won't admit it, but I knew he felt better when we were finished with his healing. (Thanks for your support, Pop!)

It was the middle of October, and I still had no full time job, and my temporary summer job had ended. I was still not reinstated into the priesthood. I decided one Wednesday evening to go and talk to the leader who was in charge of the entire Chicago district. He knew me very well. We had worked together as youth leaders. The Chicago District comprises the entire Chicago area, city and suburbs, as well as Rock Island, Illinois. The states of Wisconsin, Iowa, and Minnesota are also part of this district. Our district has over twenty-five congregations in it.

    After the leaders service that night, we stood in the parking lot and talked for an hour and a half. I told him how disappointed I was with the way the whole thing was handled. After serving in a ministry for almost eighteen years, I had expected a little more respect from them. He apologized to me and said I was right. I told him I didn't understand what was so hard about this, saying "Either you would like my help or not." I told him that carrying the priestly ministry around with me and not using it was a lot like a carpenter who carries his tools from job to job, but never gets to use them. It's a tremendous burden, and I didn't want to drag it around with me if I wasn't going to use it. I said, "I'll make it easy for you. If you don't want me to serve anymore, then please accept my resignation with no hard feelings." The situation had now been going on for almost a year. He told me it was not that easy. He said that either way, yes or no, he would call me by Sunday evening and let me know what his decision was.

    The following morning my brother called me. Boy was he miserable. After speaking with him for almost two hours, the thought came to me that maybe I should go to the west coast. I would visit him for a month to see if I couldn't help Linda and him work the whole marriage thing out. I had already made plans to have lunch with my sister Ann that day, so I thought I would ask her what she thought about my plan. As I drove to Ann's, my mind was racing. By the time I got to her house, I had almost decided that I should just move out west. (Yes, things happen that fast in my life!) I prayed and asked the Lord that if He could find me a job in within thirty days after I get there that would mean that I should stay there and not come home. As I sat having lunch with my sister, I shared my plans with her. I said I wasn't sure if I should fly out there or drive. Ann said, "I just got a feeling that you will want to drive because you are going to need your car to go on job interviews." She said, "I really have a good feeling about this." (Yes, my sister is just as crazy as I am. Remember, she has a gift, too.)

    I made my plans and decided to leave one week later on the following Thursday. My entire family agreed that this was a terrific idea and gave me their blessing. Saturday night, I called my friend Mike who was the rector of the congregation I attended. Mike and I were in our church youth group together. Down the road, we also served as youth leaders together. I told him of my plans and said, "I'm calling you tonight to tell you my plans because tomorrow I'm supposed to get an answer from our head leader as to whether I will or will not be reinstated. I'm letting you know now so that if the answer comes back as a no, they won't think I'm moving just because of that." Mike said, "No problem. I sure am going to miss you." I told him I would miss him too.

Sunday came and went with no phone call. I started packing that week. On Wednesday, Ron was in my local congregation. He pulled me aside and said, "I hear you are moving?" I said, "Yes." Then he said, "We were going to reinstate you." I said, "Too late, but no hard feelings." We shook hands and parted as friends. Thursday came and there I was, driving out of Chicago on my way to the west coast!

Chapter 3

A new start…

As I drove, I thought a lot about what I had just lived through. I was one week away from my one-year anniversary when my ex-wife said; "I can't do this anymore. I want a divorce!" When we acknowledge our pain, then we can move forward. Then the healing process can start. I love saying that.

It took me three days to drive to the west coast. I moved in with Peter, Linda, and Linda's two kids. I put all of my meager possessions in a small corner of their bedroom. They lived in a two-bedroom apartment. I had the pleasure of sleeping on the pull-out couch, which I affectionately referred to as "the rack."

Before I left Chicago, I had contacted a number of headhunters in Washington. The following Monday after I got in, I had a few appointments to sit down with the headhunters and discuss what job opportunities they had for me. I continued to apply to any job I could find. Over the next few weeks, I had very little luck with job interviews. I kept reminding the Lord, *If You would like me to stay out here then please help me find a job.*

On numerous occasions, I would sit with Peter and Linda and talk with them either separately or together about their marriage problems. I am no marriage counselor. My own marriage failed. But I do have the ability to listen and help other people find the answers they are looking for sometimes. The problems they were having was that Linda didn't think she was doing anything wrong. I'm not just saying that because she married my brother. He's not perfect. A sure sign that a failed marriage is on the horizon is when one person decides to stop trying or even refuses to admit that they are at fault in some cases. They are not willing to change, even a little. I shared with them what I was seeing. I had been living with them for a while. So they made a few changes and their relationship did get a little better.

Linda's mother was suffering from stage IV cancer at the time. She was only given a few years to live. That was six years ago. Linda and I had many conversations about meditation and energy healings. I even told her about Marty, which is something I didn't usually tell anyone about. Linda came to me one day crying. She had just come from her mother's house, and her mother, who was always in constant pain, was suffering even more that day. I asked Linda if she would like me to give her mom a healing. I explained that I would try to ground out some of her pain, which could help her sleep better. Linda told me she would have to let me know, and two days later, she said yes. I made time to go see her mom.

I had Linda's mom sit in a chair, which was extremely difficult for her to do. I began to tell her what the process would involve. She looked at me and told me that she would appreciate anything I could do for her. I spent over an hour grounding her and running energy through every part of her body. When we were finished, she couldn't believe how much better she felt. I told Linda and her mother that two things might happen. One, Linda's mom might sleep a lot, and two, she might end up going to the bathroom a lot. I warned them because an energy healing has a significant effect on some people. For the body, it becomes a very real thing. Sleep is the first sign that your body is healing itself. Going to the bathroom is the second sign that your body is dumping all of the waste and toxins that the healing has flushed out.

Over the past few weeks, I had a few interviews but no offers. I was one day away from the time frame I had given the Lord, but I wasn't nervous at all. After I gave Linda's mom her healing, my brother, and I decided to go visit his friend Rick and his family for the weekend. They lived about six hours away, and I thought Peter and Linda could use a break from each other. So off we went. Rick lived in a particularly nice area; it was quiet and peaceful. My thirtieth day on the west coast had arrived. Rick was the rector for his local congregation. I asked him to pray for me, and he gladly did.

Around 1:00 PM, my brother's cell phone rang. It was Linda. He handed me his phone and said, "She has a question for you." Linda said, "Jim, my mom has been sleeping now for eighteen hours; is that normal?" I reminded her about what I said. The feeling I had was that she was just exhausted. Because of the constant pain she was always in, she really hadn't been getting any sleep over the past few weeks, and she was making up for it. I told Linda that her mom would be fine. Linda then said, "My mom wanted me to tell you that, for the longest time, she hasn't had any feeling in her hands, but since the healing, she now has feeling, and she wanted me to tell you thanks." I told her, "I really didn't do that much. Let's thank the Lord instead." Weeks later, two days before Thanksgiving, Linda's mom passed away. Linda's father then blamed me for her death. Yes, I know. Give me a break!

As the thirtieth day went on, I would quietly pray, asking the Lord to confirm for me what he wanted me to do. Around 3:00 PM, my cell phone rang. It was one of the headhunters. He told me that one of the companies I had interviewed with two times had made me an offer. It wasn't a lot of money, but I gladly accepted the offer. I ran into the house and shared the news with everyone. We immediately folded our hands and gave thanks to the Lord for His kindness. Rick said, "Well, it looks as if you got your answer, and I am very happy that you are staying." I said, "Yes, I am too, and thanks for all of your prayers."

Okay, here's the catch about the job. As I said, there really wasn't a lot of money. The other challenge was I had to drive eighty to ninety minutes one-way to get to work. I had accepted a position as an assistant manager for an upscale pizza company. I had to start work at 2:00 PM and work well into the late morning hours. I also had to work every Saturday and Sunday. But I got my answer from the Lord. I was supposed to stay on the west coast.

Now, here's how the Lord works. The weekend that my brother and I were out visiting Rick was the weekend that there were a number of other church members there from another one of the congregations in the area. Rick was the interim rector over them at the time. I struck up a conversation with a deacon named Stan. I shared with him my situation about my job and the long drive. He looked at me and told me that he had a big house all by himself and asked me if I would like to rent a room from him because he lived only fifteen minutes away from my new job. Pretty cool! I of course said yes.

I packed up my things and moved in with Stan the first week of December.

The following Sunday the head leader of our entire worldwide church organization was in New York City holding the service. It was transmitted via satellite all over the United States and a few other countries. During this service, he spoke about the Christmas tree in Madison Square Garden and how it takes 30,000 lights to decorate the tree. He told us he had a wish for the United States: that every light on that tree would represent a new soul in our church for the United States. His wish was something we all began to pray for.

As the weeks went by, I learned everything there was about the job. I also fit myself into my new church congregation. I had befriended a deacon called Stewie and his family. Over time, I came to find that I hated the new job. The hours were horrible and long. The pay was a joke and on top of all of this, it was Christmastime, and I was always missing all of the fellowships and parties.

One Wednesday evening when I was supposed to be working, I asked for a few hours off to take care of a personal problem. I went to church that night and prayed asking the Lord for an answer about my job. I told Him; *I appreciate that you found me this job, but I have the feeling that since I am missing so many church services I feel there's something else out there for me. I am, again, putting my trust in your hands, Father. I know it's kind of short notice, but if there's any way you could give me some kind of answer tonight during service, then I will know I should start looking for another job and give my current boss my two weeks' notice when I go in tomorrow.* As I sat and listened, I kept waiting to hear something that would tell me what to do. Near the end of the service, the priest said, "Sometimes, brothers and sisters, there comes a time in our lives when the Lord tests us to see if we really want to be in His house, to hear his word. We may have to sacrifice something to show Him how we feel." If we were allowed to speak out loud in our church during a service, I think I would have yelled the loudest hallelujah. The Lord had answered my prayer. Can I get an AMEN?

The next day, to my boss's surprise, I gave her my two-week notice. I told her that the money was the biggest reason I was leaving. The other problem that bothered me so much was that they had to pay the headhunter a finder's fee for me. I just couldn't let them pay a fee, knowing that I was planning on leaving. I worked my two weeks and to my surprise, everyone that I worked with told me how sad they were that I was leaving. You see I only worked for the company for a total of three weeks. It made me feel good that I left them with a good impression. I would miss them too.

The day after Christmas, my brother called me to tell me that Linda had kicked him out of the house and that she wanted a divorce. I told him that I had already spoken to Stan, my roommate, two weeks earlier about having Peter move in with us if anything happened. I'd had a gut feeling that this was going to happen, but I didn't think it would happen until sometime in January. Oh, well. I can't be right all the time. Peter moved in with us and took the upstairs bedroom.

New Year's Day 2004 was here. We had the whole year in front of us. The congregation I attended was excited because now they had two new brothers, me and my brother Peter, to help along. We both sang in the choir, so now they had a tenor and a bass. Rick, the interim rector, found out that I too was a rector and asked me to handle the visiting schedule for the members. In our church, the ministers make visits to the members' homes two to three times a year, just to see how they are doing. It is a time where members can have a one-on-one meeting with their priest and pour out their hearts. I put a schedule together of three teams consisting of two brothers per team. We made visits on Tuesday and Thursday nights.

As we made these visits, we found out that some of these members hadn't been visited for almost ten years. They were very excited when the brothers would come to their homes. After a few weeks, Sunday mornings started to see an increase in attendance. We now had an average of almost ninety people, where before we were lucky if we saw even forty people on a Sunday. It was a very exciting time.

I was still looking for work, to no avail. I found out that Deacon Stewie was out of work too. I had continued to work out every week, and when Stewie found out he asked if he could join me at the health club. I was happy to have the company. Almost every other day we would take walks together down by the bay. We would discuss our faith, our lives, and the members of the congregation and some of their needs. Stewie was on my visiting team, so we got to know each other pretty well.

One day as we walked, I asked Stewie about a certain mother and her daughter. I said, "When I look at them, I feel a great sadness around them, and I can't figure out why." I asked him if he knew what was going on with them. He looked at me with a little fear in his eyes and said, "They're haunted. There is an evil spirit in their house, and it won't leave." I said, "What?!." He then told me that, for many years, the local ministers had been going to their home and praying, but the situation would only get worse after they prayed. No one knew what to do.

I said, "We have to go make a visit there!" Stewie asked me if I was crazy, to which I replied "Yes, but that's not the point." I told him "I don't know why I feel we have to go there; we just do." I called Rick and asked if Stewie and I could make a visit there. Rick told me to be careful. Stewie arranged the visit because he knew them very well. I had never really talked with Shelly, the mother, or Lannie, the daughter.

As I walked in the house, I could immediately feel something was there. It was not a spirit. It was a soul. No wonder things would get worse after the ministers would pray.

Within one of our highest ministries lays the power to bind and remove spirits. Every time,the head leader,would try this, Shelly told us things would just get worse.

For almost forty-five minutes, I sat and listened to Shelly pour out her heart about the horror she and her family had been living through for almost sixteen years. Yes, you heard me. Sixteen years this had been going on. At the beginning, the family never spoke openly about this problem to each other.

It was only the past five years that they acknowledged to each other that there was a problem in the house. Shelly told us that, on many occasions, this thing would knock pictures off the walls and turn their heat all the way up. It would break things, and on one occasion, he appeared right in front of Shelly and scared her. She looked right at me as I sat across the room from her and said, "I'm at my wit's end, and I feel like I'm losing my mind and no one can help me!" I sat forward in my chair and said, "I think I can help you. I just need to make a phone call. Stay here, I will be right back."

I went outside and stood on the front porch. I could feel this thing's rage. I called my friend Tina back in Chicago. I told her that I was at a member's house, and I needed her to confirm something for me. I told her that everyone in this area thought this thing was a spirit but that I thought it was a soul. She told me to give her a minute. I quietly waited for her answer. She said, "You are right it's a soul and is he angry. He's been there for over ten years, and he is lost. He doesn't really mean them any harm. He's just looking for someone to help him." I said, "I know you have helped my sister Ann remove two spirits out of her home in the past. I know he's not a spirit, but do you have any ideas?" She told me yes, but there were a few things I would need to pick up and that I should call her back in the morning.

As I walked back into the house, the hair on the back of my neck stood straight up. This soul knew that I could sense him. I'll be honest with you: I was really scared! I couldn't show my fear to Stewie and Shelly. I calmly sat back down and told Shelly that I could help her. I told her I would be back in two days because I needed to get a few things. I then told them, "Before we do anything more, let's flip open the Bible and see what the Lord has to say about all of this."

Have you ever been going through a difficult time in your life and you really needed an answer from God? I would recommend this to anyone who has faith. Grab your Bible and say a small prayer asking the Lord to help you. Stick your finger anywhere you feel may be a good spot in the pages of the Bible and flip it open. Wherever your eyes land, start reading. It is amazing at times how quickly the Lord will give you an answer by doing this. I grabbed the Bible and flipped it open and read the following:

(Matthew 8:1-4 NKJV)
And as Jesus came down from the mountain, a leper approached him and said, "Master, will you heal me? And Jesus said, yes, but tell

no one. Go show yourself to a priest and bring an offering of thanks to the Lord.

I looked at the two of them and asked, "Do you know what this means?" They both shook their heads, saying no. I said, "God is going to heal your home, but we can't tell anyone. If our church leaders find out that I'm doing this, they won't understand, and they will go nuts. But I will call your rector Rick and share this with him when we are done. I am going to take all of the responsibility for this so if anything goes wrong it won't fall back on the church, it will fall on me. Now, all of us will bring an offering to thank God for his help. Do you understand?"

They both said yes. I told Shelly that Stewie and I would be back in two days on Thursday at 7:00 PM. Shelly looked at me and said, "Are you sure you can help me? I said, "Yes. The 'thing' in your house is not a spirit. If it were a spirit, everything the ministers tried would have worked. This thing is a soul; he's angry because he's been stuck here for a long time." I asked her, "Can anyone force you to do something against your own will?" She told me no. I said, "Dead or alive a soul still has its own free will to make its own choices. Every time the ministers prayed to force him out, it just made him even madder. Where was he to go? He came to you looking for help, but there was no way you would have known that. I will be back in two days, and we will help him. Please be patient."

As I drove Stewie home, he asked me how I knew about all of this. I told him about the clairvoyant training I went through in Chicago and basically said "I really don't have a good answer. I just know this is what we should do." He told me that he was in it with me 100 percent.

As I slept that night, around 3:00AM in the morning our smoke detector went off. As I sat up in bed, I could see through my closed bedroom door into the hallway that it was the soul from Shelly's house setting off the alarm. Don't ask me why; I could see him through the door. This was a whole new experience for me. I talked to him clairvoyantly, which means I used my mind to communicate with him. Yes, I know how crazy that sounds, but I did.

I said, *Dude, you can't be here. Please go back to Shelly's house and in two days I will come and explain everything to you. You are going to have to trust me. I don't mean you any harm. Now, please leave.* As he turned to leave, he looked back at me very angrily and then left. I heard my roommate Stan open his bedroom door, drag a chair into the hallway between our bedrooms, and while the smoke detector was still sounding, rip it off the ceiling. Peace and quiet was restored once again. You see it wasn't battery-operated. It was hardwired into the house's electrical system. I heard Stan drag the chair back to its place and close his door. I laid back down, smiling to myself. Actually, I was laughing to myself. I said a small prayer and then fell back asleep.

The next morning, I shared everything with Stan and Peter. I believe Stan's remark was that the next time some angry soul comes and visits me, could I tell them to do it during the morning hours? Then he just started laughing. I picked Stewie up that morning and headed out to the store to pick up the things we were going to need for Shelly. Stewie wanted to know what we needed to get. I told him, "Apparently we need to buy some black candles, white candles, wheatgrass, and sweet grass; that's what Tina told me to get." Lucky for me, I was living on the west coast where all of these weird grasses could be found. Stewie just said, "Okay, you know what you're doing." I quietly said to myself *I hope.*

That night, I went to church. As I sat there before the service started, I prayed, *Dear Heavenly Father, you know of our plans for Shelly. I am in over my head and haven't got a clue what I'm doing. I'm kind of scared about this because I've never done anything like this before. Please help me!* During the middle of service, I heard a quiet voice speaking behind me. All it said was, *"Ask Shelly to forgive him. Ask the Lord to send an angel to guide him out of the house and tell the soul your plans."* I sat there asking myself if I had really heard a voice tell me all of that.

After the service, I approached Shelly. Before I could say anything, she said, "I have to be honest with you, Jim. I'm really nervous about this and scared." I said, "I've been praying, and you've been praying. We are just going to have to trust our Heavenly Father. He will help us." I then said, "You are going to have to forgive the soul. If you can't, there is no reason for me to come over. If you can't forgive him, Shelly, then you will bind him here and there isn't anything I can do." She glared at me and said, "Do you have any idea what he has put my family and me through?". For sixteen years, he has tormented us, and now I have to forgive him? Are you serious?" I told her, "Yes, I will ask you tomorrow, and if you can't forgive him, then we will call the whole thing off."

The following morning as I sat drinking my coffee, I thought a lot about this soul and all of a sudden the name Thomas came to me out of nowhere. I immediately called Tina, who was going to tell me how to use all of the items I had bought,. I told her that I thought this soul's name was Thomas. She said she had the same feeling. Tina then explained to me how to use all of the items. I told her I would call her when I was finished. As I sat and meditated that afternoon, I could sense that someone was standing in the doorway between the kitchen and the family room I was sitting in. I opened my eyes and there he was, standing in the doorway. I said *Thomas*. He looked at me surprised. I said, *Yes I know your name is Thomas. I told you that I was going to stop by today to help you. Please leave my house and in three hours, I will come and explain everything to you. Now, please leave. I have to get ready.* He turned and without a word; he left.

As I pulled into Shelly's driveway that night, Stewie asked me what I wanted him to do. I told him to stay by Shelly's side and not to leave her alone for a minute. He was relieved that he didn't really have to do anything. As I walked in I could see Thomas through the basement walls standing near the corner. Shelly's house was a three level home. Thomas spent most of his time in the basement, and the women of the house spent most of their time upstairs.

I walked over to Shelly and asked her if she were able to forgive Thomas. She looked at me and said; "Who's Thomas?" I told her "That's the soul's name and please don't ask me how I know that…I just know it is." With tears in her eyes, she told me that yes; she did forgive him. It was the hardest thing she'd ever had to do, but she forgave him completely. I then explained to Shelly and Stewie what I was going to do.

I lit two white and two black candles. White candles move energy and black candles clean energy. At least, that is what Tina told me. I really didn't care if it were true or not.

I then prayed, thanking the Lord for His help and protection. I then asked the Lord to send an angel to help usher Thomas out of the house into the realm where he would receive the help he needed, then finishing my prayer with *Thy will be done. I love you and thank you for hearing me.*

At this point, I should probably tell you what a realm is. Ever since I was a small boy, my church has always celebrated what we call "The Service for the Departed." Three times a year, we pray for all the souls, no matter who they are or what they have done, no matter what condition they may find themselves in. It is not a séance where we try to communicate with the dead. We simply pray to God on their behalf and ask Him to extend to them grace and mercy, as He has done for us. We celebrate our three sacraments with them, Holy Baptism, Holy Sealing and Holy Communion.

When you die here on earth, you do not go to Heaven. You are taken by whatever spirit you served here on earth to a realm. That may be a good situation or it may be what some people have called Hell. I tell people, the easiest way to comprehend the realms is to think of the old saying, "Birds of a feather flock together." The murderers are with the murderers; the liars are with the liars; rapists are with the rapists and so on. If you would like to get a pretty good idea of what the realms of the departed are like, I would encourage you to rent the movie *What Dreams May Come*. I can tell you that it is almost accurate.

Everyone seems to think that when Jesus told the malefactor next to him on the cross, "Today, you will be with me in Paradise", that Jesus took him to Heaven. If all we have to do is ask for forgiveness and repent before we die to get to Heaven, then why would Jesus be coming back for a select few? Jesus took the malefactor to a realm in Eternity called Paradise. I ask you this question: where did Jesus go for three days after He died? Jesus, The Son of God, didn't even go to Heaven after He died. The Bible states in I Peter 3:18-20 (NKJV):

For Christ also suffered once for sins, the just for the unjust that He might bring us to God, being put to death in the flesh but made alive by the Spirit, by whom also He went and preached to the spirits in prison, who formerly were disobedient, when once the Divine longsuffering waited in the days of Noah, while the ark was being prepared, in which a few, that is, eight souls, were saved through water.

Why did He do that? When the people were about to drown, they repented with an open heart and their pleas registered at God's throne. Jesus' death ushered in a new era called the time of Grace. God sent His own Son to tell these souls that soon they would be redeemed. When Jesus arose from the dead three days later, He spoke to Mary Magdalene in the garden.

It states in John 20:17 (NKJV):

Jesus said to her, "Do not cling to me, for I have not yet ascended to My Father; but go to my brethren and say to them, 'I am ascending to My Father and your Father, and *to* My God and your God."

Not all of these realms are bad. Please, I don't want to give you the impression that all of them are horrible places. They are not. We actually know very little about them. All I do know is that they do exist.

Now, as I was praying, I could sense that an angel showed up and was standing on the front lawn. (Perhaps you are wondering what angels look like? I will tell you later on.) When I finished my prayer, I said: *Thomas, I know this all seems strange to you. I am not forcing you out of this house. I am asking you nicely to leave. You are going to have to trust me. I know you don't know me, but if you look outside, there is an angel standing there who when you are ready to leave will take you to a place where you will then get the help you need. I give you my word that if you go with him, in three weeks when my church has our special service, you will get the help you need. I promise you that Shelly, Stewie, and I will pray for you every day and bring offerings for you. Once more, I am not forcing you to leave. Please trust me.* I then lit the wheatgrass. Tina told me the wheatgrass removes harmful energy. I took the smoldering wheatgrass and walked by every wall, opened every closed door, every closet, every cabinet, every room in that house. Halfway through the house, I watched Thomas leave with the angel. Prior to his leaving, I was so scared that I felt as if I was going to jump out of my own skin. I kept praying quietly, *Lord, please help me. Please help me!*

I then lit the sweet grass. Which Tina had told me draws in good energy. I took the smoldering sweet grass and did the same thing with it as I had with the wheatgrass. I called Tina next and asked her what she felt. She then, in turn, asked me what I felt. (I hate when she does that.) When I finished talking to Tina, I walked over to Shelly and Stewie were and asked Shelly how she was. She asked me if he were gone. I told her yes. She then broke down crying. I have never seen someone cry as hard as she did. With tears streaming down her face, she said, "I can't believe it's finally over. For sixteen years, we have been in Hell. We asked the ministers for help, and it never worked. Now, God moves you, Jim, from Chicago and in less than an hour, it's all over." She then began to thank me, to which I stopped her and said, "Please don't thank me. I didn't do anything. Let's pray and thank our Heavenly Father," which we did. I then reminded Shelly and Stewie about our promise to Thomas, that we would pray for him and offer for him. They both agreed. I told Shelly that our rector, Rick, was coming the following weekend to hold service on Sunday and that he was planning on staying at my house Saturday night. At that time, I would share with him what had happened. As I drove Stewie home that night, he asked me if I had done that before. I told him no, it was the first time I had done anything like that. He was wondering if I were scared at any time, to which I told him, "Yes, every minute!"

As I shared everything with Rick on Saturday night, his eyes just kept getting bigger and bigger. I told him everything. I also asked him to pray for Thomas. He seemed to take everything I told him remarkably well. One week later, on a Monday night, my cell phone rang. It was Clark, the number two church leader for the area. He said, "I have warned you about your strange ideas." I said, "I don't know what you are talking about!" He said, "It has come to my attention that you are practicing esotericism. I am calling to tell you that you are no longer a representative of the church. You are no longer allowed to visit the members, and I am going to limit your time with the members because I won't let you hurt them! You are dealing with powers and principalities that you can't possibly understand, and I am warning you to be very careful about what you do from this point forward. I don't know what you think you did for Shelly, but time will tell. So, I am warning you once more to be very careful with your crazy ideas."

I listened quietly, almost dumbfounded by what I was heard. I replied, " You do not have the authority to tell me that I am no longer a representative of our church. I am a brother. I carry no ministry. Out of respect for the ministry that you carry, I will not go visiting anymore. I am *beyond* offended that you would think I would go out of my way to hurt God's children and that I would have anything to do with Satan!" To which he replied, "Well, maybe you didn't go out of your way to hurt God's children, but you are dealing with powers and principalities that you couldn't possibly understand." I said, "I am not dealing with any powers and principalities! You just don't understand what I did. By the way, *I* didn't do anything. The Lord God was the one who took care of this. You accuse me of practicing esotericism? Do you even know what that word means?"

Here you go folks, here's the definition according to Wikipedia, the open-source public encyclopedia:

Esotericism

Esotericism refers to the doctrines or practices of esoteric knowledge, or otherwise the quality or state of being described as esoteric, or obscure.

Here's the definition according to Merriam-Webster Dictionary;

Esoteric

Pronunciation: "e-s&-'ter-ik,

1a: designed for or understood by the specially initiated alone legal doctrine
1b: requiring or exhibiting knowledge that is restricted to a small group: difficult to understand.
2a: limited to a small circle
2b: PRIVATE, CONFIDENTIAL
3 : of special, rare, or unusual interest

Do you see anything there about worshipping Satan? Working for Satan? Nope. Me neither. But that was what he was implying. I said, "If you think lighting some candles and walking around with some smoldering weed had anything to do with what went on there, then your faith is weaker than I thought. I practice hardcore Christian. I prayed, offered, and used my faith! I think we need to call Phil." Phil was the number one church leader in the area and coincidentally my former sister-in-law Linda's brother-in-law. Like I was saying, "We need to call Phil and have the three of us sit down and talk about this." Clark then proceeded to tell me that he had spoken with Phil and Phil told him to call me. I said, "I'm going to call Phil anyway, and if you think I'm going to sit by quietly and let you smear my family name, I have news for you. I will not. Now do me a favor and call Shelly and tell her that what I did for her was wrong. Better yet, tell her that what the Lord did was wrong. Admit it, Clark. Your egos were bruised. God moves some nobody, without a ministry, 2200 miles to fix a problem that all of you couldn't, and you can't handle it. I would encourage you to call Phil so that we can all sit down and talk about this before this whole thing gets blown out of hand." He then told me just to do as he said.

I then called Phil and explained to him what Clark and I had just talked about. He told me that he was aware of everything and that he wasn't going to do anything about it at that time. I then pointed out the fact that I'd given his mother-in-law a healing and he didn't seem to think I was practicing esotericism at that time. I received no response from him. I continued to ask him to sit down with me so I could tell him what actually happened. He said not at this time; he would let me know when.

Then I called Shelly because she had invited, Peter and Stan me over for dinner that night to say thank you. I shared my conversations with her and told her that it would be better if I didn't come over. I didn't want them to find out and then think I was being defiant. She told me to get my butt over there for dinner because she had been killing herself all afternoon cooking, and it would not go to waste.

As we ate dinner, Shelly kept apologizing for getting me in trouble. I told her I didn't need her help to get into trouble; I had the gift of doing it all by myself. I reassured her that everything would work out in the end and that I had already forgiven Clark and Phil for what they were doing to me. I told her, "This is just a big misunderstanding, and we just need to put our trust in the Lord and it will all work out." Suddenly, my cell phone rang. It was Rick. I had left him a message to call me because I wanted to tell him what was going on. I told him everything. When I was done, I asked him how the leaders would have found out. I reminded him about the Bible text I read where we were told not to tell anyone but to keep it to ourselves. He then paused and said; "I couldn't sleep for three days. I called Clark and told him everything." I stood there in shock. I couldn't believe what I heard. I asked Rick why he hadn't called me. He said, "You were so arrogant when you were telling me everything." I was arrogant? I said, "How many times did I say that I didn't do anything? That everything that happened was due to the Lord. I never took credit for anything. Did you tell him that I prayed, offered and that the Lord sent an angel?" He said, "I told him what I could remember."

I asked him why he would do that to me. He then told me that he didn't want me to get into any trouble, but I should have included the church in this matter from the start. I told him I didn't include the church because if something went wrong, I didn't want anything to come back on the church. I said, "Do you actually think that I was working with Satan? Why would Satan work with me to help a soul leave someone's home?" Rick said, "Jim, in the short time I have known you, I would have to say, no, I don't believe that for one minute. But you have to understand something; we are not used to things like this happening in our area." I said, "Things like this? You have had a 'thing like this' in your area for over sixteen years. Do you have any idea how much Shelly has suffered because none of you knew what you were dealing with? One of your leaders told her that maybe God was punishing her for something she did. Are you guys out of your minds? The God I know, which I'm pretty sure is the same one out here, doesn't punish anyone."

I would like to point out that during this whole conversation I never yelled or even raised my voice. I did emphasize certain words and points I was trying to make. (Yes, I was surprised, too, at my own restraint.)

Near the end of our conversation, I made one final point. I said, "Rick, please ask yourself this question: why would God move some guy from Chicago who has no ministry and was able to do in one hour what four leaders were not able to do in over sixteen years? I think everyone's egos are bruised, and maybe God was trying to teach all of you a little humbleness. Because as everyone knows, accusing somebody of Satan worshipping is always the best way to rationalize something you can't understand or are afraid of." I said, "If anyone was serving Satan, it would be you guys." Rick said nothing. I told him that I had forgiven him for turning me in. He seemed surprised. I finished by saying, "When all of this blows over, the truth will be known, and the leaders will know that God was the one who did all of this, not Satan."

I kept praying every moment I had, asking God to help me. On Wednesday evening, I walked into church and the number three church leader, Parker, was there. Parker asked if he could have a word with me. I followed him into an office, and he closed the door behind me. He then said, "Jim, I hope we can all remain friends when this is all over." I said, "Parker, I have already forgiven all of you. Do you even know why you are here talking to me?" He got really quiet and said, "I understand that you were practicing esotericism." I said, "Do you even know what that word means?" He said he didn't, so I told him he should look up the definition because what I did had nothing to do with that. I then said, "Can you please do me a favor? When you talk to Clark, please tell him that I think he's really spineless for not coming this evening to talk to me and that he has a plenty of nerve sending you here without telling you why. Tell him that I am waiting for him to call me so that he, Phil, and I can sit down and clear this whole mess up." We shook hands, and I took my seat in the congregation and waited for the service to start.

At home after service that evening, my brother and Stan told me that Parker had pulled all of the ministers into the office after I had left to announce that I, Jim, was "practicing esotericism" and was no longer allowed to go visiting, and they should all limit their time with me. My brother said, "You should have seen all of their faces. All of them said there is no way that Jim would be involved with anything like that!" That kind of made me happy. I said, "You have to be joking!" They told me that they weren't. My brother then told me that he pulled Parker aside after everyone had left and asked him if he knew the definition of esotericism, to which he also responded to Peter that he didn't actually know. My brother encouraged him to have Phil and Clark sit down with me to clear the whole mess up. He said he would try. After speaking with my brother, I called Rick and shared all of this with him. I said, "Clark took something that was between him and me and made it very public. If you think I'm going to let him spread rumors and lies about me throughout this entire area, I have news for you. If anyone asks me what happened, I will tell them the truth. When I am done, the only one that will look like a fool will be Clark. Please Rick, call Clark and ask him to sit down with me, so we can fix this."

I have a saying that I like to use when I know something is not going to happen for a long time. Ready? "I guess I will just hold my breath until I pass out and hope I hit my head on something, so the time goes by faster." Rick never called me back.

I went to my bedroom and knelt down and prayed out loud. "Dear Father, you know what's going on here. I don't understand why you are doing this to me. My own church, which I have been a member of my whole life, is accusing me of working with Satan. I feel as if I am about to lose my mind." As I prayed, I was crying so hard that the bedspread in front of me was soaking wet. At times, I cried so hard that I couldn't even find words to say. I continued praying, "I don't even know what to ask you for, but you are going to have to do something for me. I can't take much more of this! Please help me, Father! Please!"

Chapter 4

Phase 1

When I woke up in the morning, the house was empty. Stan and Peter had already gone to work. I decided to meditate to see if I couldn't get rid of everything that I was feeling. As I sat in the family room, I started to take deep breaths and focused all of my attention on going into the center of my mind. As I entered the center of my mind, I found myself floating on a wooden raft drifting down a stream. It was very peaceful. I looked around me; there were hundreds of thousands of people standing on either side of the banks of the river, and they were cheering as I drifted by. As I passed, I noticed that some were my family, friends, and members from my church. I also noticed that all of them were people who had died. I slowly drifted downstream, asking myself what this all meant.

As I turned to my left, I saw an angel standing there. He looked at me and said, *"Jim, you have done nothing wrong. God has been waiting for you to come to this area so that He may implement His plan for you. You have a very special place in His heart, and I have been sent here to protect you. No one can harm you."* I fell on my hands and knees and began to cry intensely. He then said, *"Very few people reach the level of faith that you have reached. God loves you very much, and He sent me here to protect you. He has chosen you and has a plan for you. What I will tell you now is just the tip of the iceberg. In time, the Lord will reveal more to you. If you look around you, all of these people support you and know you. But what's more amazing than that, is that He knows you and supports you."* The angel pointed to the sky and continued, *"Before time began, for millennia, God chose you for this task. He has been waiting for you to come here. And now is the time."*

I looked up at him and said, *"You've got the wrong guy."* The angel said, *"No, He doesn't."* I said, *"Yes, He does. You've got the wrong guy. I sin so much. Here are some of the things that I do."* I started to list all of them off. He said, *"God knows all of your sins and He has forgiven you."* He said, *"Jim, when you gave Him your free will and told Him that you trusted him no matter what, you found a very special place in God's heart."* I said, *"This is too much you've got the wrong guy!"* I started listing off other wrong things that I had done. The angel said, *"It doesn't matter to Him. He has forgiven you. God wanted me to tell you that he will return to you tenfold what he has taken from you."* I said, *"I don't want anything from Him. I would like Him just to take me now."* He said, *"It is because you expect nothing from Him that He will give you back everything tenfold."* I stood up and walked over to the angel and said, *"This is too overwhelming for me. I need a hug."* (Yes, I honestly did that! You need to know, I am not a small person. I am six feet five inches tall, and I weigh 255 pounds. I look like a linebacker.) I wrapped my arms around the angel, and we just stood there. He graciously patted me on the back, kind of as if I was a diseased nuisance. Now, just to give you an idea of how tall he was, my head was in the center of *his* chest! He had to be nine or ten feet tall. After a few moments, I let go of him and stepped back. I felt like I was a little child looking up at his huge father. I stared at him; there was something truly commanding about him. He exuded authority and seemed very regal.

Do you remember that I was going to tell you what angels look like? This one had blond hair that fell over his ears and hung down to the back of his neck, just above his shoulders. He had a chiseled face, with the bluest eyes I have ever seen. Hey, I am secure enough in myself to say that this angel was exceedingly handsome. He looked like that action figure He-Man, Master of the Universe. He wore an armored breastplate that seemed to be solid gold. He had the coolest sword I have ever seen. The handle was encrusted with all kinds of jewels. The blade was like polished titanium. He wore a shield behind him. It looked like it was about five feet around and appeared to be a solid piece of transparent glass, with gold markings on the surface near the edges. He wore what looked like beige pants with no seams or pockets. The pants were tucked into a set of boots. I looked at him and asked his name. He said, "My name is Michael." I said, **"YOU ARE THE ARCHANGEL MICHAEL?!"** I fell down on my hands and knees again. He said, *"Yes, I am God's General, and I have been sent here to protect you, NO ONE can harm you."* I said, **"I am telling you, you've got the wrong guy. I can't do this!"**

He said, *"Kneel down in front of me. God has a blessing for you."* I knelt down in front of him, and as he put his hand on my head I could feel a rush of energy fill my body as he said, *"Receive your blessing from the Living God! He gives you strength, courage, and wisdom beyond your years. He removes from you all fear. He opens your eyes to see everything around you. He fills your heart with understanding and will share with you the mysteries of Heaven. You will fear no evil. He binds your heart to His and makes this covenant with you that He will always be with you and you are never alone. Receive the peace of his Son, Jesus Christ! It fills your heart, body, mind and soul. Jesus, too, makes a covenant with you that He will always be there for you! Receive the blessing of the Holy Spirit he will be your counselor and your guide. May you know from this day forward that you are loved deeply by God and His Son."*

While all of this was happening, I was still fully aware that I was sitting in the family room meditating. I make this point so no one thinks that I was dreaming or hallucinating. I stood up and he told me that the plan that the Lord had for me would affect the United States first, and then it would sweep across the whole world. At this time, he didn't give me any information. All he told me was, in time, the Lord would explain things to me, and that I should just continue to trust Him. He spoke of a meeting that was coming up in the next few weeks and that I shouldn't worry; the Lord would put the words that I should say into my mouth.

I looked at Michael and said, one more time, *"You've got the wrong guy. I can't do this!"* He said, *"Kneel down once more. The Lord will give you another blessing."* I knelt down in front of him, and then he put his hand on the top of my head. As he gave me another blessing from the Lord, I could feel even more energy surging through my body. Michael then stressed once more to me that he would be by my side to protect me and that I had no reason to fear anything.

I opened my eyes to see the clock sitting on the bookcase in front of me. Michael and I talked for almost an hour. I fell on my knees and began to pray, thanking the Lord for His blessings, protection, and help. I asked Him once more if He actually had the right guy. I told Him that I would not fail Him and that I still trusted Him.

I got up, and as I walked into the kitchen, I could feel Michael walking behind me. I turned to look at him, and he just nodded at me. As I poured myself a cup of coffee, suddenly it was as if I were watching a movie. I saw Michael, with his back to me, standing in front of a set of steps. There was a blurry figure of an extraordinarily large man sitting on a throne, and to Michael's right was another blurry figure of an unusually tall man dressed in a white robe. I couldn't hear what they were saying. I just knew they were talking. I suddenly realized that they were talking about me! I got weak in the knees and had to grab the counter to hold myself up as I began to cry. Michael came up behind me and said, *"You just witnessed the conversation I had with God and Jesus. We were discussing how I would contact you so that I wouldn't scare you. That is why God had you learn how to meditate and go through the training you went through in Chicago."* I just stood there while I tried to absorb what he just told me.

I called my parents back in Chicago and asked Dad if he would lend me the money to get an airline ticket so that I could fly home for a week.

He of course asked why. I said, "Pop, please get Mom on the phone, and I will tell you." As I told them everything, they both listened quietly and said nothing until I was finished. My dad said, "Do you have a pen, son? Here's my credit card number. Book your flight and rent a car so you will have the freedom to visit whoever you need to while you are here." I, of course, thanked my dad.

I asked my mom if she were okay. She said, "I don't know, Jim, if I ever told you this. We never planned on having you. You just showed up one day without any notice. Your dad was even surprised when I told him that I was pregnant again. I have to tell you that from that day on I always said to God, *You must have a plan for this little one I'm carrying.* I'm not surprised at all. When are you planning on coming?" I said, "I will be in on Monday." That whole day, I was kind of in a daze as I tried to get my head around everything I had experienced that morning.

My brother came home from work in the evening and he found me sitting at the kitchen table. He walked in and said, "Oh crap! What's the matter?" I said, "Have a seat, I need to tell you something." As I shared everything with Peter, tears welled up in his eyes. At one point, I looked at him and said, "Do you believe me?" He said, "Yes, your imagination is not *that* creative!" As we both sat there with tears running down our faces, my incredibly astute brother asked me a question: "Is Michael wearing one of those gladiator-type skirts or is he wearing pants?" I said, "Out of everything I shared with you, *that's* the question you ask? He's wearing pants! Man, are you a bonehead!" We both laughed for what seemed like ten minutes. We both got up and hugged each other. He asked me what I was going to do. I told him I was flying home for a week so that I could spend time with the family and share this with them. He told me that he would pray even harder for me, and I thanked him.

Later that evening, I went to Shelly's house and shared everything with her. When I finished, I asked her if she believed me. She said, "Yes. I can see it in your eyes, and I can feel the emotion in your voice. Why did you share this with me? I am honored that you did." I told her that I could feel that she was beating herself up over the fact that she thought she got me in trouble. I told her because I didn't want her to feel guilty about anything that had happened. From that point on, Shelly and I were extremely close friends.

Later that night, I tried to sleep but I just couldn't. I found myself driving around town talking to the Lord. I was still not accepting any of this and continued to tell him, "You've got the wrong guy." Around 2:30 a.m., I found myself still driving. I had the radio on very low when an unfamiliar song came on. I've since learned that the song is "Here I Am" by the Christian artist Rebecca St. James. Intrigued by the very pretty piano part at the beginning, I turned it up. Here is what I heard:

> **God asks the question, "Whom shall I send?" Now, what will we answer?**
> **Will we go and do as He says? All that He wants is a heart, ready, willing and waiting.**
> **Here I am, I surrender my life to the use of your plan. Here I am. I will do as you say; I will go where you send. Here I am.**

I had to pull over to the side of the road because I was crying so hard that I couldn't see anymore. I just sat there still exclaiming to the Lord, *"You've got the wrong guy!"*

I drove down to the bay and parked. As I got out of the car, another angel appeared. Michael told me that the new angel would protect my car while I took a walk. I thought to myself, *No way. That's pretty cool*. As I walked I tried really hard to accept all of this. I kept thinking to myself, *this is nuts, this kind of stuff happens in the Bible; not now, not today. This is the twenty-first century!* I walked for almost an hour, then suddenly stopped, right where I was and shouted; "Fine, I'll do it, but I'm going to need another blessing!" Out of nowhere, a stern voice said, *"**You have plenty. Now just do it!**"* I was pretty sure that was God Himself enlightening me.

As I walked back to my car, I felt like a little kid who'd just been reprimanded so I began to pout! I thought to myself, *Fine, okay, yeah. He didn't have to talk to me like I'm some little kid; I just wanted another blessing. No, No. I'm fine! I'm going to do this for You. No, I'll be fine, really!*

When I got back to my car, there was the other angel, standing guard. I tell you; I have never felt so safe in my life. I got in and felt Michael sitting behind me. There was a long silence where I wasn't thinking anything. So I would occasionally look to see if Michael were actually there. After a while, I said, *"Michael, you look bored."* He said, *"I am fine."* I said, *"Would you like a video game or something to keep yourself busy?"* I was just trying to make a joke and lighten things up a bit. He leaned forward and put his hand on my shoulder and said, *"Jim, I have plenty to keep me busy; I am watching you."* I said, *"I really appreciate it Michael."* He said, *"Do not thank me; thank God."* By the time we got home, it was almost four o'clock in the morning. Good thing I was unemployed at the time. I slept in.

On Monday, I flew into Chicago. I had made plans to stay with my parents, Ann, and Ellen while I was in for the week. As I drove to Ellen's house, I realized that I had left Chicago almost four months before, and it felt weird to be back. It was good to see Ellen, Fred, my nephew James, and my niece Sydney. When I finished telling Ellen and Fred everything, Fred, who was a priest in our church, assured me that he would pray even harder for me; Ellen did, too. I stayed a few days with them and just relaxed.

I called Tina and asked if we were still going to Chicago to get healings. We made our plans and drove in together. On the way into the city, I shared everything with Tina. She looked at me while I was still telling her things and said, "This task the Supreme Being is using you for is huge! I can see that it will start on the west coast of the United States and spread across all the way to the east coast. After that, it will spread around the world." She then said, "Jim, you are under the impression that Michael is here protecting you from your Church. There is someone else that is fully aware of you and what God's plans are. You have never really given him a second thought your whole life." I looked at her, puzzled. She said, "What about Satan! Michael is also protecting you from him." I smiled and said, "You're right. I have never really been afraid of him. I doubt he will even care about me." She said, "Do not underestimate him. I can see in the future that he is filled with rage against you." I said, "As long as I have God, Jesus, the Holy Spirit, and Michael keeping an eye on me, I really don't have anything to worry about." As we walked into the room where the healings were taking place, I saw a lot of my old classmates from my training days. One of them ran up to me and said, "We heard you helped a soul to move on." I told her it was very exciting; that was putting it mildly. When it came time for my healing, one of the students who Saleena was mentoring asked if she could do my healing. As I sat in the chair, I wondered if the student would see Michael. The whole time I was there, I caught Saleena always looking at me, trying to figure out what was going on with me. At one point, she asked the student to come near her. The two of them whispered something to themselves, and the student walked back. She said, "Saleena asked me to try a special kind of healing energy on you." I thought to myself, *Okay. Whatever.*

As Tina and I drove home, I asked her if she thought anyone saw Michael. She told me that while I was receiving my healing she could see him hiding from them. She then told me that Michael is never more than a few feet away from me at a time. I told her that I could feel him near me all the time. Tina asked me if I wanted to come in and talk with her and one of her friends, Christine, whom I knew very well. Tina asked me to share everything with Christine because she told me I could trust her. So I did.

Later, as the evening was winding down, I sat and listened to Christine tell me about what she had been doing for the past few months. All of a sudden, Michael walked up behind me and shoved my shoulder forward, and said, *"We have to go, NOW!"* I clairvoyantly said; *"I can't leave right now; we are talking."* He said, *"We have to leave NOW!"* I said, *"It would be very rude of me to get up in the middle of the conversation and leave. I can't leave now."* He turned, and with his back to me grabbed his shield and pulled out his sword as three other angels appeared. They formed a circle surrounding us, as Michael said, *"Fine! Then we will stand our ground here!"*

The whole time this was going on, Christine just kept on talking, not knowing that anything was about to happen. I could feel something huge was coming our way. It was a particularly strange energy that I had never felt before. Michael and the other three angels closed in around us as Michael said, *"Nothing is getting through!"* I sat facing Christine. Never once did I let on that we were about to be attacked by something with my trustworthy angel close by my side the whole time. I could hear strange noises coming closer to us, and then everything went quiet. Michael stepped one foot forward as the other three once more closed in around us. Michael yelled out, *"Not today!"* The next thing I felt was Michael's hand on my shoulder as he said, *"Jim, we need to go."* I calmly ended my conversation with Christine, gave Tina a hug, and walked to the car. As I climbed into the driver's side, Michael sat behind me again. He said nothing. I could tell he was irritated with me. Before I could even draw in a breath to say something, he spoke, *"The next time I tell you to do something, you do it! This is not a game we are playing; this is real, real danger!"* I said, "Michael, you need to cut me a little slack, here. This is all kind of new to me. I apologize for upsetting you. The next time you tell me to do something, I will. Hey, what was happening anyway?" He looked up at me and said, *"Your friend, Tina, reminded you that Satan is aware of God's plan for you. Satan sent a small army to destroy you. All you saw were the four of us. What you did not see was the legion of angels God sent standing between you and them! Can you now understand how important you are to God?"* I just sat there frozen and as a chill ran up my spine. I said nothing.

Perhaps you are wondering how many soldiers make up a legion. It's anywhere from 4,200 to 5,500 soldiers. As I read that, on the Internet, I couldn't believe it was that many.

Out of the blue I received a phone call from Trish. She told me that she had heard I was in Chicago for a visit. She was thinking about me, so she decided to call and say hi. I told her that things were kind of complicated. She told me she had time if I was willing to share it with her. I told her everything. When I finished she said, "You are not the same person I married. I will pray even harder for you. Please keep me in the loop. I want to know what's going on with you." I thanked her for her prayers and told her I would call her and let her know as things happened.

As the days went by, I stopped in on my best friend Quentin and his wife Ann and their two boys, Chill (a nickname) and Nathan. I also shared everything with them. As they sat there absorbing everything I had told them, Quentin said, "Please, don't get me wrong. I believe you, Jimmy, but I don't really think this is going to affect the whole United States and then the world." Quentin has always been a little skeptical. Ann leaned forward and patted my knee while she said, "I think it will, Jimmy." I smiled at both of them and said, "Time will tell."

As I was driving to church on the Sunday morning before I was to leave, I thought to myself quietly, *I know that I am protected from Satan's forces, and he can't touch me, but what about my family and friends?* As I drove more, it was as if I were watching a movie; there right in front of my eyes appeared my family. One by one, I could see each one of my family members and my closest friends exactly where they were at that moment in time.

Standing behind each of them was an angel watching over them. I started to cry as I thanked the Lord once more for His love and kindness.

When I got to church, it was another heartfelt service, which was something that I missed and needed. My short trip was over, and I was headed back to my home on the west coast. I said my goodbyes to my family and assured them they would all be safe. The next day I boarded the plane.

As the plane landed, Michael turned to me and said, *"Satan knows you are back."* I said, *"Okay."* That's all he said to me, nothing else. As I came in the house, my brother and I embraced. Peter and Stan wanted to know how my trip went, so I told them. They were just as amazed as I was. They told me that the rumors had already started and that the members that knew me were standing by my side. They all thought Clark has blown the thing way out of proportion. Peter said, "Shelly asked that when you have a minute to please call her."

As I talked with Shelly, I could tell that something wasn't right. I asked her what had happened while I was gone. She told me that Clark pulled her aside and was questioning her about everything. She told me that she was so nervous because she didn't want me to get into any more trouble. I asked her what she told him. She said, "I told him the truth." She told me that the whole time he talked with her he kept trying to convince her that I was a dreadful, evil person. She said, "At one point, I had finally had enough. I looked Clark straight in the eyes and said, 'You've got a lot of nerve! I asked you and the other ministers for help, and it only got worse. You even told me that God was punishing me! Do you have any idea how much that hurt me? And now you want me to agree with you and help you persecute my friend Jim! He's the only one that could help me! I will not help you hurt Jim in any way!'" Folks, if you knew anything about Shelly, you would know that she is not someone who usually would stand up for herself! I thanked her for defending me, and told her once more the only thing we can do is trust in the Lord.

The following Saturday, I was sitting on the back patio; for February, it was a remarkably pleasant 70 degrees. I was extremely lonely and started to feel sorry for myself that I had no woman in my life. So I began to pray, I said, *"Father, I am not looking to get laid or even need to be that intimate with any woman right now. I just wish there was someone I could kiss or hold or just be close to. Please tell me that I'm not going to be alone the rest of my life. You know me, Father, please I don't want to be alone."*

Suddenly a living, moving picture appeared in front of my eyes. There I was, standing on the top of a hill, dressed in a black suit, with a white shirt and a black tie, which is what all of the active ministers wear in my church. Behind me were thousands of people smiling and standing in support of me. Next to me was an incredibly beautiful woman in her late twenties or early thirties. She had brunette hair that hung past her shoulders, the most incredible eyes with the sweetest face. She was gorgeous. She was about five feet six inches tall with a very shapely figure. Next to her were two young boys. As I stared at this picture, she reached up, pulled my face toward hers, and kissed me on the cheek. She then held my hand as these two young boys ran over to me and hugged me.

As I sat there staring at this picture, I said to the Lord, *"Is this my wife and children? I have no idea who she is. Father, thank you for answering my prayer. I have a question. When will I meet her? When will all this happen?"* I was never given an answer. To this day if I concentrate, I can still see my family standing by my side. There had been times in my life when I wished the Lord didn't show me all of this. It is extremely hard waiting to meet someone that you have seen and have no idea who she is. I am still patiently waiting to meet her.

Three weeks had now almost passed by. I had told the soul, Thomas, there would be a special service around this time, and it was only a few days away. I had continued to pray and offer for him over the past weeks. I also thought about a few more groups I would pray for: those who were hunted down in witch hunts, those who were persecuted because of their faith, those who felt they were utterly alone, those who were in the deepest darkest realms where no light reached them, and those who felt they were forgotten. Because I could feel for these souls' situations, I prayed extremely hard for all of them to find grace.

On March 7, 2004, we were all assembled in a big hall for the service. I decided that I should run to the bathroom before the service started. As I walked back up the stairs, I passed Linda's dad, the father of my former sister-in-law. He turned to me as I passed by him and said; "You'll be getting what's coming to you, Satan worshipper!" I was stunned. I thought, *"Satan you are going to have to do better than that if you think I'm going to let you rob me of my peace!"*

While I was standing during the congregation hymn, I felt someone walk up behind me and put his hand on my shoulder. It was Thomas; he just wanted me to know that he was there and thanked me for my prayers. As we continued to sing tears rolled down my face. (If you haven't figured me out yet, I'm an emotional kind of guy! I'd like to see anyone of you go through all of this without crying! Any takers?)

During the service, I closed my eyes and got into the center of my mind. As I looked around the auditorium, I almost couldn't believe what I was seeing! Everywhere I looked there were hundreds of souls from all walks of life listening to the service! I was thoroughly overwhelmed by what I saw. I had always heard about this growing up. But seeing it, witnessing it for the first time, was completely amazing to me.

As I looked around, I could see some of the groups I had been praying for. They were dressed in the clothing styles of their time periods. Those who were from the witch hunts looked like pilgrims. Those who were persecuted for their faith looked as they were from ancient Roman times. The ones who were from the deepest darkest realms were completely draped with dark cloaks. I couldn't see their faces.

As with every Service for the Departed, the departed souls are given the opportunity to be baptized and sealed with the Holy Spirit. Then Holy Communion is celebrated with them. To accomplish this, two ministers are selected to be the proxies for the departed. The district apostle invited all those who had the desire to be baptized to come forth. As I watched, hundreds of thousands of souls stepped forward. After the district apostle consecrated the water in the Triune name of God, he dipped his finger in the challis while he prayed asking to releasing all of the souls, in the Triune name of God, from any curse they may have had on them, then he drew a cross on both of the foreheads of the two proxies. Suddenly, I heard chains and shackles crashing to the floor. On every soul's forehead, there appeared a watermark shaped like a cross.

The district apostle then invited all those souls who had the desire to receive the Holy Spirit; which we call Holy Sealing. Once more, thousands of souls came forward. There were small children, babies, young, and old. The two ministers stepped forward as the district apostle placed his hands on their foreheads and prayed aloud, "All those who seek grace receive the life of the Holy Spirit, in the name of God the Father, the Son, and the Holy Spirit." Suddenly there appeared on every soul's forehead a cross of fire!

He continued to pray, "You are no longer a friend of God; you are now children of God. Your names are now written in the Lamb's Book of Life. This new name of yours is known only by God. May our Heavenly Father bless you on this your special day!" The District Apostle then invited all the souls who had the desire to celebrate Holy Communion. Again thousands came forward. The two proxies held out their hands and as the district apostle placed the Communion wafers in the palms of their hands he said, "The body and blood of Jesus given for you." As the two proxies put the wafers in their mouths, I watched as all of the eyes of every soul began to shine brighter. Yes, tears were rolling down my face once again. To see these things firsthand was truly wonderful. I felt that I was truly blessed for witnessing all of this.

The following week while I was sitting and thinking about the injustice and persecution I was being put through, I became extremely sad. I thought to myself, *maybe I should call Tina and ask if she can see anything in the future to tell me how long I'm going to have to suffer through this.* Out of nowhere I heard a very quiet voice filled with disappointment say, *"Why will you not just trust in me?"* For the first time in my life, I could actually feel how much I had hurt my Heavenly Father's heart. I sat and wept bitterly for a while. I apologized to Him and asked Him to please forgive me. I told Him that I did trust Him, and I would wait quietly for His help.

On Friday, I received a phone call from Clark. He asked if I would meet with Phil and him Sunday after the service. I said, only if you let Rick join us, too. There was no way I was going to sit down with those two without having someone neutral there to hear both sides. Clark agreed and a time was set. I immediately fell on my hands and knees, thanking God for his help.

It was Saturday evening, and I was home alone. John and Stan had plans, and I honestly wasn't in the mood to go with them. I tried my best to stop thinking about the meeting planned for the next day, but I just couldn't leave it alone. I decided to pray. I knelt down in the family room and began to pray. I was extremely nervous about everything. As I continued to pray, I heard the floorboards in the kitchen begin to squeak as if someone were walking on them. I kept praying. Then I heard the steps that lead down into the family room creak. I prayed out loud, "Lord, if this is a soul looking for help, I'm really not in the mood to help anybody." Suddenly Michael said, *"It is not a soul. It is Satan."* I stopped praying and sat up on the backs of my legs. There he was standing in the doorway, smiling at me. As he pointed at me, he said nothing. Michael stepped between Satan and me. He crossed his arms as if to say, "Just try it!"

Would you like to know what Satan looked like? He was as tall as Michael, nine feet tall. He had jet-black hair and a goatee. He had a pale complexion. His eyes are kind of hard to explain. There wasn't actually any color in them. They were just filled with darkness. I guess black is a color. So his eyes are black! I could now see why he was called the Angel of Light. He was remarkably handsome. He had chiseled facial features. He seemed terribly debonair, slick, and arrogant. He, too, was wearing armor. It was totally black, from head to toe. He wore a black cloak draped off his shoulders. He had no weapons on him that I could see, which I thought was particularly strange.

He just glared at me as he stood in the doorway with his hands supported above the doorframe, arms above his head as he leaned into the room. I looked at him and said, *"You have got a lot of nerve coming into my house. Get out of my house, now! In the name of Jesus Christ, I command you to leave!"* Two angels appeared on each side of him. They also said nothing as they made the motion to him while pointing outside, as if to say, "You can leave now, or we will drag you out!" Michael never moved. He was always between Satan and me the entire time. What I think surprised me the most was that I wasn't afraid of Satan at all. Yep, I know that sounds crazy, but I'm telling you how I honestly felt.

Once Satan had left, I continued to pray. I said, *"Okay, Lord, I get it! Satan could be standing six feet away from me and he couldn't touch me, so why should I be nervous about the meeting tomorrow? I know you will be with me. Thanks for opening my eyes to see all of this and please know that I love you more than I can express, Amen!"*

It was now Sunday afternoon and the meeting place was to be somewhere neutral. We ended up going to a Mexican restaurant. As Phil, Clark, Rick, and I made small talk, the waitress took our drink order. It seemed to be a very laid-back setting. I decided to start the meeting off by saying, "If you are expecting an apology you will not get one. The first thing I would like to point out was that this *thing* was not a spirit, it was a soul, and his name is Thomas. If I can impress one thing upon you, it would be that I didn't do anything. The Lord did it all. I think you guys are upset because the Lord had some guy with no ministry come from 2,200 miles away to fix a problem that has been here for a very long time. Perhaps your egos were bruised? Maybe you seem to think that your ministries make you better than everyone else?"

Clark spoke up, "Jim, we don't think we are better than anyone else. We are just not used to someone coming here and doing what you did. We are old-fashioned out here. Why didn't you involve us?" I said, "I don't think you are old-fashioned. I think you were afraid. That's why you treated me this way. I didn't involve you because of the Bible text I read." I looked at Rick and said, "You remember, right?" He said, "Yes, I do." Rick then shared the text with Phil and Clark. Phil spoke up and said, "Well, maybe you interpreted the text wrong." I said, "No, it was very simple to understand. This is the way the Lord wanted it."

Clark said, "You are a very persuasive guy. That's what makes us nervous. You brought strange ideas, like energy healings, meditation, and that book *You Can Heal Your Life*." And kept telling the members about this, after I warned you not to."

I said, "When did it become your responsibility to censor what people do and read in the privacy of their own homes?" Clark said, "The day I accepted this ministry is the day these members became my responsibility! The Holy Spirit did not write the books you were telling people about. I said, "Do your children attend public school?" He looked at me and said, with a sarcastic tone, "Yes, Jim, what's your point?" I said, "You better pull your children out of school, because I know for a fact that none of the books that are being read in their classes were written by the Holy Spirit!" He said, "Now, you're being ridiculous!" I said, "No Clark, you are! Is your faith that weak that you felt threatened by this book? This book was about thinking positive and changing your life. Nothing else."

We went round and round on this for about twenty minutes. I then said, "When you can't understand something that's different, do you automatically assume that Satan must be involved? I thought the witch hunts died in Salem, but here we are. Is it too hard for you to wrap your head around the idea that God gives people certain gifts to help in His work? Where I come from, there are numerous people that have gifts like me. My older sister has had a gift since she was nine years old. My grandmother on my mom's side had a gift. Almost all of the women on my mom's side of the family going back six generations had a gift. I am the first male in my family to have a gift. Why would Satan step in and help someone? You were all afraid. Where was your faith? Why didn't you just ask me to explain what happened? Hey, Phil, when I gave your mother-in-law two healings, you didn't seem to object."

Phil said, "That was different." I said "Oh, because Satan wasn't involved! Do you three guys have any idea how offensive that was to me that I would be involved with Satan in someway? I can't stand him! Why didn't you use some common sense? If I were a Satan worshipper, then why would I care about what you thought of me? Why would I still go to church? I love God! I serve only Him!" At this point, I was seriously ticked off. I felt like I should just lay into all of them. I could have sworn there were occasions when Michael walked up behind me and put his hand over my mouth, because at times I would just sit there and say nothing. Oh, don't get me wrong. I had plenty I was going to say. I just felt as if I shouldn't.

As the meeting went on, they started to mock me. I threw it back into their faces. The Lord seemed to give me every answer I ever needed at the right time, every time. There were times where I would defend myself, and when I was done, they would just sit there with nothing to come back at me with. I then told them that all I wanted to do was to help out in the congregation. I told all three of them that what had occurred was a new experience for me. I had never done anything like that before and I probably never would do it again. I told them, "Just tell me what you want me to do, and I'll do it. This church means everything to me. I just want to help!

Phil put his hand on my arm and said, "I just need to know that you will support us. That if I ask something of you, you will just do it." I said, "Tell me what you want me to do, and I'll do it." He looked at Rick and said, "Put Jim back on the visiting list, so he can go visiting again." I said, "I don't know about you guys, but my prayer life and faith really have increased during this time." They all agreed that theirs had too. We all hugged each other and parted friends.

Later that evening when I got home, I called Shelly to tell her about the meeting. During our conversation, all of a sudden I felt a cold breeze on my back, like someone opened up a window. I turned to see what was happening. In an instant, Michael was gone. Shelly said, "What's the matter? You stopped talking." I said, "Michael just left; no goodbye, no see ya later, nothing. He's gone, and now I feel different. I guess I got used to him always being around me. I'm going to miss him." As I sat there for a minute, I realized why the Lord put me through hell back in Chicago with the ministers and why I never found a job. I told Shelly what I was thinking and explained to her that I felt the Lord hardened the hearts of the leaders towards me because if they had reinstated me back in my office or if I had found a job, I would have never moved to the west coast. It all made sense now. I told her that I had forgiven all the leaders in Chicago and on the west coast for what they did to me. Folks, there is no such thing as a perfect church. I don't care what religion you belong to. We are all human, and we all make mistakes. You show me a perfect church, and I'll show you a cult!

I finished my conversation with Shelly, and then I prayed and thanked the Lord for opening my eyes and helping me through those tough times. I thought to myself *I hope this is the hardest thing I would ever have to go through.* I had no idea what lay ahead.

# Chapter 5

Lana

Over the next month, I went on many interviews with no luck. Finally, in the middle of April after a second interview, I was offered a job as a buyer with a small family-owned flooring company. And wouldn't you know it, the pay wasn't half bad either.

Now, while I was dealing with my "persecution," my brother was still going through his divorce. There was a woman named Claire and her daughter, Lana, in our congregation. I found out through some of our friends in church that Claire liked my brother. She knew of him and didn't care that he was going through a divorce at the time. So, I told my brother. Soon, the two of them were dating on a regular basis. Now, because they were dating, I would cook dinner and my brother would invite Claire and her daughter to join us.

I have a little culinary background. I took some classes at the Art Institute downtown for a while because I enjoyed cooking. It was only after I added up what one year of culinary school was going to cost me that I came to my senses. Mind you, I was just doing this as a hobby, not a career. It would have cost me close to $15,000.00. So I dropped out. My teacher was extremely disappointed when I told him I was leaving. He told me that I would have made an excellent chef.

Here is where my story gets a little sticky. Claire and Lana became regular dinner guests, and soon I could tell that Lana was interested in me. She would compliment me all the time on my appearance. She would tell me that she thought I was hot. I would also respond to her in the same way. I thought she was very cute. So you're thinking to yourself, *Jim, why didn't you go out with Lana?* Folks, Lana was eighteen years old at the time. She would tell me that she wished I were ten years younger. I would say, "I wish you were ten years older." You see at the time; I was thirty-seven years old. Oh, I know what you're thinking. You can stop it now. I'll have you know that there are sixteen and a half years between my parents. My dad was forty years old when he married my mom, who was twenty-three. Neither had been married before. I am happy to tell you that they are still married to this day. So this wasn't that hard of a stretch for me.

As time went by, Lana and I found that we were both really attracted to each other. I kept telling her that it would never work out. The day came when my brother told me that he had broken up with Claire. She was too controlling, and I'll just leave it at that. Claire took it exceedingly hard. Here's a little history on Claire and Lana. Claire got pregnant with Lana and told the biological father that she didn't need to get married. Lana's dad would get to visit her every now and then. Claire was a single mom. The whole time Claire was raising Lana she never actually dated, never really had a relationship, and was never married. So you can see why Claire took the breakup pretty hard. One evening, Claire called me and asked me to have dinner with her. She needed to talk to someone about Peter, so we met.

During dinner, I tried to stay as neutral as I could. I almost choked on my dinner when she asked me if I knew what the saying "friends with benefits" meant. I told her, "Yes, I do, I'm flattered, but I'm not that kind of guy. I would have to be in a relationship before I would even consider being intimate with a woman." She told me she understood. I told her that there was actually nothing I could do for her and Peter except to pray. She said thanks.

The following weekend Rick invited our whole congregation out to his house to show everyone the new church building that had just been built in his area. Wouldn't you know it; Claire and Lana asked if they could drive with me. As we drove out to Rick's house, Claire sat in the passenger seat and Lana sat behind her mom. Seems pretty innocent, right? While I was talking with Claire, I had my arm on the center console armrest. Lana asked if she could take her shoes off, so that she could get more comfortable in the back. No big deal, right? Well, Lana placed her foot next to my arm and started to rub her toe against the inside of my arm. I started getting goose pimples while she was doing that to me. Her mother kept right on talking to me because she couldn't see what was going on. I kept looking in my rearview mirror at Lana as she would lift one eyebrow and smile at me. She drove me crazy!

As soon as Lana fell asleep in the back seat, Claire propositioned me again. I was completely blown away. I told her once more that I was flattered but not interested. We spent most of the evening just hanging out with the other members that came in for the weekend. Lana was always an arm's length away from me. At one point, Rick's wife pulled me aside and mentioned that it was pretty obvious that Lana had a giant crush on me and that I had better be careful. I assured her that I was aware of the situation, and I was handling it. Well, kind of handling it.

I was invited to stay with Rick and his family, so I drove Claire and Lana to their hotel. Claire seemed unusually cold towards me, and being clairvoyant, I could feel something was coming, and it wouldn't be pleasant. As they both got out of my car, Claire told Lana to go in and wait while she talked to me. I thought to myself, *Here we go!* She said, "I can see how Lana looks at you. I don't want you to hurt her the way Peter hurt me." I said, "First off, I would never hurt Lana. And second, I'm not my brother." She told me to be careful. I told her I was.

As I drove back to Rick's house, I felt kind of lost. I knew what the feeling was; it was more than just an attraction. No, it wasn't lust! I was trying to figure out how all of this had happened. When I got to Rick's home, I sat down with him and we talked. He couldn't understand what I was trying to say. He thought I just wanted to have sex with Lana. I tried and tried to explain it to him, but he just didn't get it. So I prayed and asked the Lord to help me and went to bed.

When I got up in the morning, I found out that Clark was there. Things were still a little uncomfortable between the two of us, but you know me, I didn't care.

I sat down with a cup of coffee next to Clark just to have a little small talk when to my surprise he started talking about everything I had shared with Rick in private the night before. He went on and on about how crazy I was for even entertaining such ideas. I thought to myself, *what ideas? He has no idea how hard I'm fighting this!* When he finally took a breath, I informed him that it actually wasn't any of his business and I thought I had told Rick in the strictest confidence. He went off on me again, so I told him, "Nothing is going to happen! I have already told Lana this!" He finally calmed down and backed off.

I tried my best to stay away from Lana the rest of the weekend, but to no avail. I was tired, so I went downstairs because I knew no one was down there. As soon as my head hit the couch, there she was. Lana sat on the other couch looking at me. She told me that she'd been having naughty thoughts about me that morning. As she started to tell me what they were, I said, "Stop!" She started to get up and come over by me, to which I said, "No, you really need to stay over there." She asked why, so I told her, "Everyone here would kill me if they even thought I was near you!" So she stayed where she was, except she kept licking her lips. I thought to myself, *I would rather put up with Satan than go through this. Dear Lord, I'm just a man. Give me strength!* Finally, a few other people came down, to my relief.

We had an enjoyable weekend. On the way home, it was business as usual with Lana rubbing the inside of my arm with her toe. You women just know what to do to drive us men crazy, don't you!

I had to stop for gas, so I jumped out of the car as fast as I could.

When I got back in, I found out that Claire was going to let Lana sit in the front seat the rest of the way home. Three hours left to go. I thought, *Lord, why have you forsaken me?* Wouldn't you know it, Claire fell asleep and left me all alone with the "foul temptress." Lana was very pleasant the rest of the way home. I felt as if we were on a date. She kept asking me questions about what I liked and disliked. So I played along and asked her the same things. When I finally dropped them off, I breathed a huge sigh of relief.

As the weeks went by, Lana just wouldn't let up. I finally told her to meet me at a local restaurant so that we could talk. I once again told her that it would never work. She didn't care. But I stuck to my guns and wouldn't give in. Yes, I know how proud you are of me, and I appreciate it. The following day was Lana's high school graduation. I was invited to go, so I went. Everyone at the party assumed that I was Claire's date. Lana kept making eyes at me the whole time. She drove me crazy. As the evening wound down, I hugged everyone I knew and got the heck out of there before I did something I would regret later and get killed for.

As the months went by, Lana and I would see each other at church. I would say hi, talk to her for a while, and then run away from her as fast as I could. Lana called me late one evening and insisted that she needed to talk with me. I kept telling her that it would not be a good idea. She said that it was extremely important and asked if I would please meet with her. I finally caved in and met her in the parking lot of a grocery store. She climbed into my car and closed the door. She told me she couldn't help how she felt about me. The only thing she could think about was me. I, again, told her that it was crazy. But she wouldn't listen. She didn't care. We talked about this for almost an hour. It was getting late and I told her I needed to get up early for work, and asked would she please just go. Nope! She kept moving toward me, so I kept moving away from her until I was squished up against my door with nowhere else to go.

She leaned over my armrest and said, "I'm not going until you kiss me." I refused for a while. No, honestly I did. You would have been proud of me. She finally wore me down. I thought to myself *she's only eighteen. What's the big deal, she probably isn't that good at kissing.* I leaned toward her. I placed one hand on the back of her head and pulled her toward me. Our lips touched gently at first, and then we kissed. I thought to myself, *Boy, were you wrong! Wow, can she kiss!* I kissed her for only a few moments longer and then I said, "Pleeeease get out of my car!" She smiled and left. It took about five minutes before all of my goose pimples went away. Beats me. I can't explain why I felt this way. There was no way I could have fallen in love with her. At least that's what I told myself.

The following Friday, we went out on our first official date. After dinner, we took a walk down by the bay. We sat on a park bench as we watched the sunset together. I am an old-fashioned guy who enjoys being exceedingly romantic.

As the weeks went by, we spent every free moment together. The most we did was kiss. We had dinners together, went to the movies, and took walks down by the bay. A few times we curled upon the couch and watched movies or TV together. It was always a very nice time.

One Friday night, I got a call from Lana. She was crying so hard that I couldn't understand what she was saying. She told me that her parents found out that she was seeing me, and they had forbidden her from seeing me again. They asked her how she could she do this to them. What would people think of them if they found out that she was dating a guy twice her age! Didn't she even think of them? It took everything I had not to comment on that! They told her that she could call me this one time. But after that, she wasn't allowed to talk to me anymore. The most they would allow her to do was to say hi to me at church. As she told me all of this, I could feel my heart breaking. It was the same pain I felt when I went through my divorce. I tried my best to hold myself together while we talked. We spoke for fifteen minutes and then she said goodbye.

The moment I hung up the phone, I couldn't hold back my feelings anymore.

My brother walked in and asked me what was going on. I told him what had happened. He just shook his head and told me that the only reason this was happening was because Claire was still mad at him, and if she couldn't have a relationship with me, now that he didn't want her, then her daughter couldn't have one with me either. I told him I thought that was a little selfish of her and that it was because of our age difference. I also thought that maybe because Claire had propositioned me a few times, the thought of her daughter being with me, after I had rejected her, was just too much to handle. I was miserable. The only thing I could do was pray for Lana and myself.

The following day, Peter, who was a professional photographer, was shooting an afternoon wedding and asked if I would like to come along and help. So I went along. No matter what I did that day, I couldn't stop thinking about Lana. My heart was killing me. I kept telling myself that this whole thing was just ridiculous. But I knew what I felt in my heart for her was real. As the day went on, I helped my brother. It was a very nice wedding, and I was glad for the distraction.

Monday evening, I got a call from Lana's dad, Art. I had met Art at Lana's graduation party a few months earlier and one other time, too. So we were acquainted with each other. Here's a little history on Lana's dad. Art was allowed to see Lana a few times a month when she was a baby and through her teen years. Claire never let him contribute financially because she was an independent woman who didn't need a man's help. Ten years before I met Lana, Art got married to another woman who was always very sweet to Lana and treated her as her own. Art and his wife never had any children of their own. I got the impression that Art always came into Lana's life when it was convenient for him or when Claire would browbeat him into taking her side when they would reprimand Lana. He always used his job as an excuse for not having time to spend with Lana. I always had the feeling that Claire regretted never marrying Art. Just thought I'd share.

As I answered my phone, my stomach tensed up. Art asked if he and Claire could meet with me at Claire's office to discuss Lana and me. I told him that I wouldn't meet them alone and that I would like to bring my brother with. He told me that Claire was still not over him, and that would just cause more problems. I told him that maybe Claire needed to grow up and move on. What I said didn't help the situation, but I didn't really care. I was fed up with all of the people in the area thinking that they could tell me what I could and couldn't do! I told him fine and I would be over in about thirty minutes.

As I drove to Claire's office, I prayed, asking the Lord for wisdom, to know when to keep my mouth shut, and for the ability to restrain myself. If Art was to take a swing at me, I was pretty sure that, with one punch from me, I would shatter his jaw. I was that pissed off about this whole thing. As I walked into Claire's office and took a seat, Claire started things off. She said, "Jim, I know you are a nice guy and you would never intentionally hurt Lana. If you were ten years younger, we wouldn't have a problem with this." I hate when I'm right!

She continued, "We just don't want her to get hurt. Can you understand that? As parents, it is our responsibility to raise our daughter the way we think is best for her." Art just sat there like a bump on a log, hanging onto every word that poured out of Claire's mouth, occasionally nodding his head in approval. She then said, "Jim, what would people think if they found out that the two of you were dating?" I sat there and said nothing. I guess God heard my prayer.

To my wonder and amazement, Art began to speak. He said, "Jim, I don't know you that well, but Claire speaks highly of you, as does Lana. I am trying to understand why a guy your age would have anything to do with our daughter. It's just not normal! By the way, I called Lana's uncle and asked him to join us." Um, folks, Lana's uncle was a leader in our Church. Art was not a member of our church, but he knew everyone there. I thought to myself, *if he thinks he's going to use my own church against me, I have news for him!* Art then said, "I thought it would be a good idea to have someone neutral here in case things get out of hand." *Neutral? He's her uncle!*

I took a big deep breath as I looked up at the two of them and said, "I care about your daughter very much. As far as I'm concerned, age means very little to me. There are almost sixteen and a half years between my parents." People, the following statement that I make is going to make me sound arrogant and conceited. I would hope by now that you would know a little about me and who I am. I hope. I said, "Look at me, Art. Don't you think I could have any woman I want?" Folks, I was just trying to make a point! I then said, "Now, I'm not going to use the L word because that would just be too hard for the two of you to handle. But I care for your daughter much more than just like. I have fallen hard for her, and I'm not usually like that." At this point, Art looked at me and asked if I had slept with her. To which I told them both no.

As I spoke to them, explaining how I'd tried to prevent all of this from happening, I started to get a little emotional. I told them how many times I spoke to Lana and told her that it just wouldn't work, but then I started to have feelings for her so I didn't try to stop it anymore. I told them that I thought it was very selfish of them to be thinking of themselves during this situation, and had they even thought about Lana's feelings. They actually took that pretty well.

Art picked up his phone and started to call someone. He looked at me and said, "I'm calling Lana's uncle to tell him that he doesn't have to come. Jim, I can tell by the sincerity in your voice and the emotion on your face that you are being honest with us. I can now see why Lana likes you so much." At this point, Claire glared at him and he shut up fast. I spoke up and said, "As far as what other people would think if they found out about Lana and I? I really don't care! I have never tried to make everyone around me happy. The problem is, that for the first time in my life, I am now going out of my way to make myself happy, and that is just pissing all of *you* people off. I am trying to understand who you people think you are. I'm not your child. Your daughter is eighteen years old. You do not have the right to tell her who she can and can't be with! Mark my words, if you do this, you will be hurting your daughter in the process and driving a wedge between the three of you!"

I was very surprised that they let me say all of that without stopping me. Being as tall as I am; I can be a little intimidating for some people I guess. Claire said, "You are the adult. We are asking you to stay away from her because we do not approve of this. I am asking you for your word that you will have no contact with her. No phone calls or emails. And if she does try to contact you, we will expect you to let us know."

Almost an hour had passed, and I could see that there was no way to reason with them, so I reluctantly gave them my word. It went against everything I was feeling. They both told me that they were sorry they had to do that. I honestly wasn't listening to anything they said. All I could do was think about Lana and how I felt. I knew this was killing her too. We all shook hands, and as I started to leave, Claire asked if she could buy me a drink. I just looked at her. She knew I didn't drink so then it turned into, "Can I buy you a cup of coffee?" I think I'm too nice of a guy sometimes. I said, "Sure."

As I sat there feeling extremely uncomfortable, we talked about the weather and our jobs. Then she asked me this question, "What is it that you see in Lana anyway? She's just a kid." I sat there for a moment, remembering my mother's voice quietly reminding me that a gentleman never harms a woman. I said, "It would be very wise of you if you changed the subject. Lana is not just a kid. As far as I'm concerned, she is more mature than you and Art put together!" I wish I could describe the look on her face as she hurriedly asked me about my family back home. I thanked her for the coffee and wonderful conversation and I quickly left.

Two weeks later, at the end of July, my boss called me into her office to give me my ninety-day review. She told me that she was very impressed with how fast I picked up on things and with all of the positive changes I made to improve their processes. She said, "I don't want to keep praising you because then you're going to get a big head," so she gave me added responsibilities and a 20 percent raise. Isn't God great! I thanked Him a lot.

After a few more weeks of seeing Lana in church and not having the opportunity to speak with each other at all, it finally took its toll on Lana and she called me at work. I knew I had given my word to her parents, but I didn't care. I was in love with her, and she professed her love to me. We spoke to each other on the phone for the next few days until we couldn't take it anymore. I met her on my lunch hour. We ate something fast and then went to my car just to hold each other. It was like tearing my skin off my body every time we had to part. We started meeting each other in the evening any place we could be alone.

After a few weeks of sneaking around, my conscience got the best of me, and I told her we had to break up because I didn't want her to get in trouble with her parents. She agreed, so we did. Now, when we saw each other in church, it was like being in Hell! But we stayed away from each other for about a week, and then we started to see each other again.

At the end of August, my conscience got the best of me again, and I broke up with Lana. She took it very hard, but there wasn't anything we could do. I didn't want her to get into trouble again. Two weeks later we were back together again. Like I said before, "Love is blind and stupid!" Why do I make this statement? We are blind to everything around us. We are stupid because we know deep in our hearts these relationships won't work, but yet we ignore the warning signs. Get my point?

The next weekend, I was sitting in my family room, thinking about church and some of the rumors about me that were still going around. They were extremely hurtful, like, *Jim's a Satan worshipper, he uses a Ouija board, and Jim's just plain evil.* I didn't know why it bothered me so much. I have never let what other people think of me bother me. But this really hurt me. I finally figured it out. These people were supposed to be my brothers and sisters. We were taught that we were a big family. I kept trying to find something good about the church I'd belonged to my whole life. It was like the congregations out on the west coast were different from all the other congregations in the United States that I had been to. And I can tell you that I had been to a lot of them. While I was in our young people's group, I made friends from all over the United States and Canada. Every church I went to felt like home just not on the west coast.

When the ministers would serve, I would get very little out of the services. So often members would come to me and express the same feelings. All I could tell them was that they needed to pray harder for the ministers. I would make family visits trying to show my support of the local ministers. I never told the members what they did to me. Sometimes the members would ask me if the rumors they heard were true, only to tell me that they never believed them for a minute. I would always speak very highly of the ministers, but the members would tell me that they felt they got very little support from them, and were glad that my brother and I were in the congregation so they at least had someone they could talk to that made them feel they were loved. The best I could do was to pray with them, asking the Lord to give us strength and to open the minister's eyes to the needs of the members.

As I sat there in my living room, I became very sad. I closed my eyes and asked the Lord what he wanted me to do. I decided to meditate to see if I couldn't get rid of the sadness I felt. As I sat there breathing deeply, I found myself in the center of my head. Once again, I was on my raft, drifting down that tranquil river. But this time, there wasn't anyone else around to be seen. I was all alone. As I stood there looking around, I heard a quiet voice say; *"I need you to be yourself."* I immediately knew it was the Lord's voice. I fell to my knees and said, *"Lord I feel so alone!"* He said, *"Open your eyes and see where you are standing."* I opened my eyes and realized that I was standing in the palm of His hand.

The Lord said; *"I told you that you are never alone. I am always with you. You are always in my hand, and I will always protect you. In times of trouble, I will do this."* As I looked up He took His other hand and covered me with it. He said, *"You have no reason to fear anything. I am with you."* I said, *"Lord, things out here are not going that well in church, and I wish there was something I could do to help fix it."* He said, *"Why do you concern yourself with things that you cannot fix? I will fix them!"* I said, *"What do you want me to do? I feel so useless. I feel like I'm not helping in any way."* He said, *"I need you to be yourself. Wait and watch."* I stood up and ran over to his thumb and wrapped my arms around it. I said, *"Thank you for always being there for me. I love you so much, Father."* He said, *"Be patient. In time, you will understand. And always know Jim, that I love you."*

When I let go of His thumb, I found myself standing on the raft again. I fell to my knees and once again thanked the Lord for talking with me. When I was done meditating, I went outside where my brother was sitting. He looked at me and said, "What happened to you?" With tears in my eyes, I told him what I had just experienced. He began to cry, too. He was just as frustrated as I was. I told him what the Lord said, that he would fix everything, which brought peace to both of our hearts.

I called my sister Ann and shared everything with her. She asked me if I knew what the Lord meant when He said, "I need you to be yourself." I said not really. She said, "You are always looking at yourself in a negative way. The Lord is molding you into the person He knows you are. He can see who you are right now, but you keep fighting him. He has given you this time to become who He needs you to be for the task He has in mind for you. Even when you don't think much is going on around you, He wants you to look inside of yourself, because there is a lot going on in there. You are not the same person you were a year ago. You have grown so much, Jim, but you won't give yourself any credit. Do you realize that he answered your simple wish? I don't know of any human that has been allowed to touch Him or has stood in his hand and let them hug His thumb. You have been closer to God than any human I have read about or known. He let you touch His hand! Do you get it now? Just be the person He wants and knows you can be." As I listened to my sister talk, I felt ashamed that I didn't realize how truly blessed I was. He has always been there for me. He has always blessed me. In times that I know I have hurt Him, He has always forgiven me. I don't think I will ever feel worthy enough!

Near the end of September, Lana called me to let me know that we got caught having lunch together, and her parents were very ticked off at me for breaking my word. Next thing I know, Lana's grandmother cornered me in church and told me to leave her granddaughter alone. I quietly explained to her that it really wasn't any of her business. She looked as though she were having a heart attack as she glared at me and said, "You really are a jerk, aren't you?" I calmly leaned toward her face and said, "How nice of you to express your feelings about me in God's house. You may want to watch what you say to me, lady, because I've about had it with all of you self-centered jerks!" Wouldn't you know it? She shut up and stormed right out of the church. It was magical!

Over the next few weeks, all I heard from Lana's family and some of the leaders as I tried to get the situation resolved was, "You broke your word!" With the way I was being treated, you would have thought I had clubbed a herd of baby seals or killed someone. I told all of them how much of a privilege it was for me to be standing in the presence of perfection! They didn't like that comment too much. But as usual, I didn't care. Lana and I stayed away from each other to make everyone else happy.

Chapter 6

Unusual Surprises

It was the end of October. My mom was celebrating her sixty-fifth birthday, and my family was throwing her a huge surprise party, so Peter and I flew in to surprise her. We landed on Friday night and stayed with Ann and her family. We had been telling mom that there was no way we could make it in for her birthday, but we wished her the best. The party wasn't until Sunday afternoon. Peter and I decided to stop over at our parents' home on Saturday. We walked into the living room as Ann called both of our parents to come where she was so she could show them something. They came in and almost had heart attacks. It was great to surprise them!

Sunday afternoon, seventy-five of Mom's closest relatives and friends waited for her to show up at the restaurant that we had told her just our immediate family would be at. She walked in, and we yelled "Surprise!" She was completely overwhelmed. It was great.

Peter and I had to fly back on Monday, which coincidentally was the one-year anniversary of my living on the west coast. As we made our plans to fly out, Tina's new boyfriend Billy volunteered to drive us to the airport very early Monday morning. According to Tina, Billy was a self-made millionaire. To look at him, you would have never known.

As we drove to the airport, Billy told us that Tina had asked him to help the two of us start our own business. Peter and I had been talking about this particular business for almost twenty years, but neither of us had the capital to pull it off. He asked us what our business was. (No, I'm not going to tell you readers.) After we explained it in detail to him and why we thought it would work so well out on the west coast, he offered to put up $250,000 toward our business. We couldn't believe our ears. We were planning on being back in Chicago in two months for Christmas, and decided to have a rough-draft business plan started by then. As Peter and I sat waiting to board the plane, we were already making our plans. It was a very exciting trip back home.

The following Sunday was the week before our next Service for the Departed. As I sat in the bench during service listening to the leaders, I noticed that to my left there was a soul of a little girl sitting next to me. She looked as if she was about seven years old. She had long dark hair with big brown eyes and a very cute face. She was very slender and wore a flowered dress. I spoke to her clairvoyantly and said, *"Hi. Who are you?"* She looked up at me with those big brown eyes and smiled. I stared back into her eyes and thought to myself that her eyes reminded me of my ex-wife Trish. She placed her hand on my hand and said, *"I'm your daughter Amanda. I have been waiting to meet you, Papa. I love you."*

As I looked at her, there was no doubt in my mind that she was our daughter. She had Trish's facial features and eyes. Years ago, Trish had told me that she thought she had a miscarriage. I never believed her because there was no proof that she was pregnant. Amanda said, *"Mom was right; because here I am."* (Yep, she's my daughter all right. She has my bluntness). *"I don't blame you, Papa, for not believing Mom. You were a different person back then. I have been praying for you, Papa. I just want you to know how proud I am to be your daughter!"* She stood up, and we hugged each other clairvoyantly. Tears were streaming down my face as I sat there. My brother was sitting next to me. He leaned over when he saw that I was crying and asked, "Are you okay?" I smiled and told him I would tell him later. Amanda sat next to me the rest of the service. I put my arm around her, and she snuggled up next to me as we held hands. At the end of service, she leaned in to kiss me and give me a big hug. She said, *"I will see you very soon, Papa. I love you very much!"* I said, *"Please don't leave. I have so many questions."* She said, *"I have to go, Papa. I love you. Please say hi to Mama for me."* I told her that I loved her, too."

Do you remember when I told you back in Chapter 1 that Trish and I remained friends, and we still stay in contact today? It is because of this situation that we speak to each other often.

After the service, Lana walked over to say hi and she asked me why I was so emotional. I told her. She couldn't believe it but smiled and said, "I'm very happy for you." I even told Shelly. She told me that it didn't surprise her at all. As Peter and I drove home, I explained everything to him. He said, "I have a niece in eternity!" I said, "Yes. Please pray for her." The next day I sent Trish an email sharing all of this with her. She replied back with a bunch of questions about what Amanda looked like and how old was she? And then she asked this question: "What about Carrie-Ann?" I emailed her back and said, "I thought this was Carrie-Ann, and she changed her name." While I was emailing Trish, I was also emailing my sister Ann. She asked a similar question: "Did you see Carrie-Ann?" Trish emailed me back and explained to me that we'd had two miscarriages and that we only named the second child Carrie-Ann.

Amanda must have named herself. Ann emails back with the same information, except she told me that she remembered Trish trying to tell me that she thought she had two miscarriages, but I wouldn't listen to her. I emailed them both back and said, "Yes, I remember now."

As I sat thinking about Amanda and why she would have picked that name, I started to laugh out loud. I sent an email to Trish with the reason I thought Amanda would pick that name above any other. As I hit SEND, I received an email from Trish, explaining the same reason Amanda named herself that I just sent her. I picked up the phone and called Trish. When she answered, she was laughing, too.

Trish and I loved watching *The Simpsons* together. One of the best parts was when Bart would prank-call Moe's Tavern. In one of our favorite episodes, Bart asks Moe if he can speak to "Amanda Hugginkiss."

Then Moe says, "Hey, I'm looking for Amanda Hugginkiss! Is there a man to hug and kiss? C'mon people, can't I find a man to hug and kiss?" We were both laughing so hard that tears were rolling down our faces. I said to Trish, "It looks as if our daughter has the same twisted sense of humor that her parents have." She then said, "Carrie-Ann would be three years younger than Amanda. You didn't see her?" I told her, "No, just Amanda." She then asked me to let her know if I hear anything more about Carrie-Ann.

As soon as I hung up with Trish, Ann called. She said, "Carrie-Ann is afraid to approach you because she doesn't think that you love her or that she even exists." It broke my heart to hear her say that. I said, "I never believed Trish because I thought she just wanted some attention but now I feel horrible about this. I love both of my daughters very much. What should I do?" Ann explained to me that when I had a free moment, I should let Carrie-Ann know how I feel about her, which is exactly what I did on my lunch hour. I sat in my car and spoke out loud apologizing to my little girl for how I must have made her feel. I told her how sorry, I was and how much I loved her and how I genuinely wanted to see her whenever she was ready to come forward. I even asked her to forgive me. I then prayed and thanked God for revealing all of this to me too.

As I drove home after work that evening, I thought to myself that I should probably get a healing from Marty because it had been a while. But then I thought maybe I should go work out first and then get a healing. All of a sudden, I heard two little girls' voices yell: *"No, get a healing!"* I recognized one of the voices to be Amanda's. The other voice must have been Carrie-Ann's. I yelled out at the top of my lungs, "I'm going as fast as I can. I will be home soon to get my healing!"

I ran into the house. No one was home. I sat down and began to breathe deeply as Marty began my healing. I got into the center of my head. I was standing on my raft. All the way at the other end of the raft were my two little girls and my sister Patty. My Mom had a miscarriage between Ellen and me. I always believed Patty existed, but I had never seen her before today. She looked just like my Mom did when she was in her thirties.

As I tried to walk closer, I felt that something was holding me back, and I couldn't move. Marty said, *"Jim, we have to finish your healing first before you can go to them. Be patient."* I yelled across to the three of them, tears streaming down my face, telling all three of them how much I loved them and told Carrie-Ann once more how sorry, I was about everything. She called out to me and said, *"It's okay, Papa. I love you!"* I looked at Marty and told him to hurry up. He told me he was going as fast as he could. I turned to my right just as Michael appeared. I asked, *"Why are you here?"* He said, *"Nothing is going to prevent this from happening. The Lord sent me!"* I kept yelling to them to wait; I will be there soon. I felt in my heart that we didn't have much time. There was such a sense of urgency, and I couldn't explain it. I kept rushing Marty. He just kept glaring back at me and telling me he was going as fast as he could. Michael stepped forward and said, *"Jim, the Lord has willed this to happen. Be patient."*

As the healing progressed, I could see all of my departed relatives from both sides of my parents' families standing behind my sister and my girls. They were all smiling. I could feel Marty was almost finished. The moment he was done, I ran to the other side of the raft and embraced my girls. I held them in my arms and squeezed them so tight.

I kissed their faces over and over again. All of us were crying. And as fast as I got there my sister leaned down by me and said, *"We have to go, Jim."* I looked up at her and said, *"I just got here! Please, a few minutes more!"* Patty put her hand on my shoulder and said, *"We can't, Jim, we have to go. Your girls will be fine. You will see them again on Wednesday in church. I will keep an eye on them as I have been doing."* I stood up and hugged my sister. Michael walked over to me and held me back by my arm as they left. I kept yelling to them that I loved them and couldn't wait to see them again. And then they were gone. I wrapped my arms around Michael. He held me as I cried. He said nothing to me as I just held onto him crying. He pushed me gently away from his chest and said, *"You truly are blessed, Jim. No one has ever been given an opportunity like this one. Can you see how truly special you are to God?"* I had no words to say. I just nodded. He said, *"You will be fine. We will be talking together very soon."*

And as quick as he appeared, he was gone. When I finished meditating, I call my sister Ann and shared everything her. The next day, I called Trish and told her everything, too, especially that the girls told me to tell her that they loved her too.

Over the next few days, anytime I had a quiet moment, the name Emily would come to mind. It was the weirdest thing. I couldn't figure out what it was about. On Wednesday evening as I sat in the service with my two daughters, I turned to Amanda and said, *"Honey, for the past few days the name Emily has kept coming to my mind. Do you have any idea who Emily is?"* She smiled and turned her head looking across the aisle to the other side of the church. A little blond girl around the age of five walked over toward us and stood next to Amanda. Amanda said, *"Papa, this is Emily."* As I looked at this little girl, I stared in awe at her. She had my brother's eyes and facial features. I looked at my two girls and said, *"Come on! Are you telling me that this is Peter's daughter?"* Emily smiled and pointed where Peter was sitting and said, *"Yes, that's my dad!"* I looked at all three of them and said, *"How is this possible? You are too young to be from Peter's first wife."* The three girls nodded their heads as if to say, *"keep going."* I said, *"Peter wasn't married to his third wife long enough to have you because you look as if you are five years old."* Oh, by the way, Peter has been married three times. The girls kept nodding their heads again with a look of "you're almost there." I said, *"Oh, come on.*

His second wife was ten years older than he was. You're telling me that you are Jill's daughter?" Emily looked up at me with tears in her eyes and said, *"They had no idea they had me. I was only here for a second, and then I was gone. I have been trying to get my dad's attention for the past few days, but he just can't see me. I decided to try and get your attention. That's why you kept hearing my name. Uncle Jim, can you please tell my dad that I love him and that I exist?"* She walked over to me, and I held her while we both cried. My brother leaned over to me and said, "Why are you crying? It's not really an emotional service." I said I would tell him later. I let go of Emily. As she walked past me, she sat down next to Peter. She put her hand on his and leaned into his side. Peter had no idea that his little girl was sitting next to him during the service.

After service, one of our friends, Matthew, asked if we would like to go out and get a cup of coffee. I told him yes. Peter had to help with something around the church, so Matthew and I went on ahead without him. Matthew pointed out to me that he noticed I was crying. I explained a little about what had happened and said, "My brother is going to have a rude awakening when he gets here." We both decided to order him a beer instead of coffee. As Peter sat down and started to drink his beer, he looked up at me and asked what was going on. I said, "Brother, here's what happened." As I told him why I was crying, he just kept looking at the floor, shaking his head back and forth. I grabbed his shoulder and said, "Congratulations! You're a father!" He looked up at me with tears in his eyes and said, "I have to be honest with you, Jim. When you told me that you had two daughters, I was jealous. Do I really have a little girl too?" I said, "You sure do!" I told him that, for a while now, Emily had been trying to get his attention. He stopped crying and said, "It has been so weird lately. Every morning as I would wake up I could swear that there was a little blond girl standing in the corner of my bedroom. I just thought it was my eyes." I said, "Well, apparently you have seen Emily, because I haven't told you what she looks like. She has blond hair like your ex-wife Jill." I then described her to him in detail. It was really a wonderful evening. Our friend Matthew was used to all of this by now. He was one of the brothers that came up to me after the announcement was made that I was practicing esotericism and said, "Jim, when I heard that, I thought to myself there is no way you would be involved with anything like that." He told me that his dad thought it was crazy too. Later on I realized why Matthew became close friends with Peter and me…but you are just going to have to keep reading.

    The following Sunday was our local Service for the Departed. I was praying for the same groups I'd prayed for before. As I looked around, I saw all of them again, but this time there were more. The church was filled to the brim. There were so many souls at this service that they were standing outside the church. As far as I could see in all directions there was no end to how many souls I could see. It was a wonderful service.

    The first week of December as I was meditating, Michael showed up. He reminded me of the task at hand and to stay focused. I told him that things seemed a little quiet. He told me to be patient and to plan our business. It was an extremely short visit.

    On December 23, we flew back to Chicago to spend Christmas with our family. While we were there, we sat down with Billy and went over our rough-draft business plan. He thought it was a brilliant idea, but $250,000 was not going to be enough, so he offered us $500,000 to start our business. We were both overjoyed.

    The old year 2004 was at an end, and I was glad to see it go. I felt in my heart that even though the Lord had put me through a number of things to test me, it only brought me closer to Him and strengthen me. I have another saying, "Out of every bad thing that happens, there is always some good; you just have to find it." Life is always a matter of perspective!

As the New Year began Lana, and I tried our best to stay away from each other. It was extremely difficult for us when we would see each other at church. We knew that one of her aunts was always spying on us, just waiting for us to slip up so she could run back to the evil queen and report on us. I'm sorry; I always felt like her aunt was one of those evil flying monkeys in the Wizard of Oz and Lana's mom was the evil queen.

Occasionally we would have lunch, but then I would remind Lana that I had broken my word, and I didn't want all of the crap that was associated with her family. So we would go back to not seeing each other outside of the church, which I affectionately termed "our tormented little place in hell," to keep everyone happy. In life, I found that it was my responsibility to make everyone else happy and make myself miserable. At least that's what it felt like at the time. Rick would always say to me, "Jim, you sure do have a lot of drama in your life." I would reply with, "Rick; it's not drama; it's called life. Your problem is that you live a very boring life." He agreed and told me he wouldn't change anything, and I told him I felt the same way about my life.

A few weeks later, I received a phone call from Shelly. She was crying. I asked her what was going on. She said, "I can't go through this again, Jim. I will lose my mind if I do." I asked her what she was talking about. She said, "It's been a year since Thomas left, and now there's something else in my house! I can't go through this again! There isn't anyone else I can call. Please help me! Jim, Please!" I said, "Shelly, I will be right over. My first impression is that this thing means you no harm. I will be over in five minutes!" As I drove to Shelly's house, I prayed as I have prayed so often: *"Father, please grant me your grace and insight so I can help. Shelly has been put through so much, Father, and yet she has remained faithful. Please help us! Oh yeah, and I really don't need the crap scared out of me, so please protect me!"* As Shelly opened the door, she had tears in her eyes. I put my arms out and held her as she repeated what she had told me on the phone. I said, "Shelly, I don't believe that the Lord would put you through this again. Before we jump to conclusions, let's pray and see what happens, okay?" We folded our hands, and I prayed a small prayer, thanking our Heavenly Father for his help. She took me into the basement. The minute my feet hit the basement floor, the hair on the back of my neck stood straight up. I prayed to myself, *"Lord,* remember I really don't want to be surprised by something and freak out." Shelly took me into the back bedroom and said, "I was in here just cleaning a little when the clock radio turned on all by itself. The music was blaring so loud, and the song that was on the radio was 'Hard to say I'm Sorry.' I screamed and ran upstairs. I could feel something was following me. It stopped at the bottom of the stairs. I just kept running, and then I called you." As I stood there listening to Shelly, my neck hair was standing straight up to the point that I could have scrubbed the paint off the walls with it. To look at me, you would have had no idea that I was on the verge of soiling myself. I just stood there looking around the room with cat-like readiness waiting for something to happen. All of a sudden, I felt something walk up behind me and breathe deeply out through its nose as if it was snorting. No, I didn't dare turn around to see what it was. I calmly told Shelly that maybe we should go into the family room. As we walked to the couch, I quietly prayed to myself, *"I'm getting freaked out over here; a little help would be good about now!"* I sat her down on the couch and asked her what she was thinking about when this happened. It has been my experience that, in most cases, a person's first impression of the situation is almost always correct. She said, "For the past few days all I have been thinking about is my dad." I said, "Did your dad breathe through his nose like this?" I made the same breathing noise through my nose as I heard in the bedroom. She stared at me with her eyes wide open and then started to cry. She said, "How did you know he made that noise?" I said, "Oh, your dad walked up behind me while we were in the bedroom and scared the crap out of me by breathing that way!" Thanks a lot, Shelly's dad! Her dad then appeared, standing behind her. He said nothing but motioned to me to keep talking to her. I remembered having seen a painting of Shelly's parents on her living room wall. That's how I knew it was he. It was the weirdest thing. He never said a word, but I knew exactly what he felt. I said, "Shelly, your dad is trying to apologize to you for the way he treated you when you were a little girl growing up." She began to cry even harder. I looked at her dad. He just nodded his head at me. I said, "He has been trying to get your attention for the past few days. He stood next to your bed while you slept try to get his message across, but it was no use. He didn't mean to scare you, but he needed to speak with you. That's why he turned the radio on in the room, because he knew that song was playing. Remember? The song 'Hard to Say I'm Sorry?' I looked at her dad and said, "Very clever." He just smiled and motioned for me to continue. "He's been waiting to come and ask you for forgiveness for a while. He feels terrible with the way he used to yell at you all the time and treat you. He figured that if you could forgive Thomas for everything that he did to you then maybe you would find it in your heart to forgive him, too." I looked up at her dad. As he nodded, tears were running down his face. I said. "Shelly, it's not easy for him to come to you and ask you for forgiveness. Is it?" She said, "He was such a hard man to please. I could never do anything right. No matter what I tried to do, he was never happy with me. He never would tell me that he loved me. That's all I ever wanted from him! He hated our church too. He was never a member, but he would go out of his way to criticize us about it." Her dad looked at me as if he were pleading with me. I said, "Shelly, your dad feels terrible about the way he treated you. He knows he was wrong, and he would give anything to change the past and make it different if he could. He loves you so much and is asking you to forgive him. He is not in a pleasant realm and would like you to help him, if you can." He nodded yes once again. Shelly just sat there for a while crying. I put my hand on her hand and said, "You always tell me that you don't think you have a special place in God's heart. Can you see how much God loves you that He would allow your dad to come to you and ask you for forgiveness? Service for the Departed is less than two months away. Not many people in this world or the next world get this kind of opportunity. It is because of your faith that the Lord has allowed this to happen. Pretty sweet if you ask me! Your dad is not rushing you. He knows this may take some time for you to work through." Shelly looked at me and asked, "Where is my dad standing?" I said, "Right behind you. I should tell you that he has been crying the whole time we have been talking." She turned and looked up to the place I was pointing at and said, "Dad, all I ever wanted was your approval. I just wanted to know that you loved me." She began to cry hard and then said, "Dad, I forgive you!" I began to cry. (Hey, it was a very touching moment, okay?) He leaned over and kissed her on the top of her head. All of us had tears streaming down our faces. We all just hung out for a while and cried. It was such a neat experience.

    Her dad motioned to me thanking me for my help. I told him not to thank me, but we should all thank our Heavenly Father for His help. I said, "We will both pray and bring offerings for you, every service." He smiled with tears in his eyes and then motioned to me that he had to leave. Then he was gone. I held Shelly as she cried, trying to offer her words of encouragement. We sat and relived the whole Thomas experience. We confirmed to each other that we were still praying and offering for Thomas, too. Shelly thanked me again for helping. I once again told her that I didn't actually do anything; all the thanks go to God!

At the end of January, my sister Ellen called me. She was highly emotional as she spoke.

She said, "Jimmy, for a while now, I have felt that I was pregnant again with our third child. I had all of the telltale warning signs that I had when I was pregnant with James and Sydney. I took the test, but it came back negative. I knew in my heart that I was pregnant. Last week, the feelings, went away, and I thought to myself, I must have had a miscarriage." Then Ellen said, "I broke down and cried. I told Fred, and he began to cry too. For days after, the name Ian kept coming to mind. As I was sitting and thinking about this name, all of a sudden a little boy appeared in front of my eyes and said, 'Hi, I'm Ian.' Jimmy, I couldn't make out the face, but I knew he was my little boy. Don't ask me how, I just did." See folks, I belong to a family of freaks. I'm cool with that. She said, "A few nights ago, I had a dream that Patty was holding a little infant in her arms. She smiled at me and told me that she would take care of him for me. Jimmy, you're an uncle again." I said, "See, Ellen how blessed you and Fred are? The Lord knew that at this time in your life, you too couldn't actually afford another child. But because you prayed so hard, He answered your prayer." Life is always a matter of perspective. I said, "You have a little boy in eternity that you can love and pray for. Someday, you will hold him in your arms. I will pray for Ian and your family. I am truly happy for the two of you. Please tell Fred I say hi."

Chapter 7

Phase 2

It was now the first week in February and almost a year to the date that I first spoke with the archangel Michael. I was sitting in the living room having Marty give me a healing when Michael shows up. I could see him with my eyes wide open standing next to the fireplace. He appeared to be transparent, but I could see him in detail, color and depth. He looked at me and said, *"When you are done with your healing, meet me on the raft."* Marty spoke up, *"Michael has something special for you."* Michael looked sternly at Marty then Marty said, *"I'm going to shut up now!"* I looked at Marty and said, *"Nice, Marty. Thanks for stealing Michael's thunder."* Marty just looked down at the floor shaking his head and smiling.

As I stepped onto the raft, I could see a bust behind Michael with some kind of armor on it. Michael said, *"Please come here and I will help you put this on."* I walked over to the armor and Michael held it up. I slid my arms into it. It fit like a jacket, but it had almost no weight to it. Once I was wearing it, I held my arms out and looked at it in total amazement. Michael helped me fasten each clasp on the front. He then placed a helmet on my head that covered the sides of my face. The helmet matched the armor in texture and color.

Would you like to know what my armor looked like? It was made of what looked like black chain mail covered in all kinds of different-sized jewels: diamonds, rubies, and other precious stones. Before I could ask, Michael said, *"Jim, each stone represents your offerings and sacrifices. They will now protect you."* He walked over to the bust. Next to it was a sword. He picked it up and handed it to me and said, *"Jim, this sword was forged out of the fire of love that burns in your heart for God. It will now fight for you."* I held it in front of myself; it also weighed very little in my hand. It looked like an Old English Mason sword. The hilt has a pommel with a live burning sun embedded in it. From the cross-guard to the pommel, the inside of the blade was solid yellow gold and the outer edge was white gold with black onyx inlaid as the handgrip. The blade is five feet long. A very handsome and deadly sword, if I may say so myself.

Michael pulled me by my arm in front of a mirror and said, *"Look and see how well you are prepared! You will fear no one!"* He said, *"I will talk with you in your living room."* I opened my eyes. As I sat on the couch, I looked to my right. There he was, standing right next to me. He said, *"Because Satan is aware of God's plan, and knows who you are, the Lord has decided to assign a group of special angels to guard over you."* As he spoke, six more angels appeared in different parts of the living room. They were all as tall as Michael, clad in armor and carrying a sword and shield.

One of the angels stepped forward in front of me. Michael said, *"Jim, this is Anthony. He is your lead angel. He will direct you in time of need. Do as he asks."* I waved at him and nodded my head. He smiled and nodded back. The other angels formed a circle around me. As Michael introduced them by name, they each nodded their heads. He said, *"This is Thomas, Jonathan, Michael, James, and Peter. They have been assigned to protect you. They will keep you safe."* All of a sudden, something appeared behind them. They all drew their swords and shields. As they turned to face it they tightened the circle around me.

I stood up to see what it was. He was tall just like my angels but he was extremely thin and bony. He was twisted and had a slightly hunched back that made him lean forward. He had bright red hair. His face was thin and his chin came to a point. He had a red beard. His complexion was also dark red. He too, was clad in armor, but it was intensely dark, black and red. He looked like what everyone thinks Satan looks like. You know that common picture of Satan when he appears all red with a pointed tail? He was just like that except he had no tail. As he spoke, his voice was raspy and quiet. He pointed his bony finger in my direction as he pulled out his sword and made a motion across his neck as if he were cutting my throat. He said, *"Supplanter, we know who you are. Your days are numbered so be careful!"* I looked at him and said, *"Get out of my house! Now!"* With an evil grin on his face, he turned and left.

I looked at Michael and asked, *"Who was that?"* He said, *"His name is Andreus. He is Satan's number-two man. He controls the entire west coast of the United States."* I asked, *"What was that all about?"* Michael explained, *"I told you, Satan will try to stop God's plan. But he will fail. The Lord's plan will be fulfilled, and you are a big part of that. Always be mindful of the task at hand. Anthony and others will always protect you."*

I questioned, *"Why did he call me Supplanter?"* He said, *"The name James was given to you by God. It is not a coincidence that you have that name. The Lord moved your father's heart to choose that name for you when you were born. Before time and for millennia the Lord chose you for this task. He has been waiting for you to fulfill His plan. When you gave up your free will and trusted Him, He put you on the path that you now walk. He has big plans for you, Supplanter, and you will not fail him! Look up the meaning of your name and you will see what I am talking about." I said, "Michael, I don't know how to use the weapons I have." He said, "Take heart and trust in the Lord. While you sleep, I will train your spirit. It will help protect you, and you will become a mighty warrior for God's work! I must take my leave of you now. Take heart. God loves you very much and you are never alone." With that, he ran off and disappeared. I ran to my computer and looked up the meaning of my name:

<u>James</u>

Meaning: Supplanter

Let's see what Dictionary.com says about supplanter,
Sup-plant-er, noun
1. To take the place of (another), as through force, scheming, strategy, or the like.
2. To replace (one thing) by something else.
3. To trip up, overthrow. Synonyms 1. Remove, succeed.

I then tried to find information on Andreus. As I typed, Marty said, *"You're not going to find anything on him."* I said, *"Wait, I'm still checking."* He said, *"You are wasting your time. No one knows he exists."* I said, *"I'm checking other sites. Hang on!"* He said, *"You're not listening to me. Hello. I'm telling you, you are wasting your time."* I said, *"Fine!"* I sat back in my chair, rubbing my eyes. I opened them and looked around the room. Anthony was standing right by my side. The other angels were standing in different parts of the family room, looking out and occasionally turning their heads from side to side. Anthony said, *"We will keep an eye out for danger. You have nothing to worry about. We are here to protect you."* I looked at Marty and said, *"Okay, give!"* He asked, *"Give what?"* I said, *"Don't play dumb with me. What's Andreus's story?"* He said, *"Fine. Andreus is a demon, one of the fallen angels who were kicked out of Heaven with Satan. You already know that he's in control of this area and that he doesn't like you very much."* I said, *"Tell me something I don't know!"* He said, *"He has a brother named Antonius, who is just as evil as he is."* I said, *"You have got be kidding me. What's with their names? Are these guys Greek or what?"* Marty said, *"This isn't a time to make jokes. This is very serious, Jim! I am trying to help you.*

That's why we were put together!" I said, *"I think you got a lot more than you were expecting when we were paired together."* He said, *"Jim, I serve God first and then you. It has always been a pleasure to serve you. I don't regret anything, and I'm glad we are friends."* I looked at him and said, *"Wow, Marty. I never knew you felt that way. Is this the part where we hug each other?"* It was, so we did.

Okay, here is the hierarchy in the Spirit world, just in case you were wondering. Some people are under the impression that when you die, you earn your wings and become an angel. Sorry, that does not happen.

Humans are three-part beings: body, soul, and spirit. God also gave us our own free will. Angels are two-part beings: body and spirit. They have no freewill and have always existed with God before the Universe was even created.

And the hierarchy is as follows:

1. **God**
2. **Jesus**
3. **Holy Spirit (HS)**
4. **Mankind (Yes, mankind. We are the "Crown of God's Creation.")**
5. **Archangels**
6. **Angels**
7. **Good Spirits**
8. **Dog Excrement**
9. **Satan**
10. **The Anti-Christ**
11. **Demons (Fallen Angels)**
12. **Evil Spirits**

Now back to the story. I just sat there feeling extremely comfortable for some reason. So I decided to take a mental inventory of my situation:

1. Personal armor, helmet and sword. **CHECK**
2. Six angels. **CHECK**
3. Trusty sidekick Marty. **CHECK**
4. God's plan. Although I honestly have no idea what it's all about! **CHECK.**
5. Satan knows who I am and is ticked off at me. Why? I have no idea! **CHECK.**
6. My name means to remove or replace by force. (Don't know what that's all about!) **CHECK.**
7. Homicidal big red demon-maniac named Andreus who threatened my life! **CHECK and DOUBLE CHECK!**

Yep, just another ordinary day in the life of Jim. Pretty sweet!

Three days later as I was working out at home, one of my fans decided to drop by and say hi. You remember Andreus, right? He just appeared out of nowhere, but a split second before he showed up, my angels surrounded me. I used this opportunity to make a mental note for the future. *"Note to self, when your angels form a closed circle around you with swords drawn and shield poised, crap is about to hit the fan and knock it over!"* In true fallen angel form, Andreus began to repeat his threats to me. I looked at Anthony and the other angels and said, *"Okay, there he is, get him!"* They just kept protecting me. I said, *"If you're waiting for the suspense to build I think we're there. Okay, now!"* Nope. Nothing; they didn't move an inch. The whole time Andreus just kept talking so I decided that I should probably try to listen to what he was saying. All I caught was the tail end, because I prayed quietly to myself that the Lord would step in. Andreus said, *"I will not rest until I have destroyed you. You will fail! Never forget that you are just a human; a small and weak human!"*

As he finished, two more angels showed up and escorted him out of my house. As he left, I couldn't help myself, so I spoke up and said, *"Are you leaving so soon? Maybe you should seek therapy for those rage issues you have. Well, I'm sure I will see you again very soon. Bye-bye!"*

Anthony turned to me and said, *"Jim, do not provoke him. You are a representative of the Lord. Remember that."* I apologized to the Lord for being an idiot and thanked Him for His protection.

One week later, Michael showed up once again and said, *"Meet me on the raft."* I meditated, and in an instant, I was in the center of my mind on the raft. I walked over to him and saw that he was holding something. It was a shield. He hooked it onto my back. It looked just like his. He said, *"Jim, this shield was forged out of your faith. It will now protect you. Next week, you are going to Chicago for your sister Ann's wedding. Enjoy yourself. Anthony and the other angels will always be with you. When you come back from Chicago, Phase 3 will start."* He put his hands on my shoulders and pulled me towards him. As he looked me right in the eyes, he said, *"Always remember, nothing can harm you."*

As Peter and I flew into Chicago, I put the final touches on the lyrics I had written for a song I was going to sing at Ann's wedding. She had asked Ellen and I to sing a few songs. I was alone once again in my life, not seeing or dating anyone. I was inspired one day thinking back almost a year earlier when the Lord had showed me the woman of my dreams with my two sons. Remember? I was standing on a hill and they were there with me.

One day on my way home from work, I had started scribbling lyrics down on a napkin I had in my glove box. Presto, three days later, I finished it. So I took it upon myself to surprise Ann and her would-be-hubby with this song. I took the music from a Josh Groban version of the song "Broken Vow". I changed the title to "Answered Prayer". Pretty ironic, I thought, but you kind of know me by now. My singing range is pretty close to Josh Groban's and I enjoy his music. Here are the lyrics I wrote and sang at my sister's wedding. You will see later why I'm telling you this.

Answered Prayer

1st Verse

For many years, I prayed and asked
To find someone; I would be blessed.
I looked around and saw what others had, and sighed.
Would my one wish just be denied?

2nd Verse

He showed me you and I did smile.
A glint of love did fill your eyes.
I said, "Oh, Lord, is this, the one that you have sent?
We'll share a love that will not end."

Chorus

I thank the Lord. I thank him now.
For all the tears that I have cried
My heart is yours. All that I am. Given from His own hand.
Answered my prayer, He has.

3rd Verse

I cup your face and hold my breath,
The love I feel; want to express
How few the words, they vanish, run and flee from me,
To spend my life with you how sweet.

Chorus

I thank the Lord I thank him still
For all the tears that I have spilled
My heart is yours. All that I am. Given from His own hand.
Answered my prayer, He has.

Bridge

I pull you close…and lose myself as I gaze into your eyes,
The love I feel for you will last throughout all time…I hold you tight.
I kiss you deep and pray to God that it won't end,
My love for you will never end!

Chorus

I thank the Lord…to him I'll sing
For all my hopes…He saw my dreams
No more I need…no more I ask. For on this day I'm blessed.
Answered my prayer, He has.

As with any wedding, there is a rehearsal and a dinner a few days before. Friday night, we gathered at the church. After meeting my soon-to-be brother-in-law's family, all of us then stood around waiting. I was off to the side of our big fellowship room by myself just watching and listening to people talk when all of a sudden, I heard Anthony yell, *"Get him back!"* Within seconds, I could feel the angels crushing in around me to the point of suffocation. All I saw was their backs. I could hear them fighting with their shields and swords. I could hear swords hitting swords, but I couldn't see past them. Anthony yelled again, *"Get him back! We didn't anticipate that they would attack him here. Protect him!"*

As I stood there, freaking out, I thought to myself, *"Didn't anticipate they would attack me here? You're freakin' angels! You know everything. What the hell is going on?"* When to my surprise, I could feel little hands reaching past the angels touching me and grabbing something from me. With each handful they grabbed from me I felt as if something was leaving me. I felt like part of me was missing. I started to feel weak.

Anthony yelled again, *"Go after them! Go now!"* He turned around shoving me backwards. When I physically hit the back wall of the church, I looked past him. All I saw was a group of angels, fifteen or so, battling something. I couldn't see what it was, but there were many of them. Anthony said, *"I'm sorry, Jim. We knew they were planning on attacking you. We just didn't think it would be here. We are in control now. Don't move. Stay here."*

Lucky for me, everyone was so engrossed in their own conversations that no one noticed that I had moved about thirty feet from where I was standing before. I didn't even realize I had moved that much myself. I just stood against the wall with Anthony's hand on my chest trying to catch my breath. My brother looked over at me and mouthed the words, "Why are you standing all the way over there?" I just motioned for him to give me a minute. Anthony apologized to me again and told me that they increased the security around me. I asked, *"What just happened?"* He said, *"You will be told in time. You are safe now. They won't attack again!"*

Folks, there comes a time in all of our lives where we just don't get all of the answers we may be looking for. Welcome to that time in my life. I kept asking him questions, and he kept saying the same thing, *"You will be told in time."* So I did what everyone does right after they feel they may have been violated in some way. I sang for my sister's wedding rehearsal. I thought to myself, *I feel a little off with my singing. Only because I was just attacked by some mutant little demons or whatever they were!*

Everyone told me I sounded good, so I just took it in faith that in time I would be told what had happened to me. At the dinner, my brother asked me what had happened, so I told him. You should have seen his face. His response was the same as mine. "They're angels. How could they not have known this was going to happen?" I smiled and said, "You know what, Brau?" (Brau is my nickname for Peter. He calls me Chubby because I used to be chubby.) I continued, "I'm sure I will be told in time." He said, "Well, you better let me know when you do find out, because this is just crazy!" I told him I would tell him as soon as I found out and I agreed that this was insanely crazy.

I was staying with my sister Ellen. On Saturday morning, Marty walked right in front of me and just stood there. I said, *"Yes?"* Marty said, *"I need you for one hour. You need a healing and we will explain to you what happened yesterday."* I said, *"If I go downstairs, the kids are going to come down with me and expect me to play with them."* He said, *"Not this time. There will be an angel who will stand at the top of the stairs, and he won't let anyone down until we are finished."* As I walked to the doorway that led downstairs, I passed an angel. He nodded at me as I passed by him. He stood in the doorway with his arms crossed. Marty said, *"He won't let anyone down to bother us."*

I sat in a chair in the bedroom I'd stayed in when I lived with Ellen and her family. As I sat there, Marty started the healing. I could feel the energy rushing through me. I was still extremely tired from the attack. I asked

Marty what had happened. He said, *"Jim, please be patient. I will explain it to you in a few minutes."* He continued to ask me to take deep breaths. I said, *"Marty, I feel like a part of me is missing. It's just so weird."* He told me to hang on a minute and to take one more deep breath. All of a sudden, my spirit was transported to another location. I was still aware that my body was sitting in the chair in my sister's basement. But my mind, my consciousness was looking all around me, and as I saw hundreds of angels lined up in formation, row after row, standing at attention and cheering.

There were just too many for me to count. They were cheering and yelling *"SUPPLANTER, SUPPLANTER!"* I asked Marty what was going on. He said, *"You are in a realm where the warriors of God gather and prepare for battle."* I said, *"Why are they cheering?"* He said, *"They cheer for you! They all know who you are Jim. You are Supplanter. You are a very important part of God's plan, and all of these angels stand behind you and support you. Yesterday while you were at church, you were attacked by a group of demons sent by Satan. They stole some of your essence. In other words, they stole what makes you YOU! A group of angels have cornered all four demons as they were trying to scatter your essence to the four corners of the earth. They have been hunting them down across the world waiting for this moment. Do you see the golden sun above your head?"* I answered, *"Yes."* He explained, *"Watch what happens next."*

As I sat there in the middle of all these angels, it was as if I had a bird's eye view of what was happening across the world. I saw Paris, France, as an angel cornered one of these demons. It was amazing to watch the swordplay as it unfolded. I watched the angel skillfully block each sword thrust that came from the demon. The demon held a golden jar. Marty spoke up. *"That jar contains part of your essence. Keep watching."* The angel reached behind himself, grabbing his shield as he turned, spinning and deflecting the demon's sword. As he spun back around, the angel lunged upwards at the demon with his shield hitting the demon's sword and leaving the demon wide open. With one more pivot, the angel swung around backwards and cut the demon right in half. In an instant, the demon was just a flash of energy, and then he was gone.

The jar hit the ground and exploded. The energy within the jar shot straight up into the sky. As I watched it race across the atmosphere, it shot right into the sun above my head. Marty yelled out, *"One down, three to go!"*

As I continued to watch, my attention was directed to the other side of the earth. Two angels had another demon cornered. As one angel fought with the demon, the other angel stepped in and knocked the jar out of the demon's hand. As the demon dropped the jar, he seemed startled and in an instant the two angels cut him in half. I watched as the demon exploded and then was no more. One of the angels smashed the jar with his sword. I watched the energy from the jar shoot across the sky and land in the golden sun above my head once again. And so it went. I sat and watched as warrior angels cornered the remaining two demons. It was just breathtaking to watch these masterful warriors as they defended themselves against the enemy, never blinking an eye, always staying focused, spinning around with sword and shield, striking blow after blow against these demons. The third demon seemed to overextend himself too far. I watched as the angel sliced off the arm holding his sword. Then the angel spun back around and took the demon's head off. The angel then smashed the jar open and once again I watched my energy fill the sun above my head.

The fourth demon was really putting up a fight. The demon was yelling something at the angel in a language I couldn't understand. The angel seemed unaffected by his words. With no expression on his face, he calmly continued to battle the demon. Back and forth, swords hitting swords, shields hitting bodies and deflecting sword blows.

As I watched, the angel pinned the demon against the wall with his shield. The demon couldn't move. The angel then swung his sword above his head with the blade pointing downward, and he thrust it into the demon's head. Immediately, the demon exploded into a ball of fire and was gone. The angel picked up the jar and held it over his head and then, as hard as he could, he smashed the jar to the ground.

Marty said, *"That demon had most of your essence. Watch."* Out of the jar shot the biggest ball of energy I have ever seen. It was like rolling flames as it shot into the air and slipped across the atmosphere. When it hit the golden sun above my head, I could actually hear a crackling sound. Marty said, *"Jim, take a big, deep breath. We are going to put you back together. Here it comes."* As I took my breath, the sun split open and its contents dropped right on top of me. It was the most incredible feeling I had ever had. It was intense. I could actually feel my body almost pass out. Marty just kept saying, *"Breathe. Keep breathing deeply. Breathe!"*

I sat there trying to recover from the most mind-blowing energy experience I had ever felt. All of the angels were cheering even louder now and banging their swords against their shields. I looked at Marty and said, *"I really don't get it. I'm no one special."* Marty said, *"What is it going to take to convince you that you are someone special! Stand up!"* So I stood up. He said, *"Jim, this how you appear to the Lord when he looks at you."* As I stood there, I began to grow taller, taller, taller, and even taller. I felt as if I was well over a hundred feet tall. As I looked down, I could see across the entire realm I was standing in. There were millions of angels. They all seemed so small and looked like toy soldiers.

Marty yelled up to me, *"Do you get it now? When you remain humble and small, you appear this big to the Lord. Always remember to remain humble. He will do great things with you."* I then began to shrink back down to my original size. Marty said, *"Please sit back down. I know this is all very hard for you to understand. God has a plan. We keep telling you that. We keep telling you just to be yourself. Jim, you are the person He needs you to be, but you just don't believe it!"*

As I sat listening to Marty speak, he suddenly stopped and stood there with his mouth open. The angels stopped cheering. You could have heard a pin drop. Row by row, all of the angels around me went down on one knee and bowed their heads in silence. I look back at Marty and watched as he started to bow and walk backwards away from me. I turned to look behind me. There was a exceptionally tall thin man dressed in bright white robes walking down the aisle. He was taller than everyone else there. As He walked up to me, He smiled and put His hand on my head. I stared at Him in awe! I turned towards Him and wrapped my arms around his body and squeezed Him as tight as I could.

He said, *"Jim, my Father and I are very proud of you. You have a very special place in both of our hearts."* I held onto him as I began to cry. He continued, *"The song you wrote for Ann's wedding touched my Father's heart very deeply. Not many people today include Him in their songs as well as their lives, but you did.*

Your song touched me, too. You keep telling everyone that you are no one special. Do you know that every time you say that it belittles my Father and me, and it also hurts us?" He then bent down next to me and put my face in his hands. He pulled my face towards Him and said, *"Look into my eyes, Jim. Can you see the love I have for you?"* His eyes shone so brightly. They were so warm and loving. He continued, *"To us, you are a very special soul, and you are a vital part of my Father's plan. Please tell people that you have a greater responsibility and leave it at that. I have something for you."*

He stood up and walked behind me. He then draped something over the shoulders of my armor and said, *"Jim, this is a mantle of peace. My peace, I give to you. It will help you with the task at hand."* He came back to my side and held my head against his body. While tears ran down my face, He said, *"I know this is very overwhelming for you. My father and I have been waiting a long time for you. You will not fail us. In time, we will tell you of my Father's plan but for now just keep your wonderful faith. I bless and increase your faith. My Father has made you a promise that you are never alone. I make that same promise to you too. Be strong, Jim, and know that I am always with you. We love you very much. Receive the blessing of my Father."*

He put His hand on my head, and I felt a rush of energy fill me. He then turned and walked away. As he left I looked back at Him and saw His hands. They had the nail holes in them. As Jesus left, the angels stood up one by one, and they bowed their heads to me. I turned back towards Marty. As he ran back to me and we embraced, he said, *"Do you get it now? I have never seen the Son of God do anything like that before! He doesn't do this kind of thing, Jim. Wow! Jesus talked with you and gave you a mantle of peace."* He jumped around and smacked me on the shoulder and said sarcastically, *"I'm no one special! Jim, the Son of God was here. He talked to you. Do you get it now?"*

After my experience, I don't feel as if I should describe what Jesus looks like. All I will tell you is that He doesn't look like all of the pictures that others have portrayed of Him. He was Hebrew! Not Caucasian, folks. If anyone who reads my book were to ask me when they meet me what Jesus looks like, then I will tell you. But for now, I will leave it like this. Sorry.

That afternoon, after I told Peter, Ellen, and Fred, I went to my folks' house and shared everything with them. My dad just sat there dazed. He looked at me and told me that he believed me; he was just letting it all sink in. Mom had tears in her eyes as she asked me what the task at hand was. I told her that I had no idea.

Ann's wedding was beautiful. Everyone enjoyed the singing. As everything started to wind down, Tina and I spoke about giving each other a healing the next day. Tina went through the same healing program I went through and had been working with her healing master for many years.

The next morning after breakfast, I went to the bedroom I was staying in, when I noticed that all of my personal belongings, my watch, ring, money clip, and tie-bar with my church emblem on it, were thrown all over the room.

I stood there for a minute and looked at Anthony. He said, *"Andreus was here. He wanted you to know that he knows where you are at all* times, and he can't wait until you come home." I said, *"What a turd! Am I supposed to be afraid of him?"* Anthony said, *"We are here to protect you, but you must not provoke him."* I said, *"He started it!"* Anthony answered, *"You are a representative of the Lord God, and He will not be provoked by anyone so too, neither will you!"* I said, *"Fine. I hear what you are saying."*

I began to look for all of my things. I couldn't find my ring; I'd had it for over twenty years. Instead of buying a high school class ring I bought a church ring. It is gold with our church emblem on it. It means a lot to me. I looked at Anthony. He said, *"It's behind the door in the corner."* Sure enough, there it was.

The next day in the afternoon, I had Tina give me a healing before I gave her one. She spent around forty-five minutes on me. I had shared with her what had happened over the past few days when we were at the wedding. She was also amazed. We then switched places and I began Tina's healing. Marty and Tina's healing master were talking and comparing notes on Tina and me. I told Marty to focus!

As I looked to my left, a spirit appeared. I saw a young, blond, petite woman standing off to the side wearing a yellow dress. She was very pretty. I asked, *"Who are you?"* Tina spoke up and said, "She's your psychic surgeon." The spirit said, *"My name is Amanda. I have been sent to help you. I will work with you the same way Marty does."* I said, *"I haven't been trained on how to use Amanda."* Tina answered, "You just plug her cord into the back of your left hand. She will tell you what to do."

So I took Amanda's cord and plugged it into the back of my left hand. The energy in my hand felt the same as it did when working with Marty. Amanda said, *"Marty's energy flushes and removes bad energies. My energy cuts and removes things. Just like a surgeon would remove a tumor from a physical body; I do the same by removing things from people's spaces. Marty and I will make quite a team for you."* As she spoke, I looked at Marty as he was smoothing down the sides of his hair and wiping a finger across his eyebrows one at a time as he looked at Amanda. I questioned Marty, *"Need a breath mint?"* Amanda just rolled her eyes and said, *"Not that kind of team, Marty!"* He looked terribly disappointed so I told him to knock it off and grow up.

Everything was going well until we got to Tina's sixth chakra, her third eye. Amanda found a locked wooden chest in the center of Tina's mind. I asked Tina what it was. She screamed, "Whatever you do, don't open it!" Tina explained, "Ten years ago, two clairvoyant friends of mine helped me trap it in this box. It's a very evil demon. We tricked him to get him in this box, and boy was he mad. He caused so many problems in my life. I can't and don't even want to think about how much he toyed with me and hurt me. I don't know how to get rid of him, so just leave him there." I looked at Anthony and asked if he could help. He answered, *"Yes, one moment, while I bring in some help."* Twenty angels filled the room. Amanda walked over to the chest. Anthony said, *"Amanda, after you open the chest, step to the side quickly. We will do the rest."*

All of the angels formed a circle around all of us. Amanda cut the lock off the chest and flipped the lid open while she jumped off to the side. Immediately a enormous orange furry beast with yellow eyes, fangs, and claws jumped out growling and screaming. Two angels grabbed him and held him between themselves while another angel pulled out his sword and thrust it into the demon's chest. The demon then just disappeared.

Tina said, *"I guess we now know why Amanda showed up today and why you have these angels close by to protect you."* Tina was so happy. She told me how this demon confused her and influenced her to do things that cost her many friendships and almost made her lose her family. We finished Tina's healing. Everything was just perfect; at least that's what I thought.

The next morning, we were going back to the west coast. I had this weird feeling in my heart that was more than just an anxious feeling to get back. Once we landed, I felt a little better until Anthony said, *"Andreus knows that you have come back."* To which I responded, *"And?"* So Anthony said, *"You need to be on your guard. We are watching you very closely, but you must always be ready."* I said, *"Okay."*

Chapter 8
Phase 3

    The next evening, it was back to planning the business. Our business comprised two types of business merged into one. Peter researched one part, and I researched the other. We made appointments with numerous vendors and suppliers. When we shared a little of our concept with some of the vendors, they loved our idea and were willing to give us an even greater discount. Because of my twenty years' experience as a buyer, I was able to negotiate exceptional pricing for us. Everything was falling into place. It was tremendously exciting to build a business from nothing and then watch the plan as it grew. Each and every free waking moment was spent on our business; every evening and almost every weekend was spent finalizing our plans.

    On Tuesday evening, Shelly invited me over for dinner, so I could tell her all about our trip to Chicago and my sister's wedding. When I was in the kitchen by the sink getting a drink of water, I turned around and there was an enormous demon standing in the kitchen doorway. He was well over nine feet tall and over four feet wide. He was enormous! He was clad in red armor and had the face of a boar. He had a black complexion with horns coming out of the sides of his head. He was extremely ugly. As he spoke, Anthony stepped in front of me and just stood there. Shelly just kept talking to me because she had no idea this was going on.

    The demon smiled and pointed his finger at me and then made the knife across the throat motion to me. He said, *"Supplanter, I just wanted to stop by to see you and let you know that I also know who you are. I will make it my business to destroy you! Lucky for you that you have these angels protecting you or I would take care of you right now! Remember, I will be watching you!"* Shelly noticed that I wasn't looking at her but that I was staring at the open doorway. She asked, "Are you okay? What's going on?" I told her to give me a minute. I looked right at the thing and said, *"I really don't give a crap about what you said, so get out of this house right now before I asked God to send someone to help you leave!"* With that, he pointed his finger at me and laughed as he left.

    Shelly looked scared at me and asked, "Jim, what's going on?" I answered, "Some big, ugly demon just stopped by and threatened me. He's gone. We are safe now." She asked if it was Andreus. I told her, "No, it was some new guy." I looked at Anthony and before I could ask, he said, "His name is Markus. He is Satan's number one general." Tell Shelly that she was safe the whole time. She has an angel that has been with her since her life began. His name is Maurice."

I shared everything with Shelly. I even kidded around a little with her when I told her they had to import a French angel for her. She just laughed. Anthony then repeated once more that I must always be ready for anything.

The following weekend was Service for the Departed again; remember, we have it three times a year. We had the service at a big hotel. Most of the district was invited for the service. Before the service started, I clairvoyantly surveyed the auditorium. I could see Thomas as well as a number of souls from the groups I was praying for. I looked across the aisle and seated in the row across from me were our church's seven previous chief apostles: Peter, Krebs, Neihaus, Bishoff, Schmidt, Streckeisen, and Urwyler. They had each been in charge of our church for certain periods of time when they were alive. I was amazed that I saw Apostle Peter from the first church. All of them looked right at me and with their hands folded they shook them as if to say, "We are praying very hard for you." I was stunned. Why would they all be praying so hard for me and what did they know? Did they know what God's plan was for me? I was completely overwhelmed. The service was magnificent, once again thousands were baptized and sealed with the Holy Spirit and received Holy Communion. It was truly a wonderful day.

During the course of the following week, my lead angel Anthony told me that he would help me work out. Every time I would look at him; he seemed a little out of focus. He told me I should just meditate; that everything was fine. He gave me pointers on how to lift and how many reps to lift. I kept telling him that this was too much weight, but he wouldn't listen until I got sick and actually threw up. He apologized to me. Needless to say, I didn't take any of his pointers anymore. Give me a break; I don't have the strength of an angel.

Over the weekend, Anthony told me that he wanted to talk with Peter and me about the future. I said, "This seems a bit unusual. We have never included anyone else in this task at hand before." He said, "Some things have changed and your brother and Shelly are now a part of it. Call Shelly and see if we can all get together this evening so that I may share everything with the three of you." I called Shelly, and we made plans to be over at her house in a few hours.

We all got together in Shelly's basement. Anthony told me that he would tell me what to say and that I should just repeat it to the two of them, so I did. As I sat there, my heart was aching and hurting me even more than ever before. I didn't say anything to the others, although I felt just like I was being suffocated. Anthony began to speak so I shared what he said out loud to Shelly and Peter. He said, "The Lord has decided to have a spiritual triad in his work. The three of you will encompass this triad. Jim, you will become the apostle for the Chicago district; Peter, you will become the apostle for the west coast; and Shelly, you will become the ambassador for the Realms of Eternity."

As Anthony spoke, my heart began to hurt more and I was finding it hard to breathe. We all questioned how this was going to happen. Anthony told us to trust in the Lord and everything would work out. I asked, "What about our business? How am I supposed to help run the business when I'm in Chicago? This doesn't make any sense." Once again Anthony told us just to trust in the Lord. He went into a little detail about how all of this was going to work. As I sat and relayed to the other two what he was saying, I had a really difficult time believing any of it, so I said. "The chief apostle doesn't even know who we are."

Anthony said, "The Lord showed the chief apostle the three of you in a dream. He knows who you are, and when the time is right he will call for all of you." I was had an extremely difficult time breathing at that point. I was also genuinely trying hard to accept all of it. I spoke up and said, "I can't do this anymore. I feel as if I'm going to pass out!" Anthony was standing behind me and said, "Fine. That will be all at this time."

Shelly and Peter came to my side because I must have looked horrible. I said, "I'm sorry, guys; this just doesn't feel right. For all of this time, the Lord has only included me in this plan. He has never mentioned the two of you. Please understand that this has nothing to do with my ego. It has everything to do with the way the Lord has been handling this. He doesn't change. Why now? Why would he change and include the two of you? Don't get me wrong, I would love the two of you to help out in this, but my heart is killing me and I can barely breathe. Something just isn't right and I can't put my finger on it."

Shelly and Peter agreed that we should just stop talking about it and change the subject for the time being. Anthony spoke up, "Jim, you felt uncomfortable because I was speaking through you. I was in your space. That is why your heart hurts and you had a difficult time breathing. The human body can only hold so much energy and then it starts to fight back. This is why you are so uncomfortable. I will withdraw from you and you should start feeling better." My breathing became better, but my heart was still hurting. The three of us agreed that we would keep it to ourselves and just see how it all played out.

The next day while I was at work, Cathy, a vendor I did business with, was trying to set me up on a blind date. I kept telling her that all of my blind dates were horrible. I have two rules: I don't date women who are bigger or hairier than me. So I told Cathy she should stop wasting her time. She then informed me that the girl used to be a model. I said, "Continue." Cathy told me her name was Jill, and she was a buyer for another flooring company, just like me. She was twenty-six years old, a tall, slender blonde with very pretty blue eyes, who liked older men, and was a real knockout. To which, I responded, "Then what's wrong with her?" Cathy said, "What's wrong with you?" I answered, "Where should we begin?" I told Cathy that I would think about it.

Here's my problem. Remember the picture of the brunette standing on the hill with my two sons and me? That woman kind of resembles what Lana might have looked like in a few years. I could never get a close-enough look at her face to see exactly what she looked like, but the woman from my vision was definitely a brunette, not a blonde.

As I drove home, Anthony told me that Michael wanted to talk with me. When I got home, I went to my room and closed my eyes. I could see Michael, but he was too far out of my range to see him clearly. He told me to stay where I was. He then told me that Jill was the woman of my dreams, and I needed to go out with her. I argued with him as I pointed to the mental picture of the brunette standing with my two sons. He told me that things had changed and that Jill is the girl for me. It just didn't feel right. We went around and around, until he got a little angry and said, "Just do it!"

Michael told me to kneel down in front of him because he had a blessing from God for me. I knelt down in front of him. He put his hands on the top of my head. As he spoke, I felt nothing as I had the other times. It was really weird. That pain in my heart was growing stronger each passing day. It felt exceedingly uncomfortable. No, I wasn't having a heart attack. My left arm never went numb! When he finished, I told him that I felt nothing. He told me that my body got used to the energy and that I shouldn't worry about it. He told me that the pain in my heart was the anxiety I felt about my date with Jill. And with that he ran off.

I called Cathy the next day and got Jill's phone number. We talked a few times and then made plans to go out the following Monday night. As I sat in my car that night, Anthony and Marty both told me to relax and that it was just a date. I told both of them that it didn't feel right. Marty told me to let it go and have an enjoyable time. Anthony then told me that when I greeted her, I must kiss her hand. I told him he was nuts; that there was no way I was going to do that on a first date. She would think I was a geek! He said, "You must be obedient to the Lord's wishes. She will think its romantic; just do it."

As I greeted Jill, I held her hand and kissed it. She looked at me as if I was nuts and said, "Oh that was kind of different." I thought to myself, "Great, now she thinks I'm a freak!" I tried my best to find a common ground of interest with her. She seemed very stuck-up and quite a high-maintenance kind of girl. I listened to her drone on about all of the fabulous places and countries she had been to and how modeling was the greatest thing that ever happened to her in her life. I thought to myself, "And now you're a flooring buyer? Something went horribly wrong for you."

At one point, she excused herself to go to the ladies' room. After she had left, I looked at Anthony and said, "This is the woman of my dreams? She's more like the woman of my nightmares! She is not at all what I'm attracted to. She's thin and very bony. I bet if I hugged her, I would snap her in half. Oh yes, and she's blonde!" All he said was, "You need to give it more time." I told him, "I don't see how this is going to work out. She doesn't even go to church. You remember God, right?? He's a pretty big part of my life. I don't see her going with me to church at all." Once again, all he said was "Just give it more time."

After about an hour and a half, I could tell that she felt the same magical energy I was feeling. None! At the end of our date, I told Jill that I would call her sometime that week and that I'd had a nice time. She told me that she would call me on my birthday, which was the coming Friday. I said okay.

The following Friday, Shelly threw me a birthday party. It was only with a few friends. I actually don't like being made the center of attention. Before everyone got there, I received a call from Jill, wishing me a happy birthday. I had such a hard time talking to her. There were moments of dead silence. I finally told her I appreciated her calling and we hung up.

Lana showed up at the party and surprised me. She told me she didn't have her parents' permission, but she couldn't stay away on my birthday. She sat next to me the whole night. We held hands under the table, and it was a very enjoyable evening. Lana gave me a kiss later that night as she left. With tears in her eyes, she told me how much she missed me and wished things could be different. I told her I felt the same way. Once everyone left, Shelly asked me if I could give her an energy healing sometime next week. I told her I would be happy to on Monday evening, and we set a time.

On Monday evening, I had Shelly sit in a chair, and we began the healing. I spent about forty-five minutes on her. She had a lot of issues from her past that she was working through. She did a terrific job of letting go of everything. After the healing, she asked if I would like to stay and talk. I said I would so we went into the kitchen. After a while I excused myself and went to the bathroom. As I dried my hands off and looked at myself in the mirror, I heard a quiet voice say, "Jim, it's me, Jesus. Look closely at your eyes and see me." I leaned in and looked closer at my own eyes. They glimmered. He said, "If you give yourself over to me, I will share with you and Shelly my plan." I paused for a moment and then said okay. He said, "Go back into the kitchen and I will talk with the two of you." I sat down and explained to Shelly that Jesus was inside me and would like to share with us his plan. She looked at me as if I was crazy. I didn't blame her. She said OK. All of a sudden, I felt something happen to my body. I lost total control of it, and was now looking through my own eyes as if I was in the backseat of a car and someone else was driving. When my mouth opened I began to speak with the most remarkably clear English accent I have ever heard. To this day, I can't even copy it close to what it sounded like.

"Jesus" began to tell us that his Father loved us very much and had a specific plan of salvation. He spoke about His return and how He would take us with Him. He then started to talk about Shelly's ex-husband and how horrible and cruel he was to her and that because of what he did to Shelly, "Jesus" was going to punish him. At this point, I felt as if I was having a heart attack. Shelly looked at me and said, "Why would you punish him? You are Jesus. You forgive!" He said, "There is also a side of me that punishes those who hurt the ones I love." At this moment, I knew something wasn't right. I started to try to regain control of my body, but the harder I struggled, the harder He pushed back.

He said to Shelly in an English accent, "Love, just give me a moment. I need to speak with Jim." With that, I could feel him turn inside of my body and stare at me. He said, "Jim, you are making it very hard for me to share with the two of you my plan. Now, just sit there and be patient." He then turned back and began to talk with Shelly again in that English accent. He said, "For so many years, I watched him treat you horribly and I have now decided that he does not have the right to live anymore." Shelly said, "How can you talk like this? Why are you doing this? What are you going to do to him?" He said, "In a few days, your ex-husband will be walking across the street and he will be hit by a truck and dragged to a very horrible death." Shelly began to cry. She said, "This isn't right. No one should be punished this way. We have been taught our whole life to forgive and to forget!"

He said, "Shelly, why are you questioning the Son of God! If I feel he should die, then he should die! You suffered so much when you were married to him, and I feel he should now suffer for everything he did to you. He is a worthless human being who only thinks of himself and no one else. I would think that you would be thanking me instead of fighting me!"

My chest was killing me, and I began to struggle again. I started screaming in my head as loud as I could to Shelly, "This is not Jesus!" He then reached out and grabbed her hands as he began to tell her that he loved her very much and that she should just let it happen. You should have seen the look on Shelly's face. In all the time that Shelly and I had been friends, I had never touched her in any way. The only physical contact we would have was a hug now and then. She tried to pull away from him, but as she did, he held on tighter and squeezed. She looked at him and said, "Jim, you are scaring me!" I screamed in my head, "It's not me!"

He held her hands tighter and said, "Jim's not here right now. It's me, Jesus, and you. Relax. You see, Shelly, I know how you feel about Jim. You are attracted to him. He's a very handsome man. Do you like the way I made him? I think you can see why Lana's attracted to him, too." Shelly spoke up and said, "I don't like this! Jesus would never talk like this! Jim, what is going on? Please stop this right now!" I began to fight again. The harder I fought, the more the pain in my chest grew. It was excruciating. He told Shelly to hold on a minute; that he needed to have a talk with "our friend Jim."

He turned in toward me again and said without an English accent, "I'm only going to say this once, so you had better listen well! If you don't stop fighting me, I will choke Shelly with your own two hands until she is dead! Do we have an understanding?" I was horrified so I backed off and prayed, "Dear God! What is happening? Please help me!" He looked at Shelly and said with that creepy English accent, "Now, that's better! Shelly, let's play a game. You had better stand up quickly because your friend Jim is going to need your help. To show you that I have total control over Jim's body, I'm going to cause his muscles to relax." He began to laugh. "If you don't support and hold your friend up, he's going to fall to the floor and break something!" With that, I felt my entire body go limp. Shelly sprung from her bar stool and grabbed me.

Folks; Shelly's not a particularly big person. Of course, most people compared to me would be small. She put her arms under my arms and tried her best to keep me on my stool. He said, "C'mon, Shelly, you're going to drop him, don't you love and support your friend?" Shelly yelled, "This isn't funny, Jim! I can't hold you much longer! You are too heavy for me, and I'm getting tired!" He toyed with her for another five minutes by almost having me fall of the stool; at the last second, he would stop me. Shelly had her arms wrapped around me as tight as she could. I could see she was getting tired. He said, "Isn't this fun!"

For the next two and half hours, he played with us. He knew all of our hopes and fears, and he played on all of them. He would start by telling us pleasant things and then he would twist them into a hellish nightmare. I have never been so scared in my life, and I could tell that Shelly was horrified, too. We were both physically exhausted. At one point, Shelly's daughter Lannie and her boyfriend walked into the kitchen while this was still going on. They could tell something wasn't right. He looked at them using my voice and held a short conversation with the two of them as if nothing were going on at all. Once they left and went to Lannie's room, I decided I'd had all I could take. I began to fight again, trying to get control of my body. He turned in toward me and said, "Jim, you don't listen very well, do you? If you don't stop fighting me, I will stand you up, walk you into Lannie's room, and have you kill her and her boyfriend, and after they are dead, I will have you come back in here and kill Shelly! NOW, BACK OFF!" I stopped fighting once again. He continued to horrify us for another hour until Shelly stood up and said, "Jim I'm not doing this anymore! It's one o'clock in the morning, and I have to get up for work! Leave now!" And with that being said, he released me and I regained control of my body.

I looked at Shelly and said, "Shelly I have no idea what just happened!" She said, "I don't want to hear it! Get out of my house before I call the cops!" I grabbed my things and ran out of the house to my car. I sat in my running car while it was still in Shelly's driveway. I was physically exhausted. I then heard an evil voice laughing while he said to me, "You are such a fool. Everything you have thought to be real is a lie! There is no God, no heaven! You sit there in fear because you are trying to figure out who I am. Don't you know who I am? I'm Satan!" I said, "No you're not. I've seen Satan." He said, "When I get done with you, your reputation will be exactly what everyone in this area already thinks of you, that you are crazy! I have destroyed you! I have destroyed one of the closest friendships you have ever had. You are a joke, and I'm just getting started!"

As I sat there, my mind was racing trying to figure out what to do. I looked to my right and there sitting on the passenger seat was a video I had rented. He continued talking. "You are a moron. You put your trust in God. He doesn't even exist. You have no armor, no sword or shield. All you have is your reputation, and I have destroyed you!" I took a big deep breath and said, "Shut the hell up! I really don't care what you say! I have to return this video, so leave me alone!" He laughed and said," I have destroyed your life and all you're worried about is some movie you rented!" I answered, "Yes, I don't want to be charged a late fee, I'm too tired to care anymore so why don't you just shut up!"

As I drove to the video store and then home, this thing kept talking to me, tormenting me. When I pulled into the driveway, he said, "If you wake Peter up and tell him anything about what has happened I will kill him with your own two hands! I control you! I own your body! In the afternoon when your brother comes home from work, he will find you dead on the floor because I'm going to force you to commit suicide! You are such a pathetic loser! And after you die, I will drag your soul to the depths of hell, where I will torment you for all eternity!"

I walked into my bedroom and knelt down to pray, but every time I tried he would keep talking. He told me that God was a fake, that He wasn't real, and that I was wasting my time. But I didn't believe him. He then told me that God couldn't hear my prayers because this thing was blocking them. All I could pray was, "Father, where are you? Please help me!" The thing just kept mocking me. I tried to sleep, but I couldn't. He wouldn't stop. He kept me awake all night. My chest was killing me now more than ever.

In the morning, he told me once more that if I tried to warn Peter, he would kill both of us. I didn't listen, though. I ran into the laundry room where Peter was and cried, "Peter, I don't know what is happening to me but I am possessed! Protect yourself from me!" With tears running down my face, I quickly told him what had happened the night before. Peter said, "This is not funny, Jim! You're scaring me!" I said, "I'm not kidding, Peter. I'm possessed! When you come home from work this afternoon, you will find me dead on the floor because this thing is going to force me to kill myself." Peter said, "What can I do?"

The thing inside of me used my gift as he looked at Peter. It told me to tell Peter this: "Peter, this thing inside of me said you are thinking of calling Tina. Don't or he will kill the both of us!" Peter said, "Yes, I was thinking that." Peter stepped toward me. I screamed, "Stay away from me! I don't want him to hurt you!" Peter looked at me and asked, "What's with your eyes? I can see they are not your eyes!" I answered, "I told you, I'm possessed! Stay away from me!" Peter said, "I don't care what this thing says. I'm calling Tina!" The thing inside kept telling me that we were both making a big mistake, and he was going to kill both of us.

    Peter grabbed his cell phone and called Tina. As they spoke, I sat on the couch clutching my chest because it hurt that much. I could hear Peter telling Tina everything, including the part where we were told we would both be made apostles and be in charge of our own districts. Peter walked into the room where I was and told me that Tina wanted to talk with me. I grabbed the phone and listened to Tina say: "Jim, you are in charge of your own space. Rely on your training. You know who you are. He can't force you to do anything you don't want to do. Take some deep breaths. Put him in a room and build a wall around him. Stay away from him. Fill the room with darkness and leave him alone. I think I know who he is. You need to go to work. I will call you this evening and tell you what I know." I said, "Go to work? I haven't slept all night! I'm exhausted! Besides, I'm already late." She said, "Jim, you need to go to work for the distraction. I can see four angels standing around you right now. You are safe. Just stay away from this thing, and I will call you tonight."

    I got dressed. I called my boss to tell him I'd overslept and then I went to work. All morning the thing wouldn't leave me alone. Have you ever had a day where you were just up to your eyeballs in work and an evil demon won't leave you alone? Yeah me, too!

    Around lunchtime I got a phone call from Lana. She wanted to take me out to lunch for my birthday. I tried to discourage her and she kept asking me why. I finally told her that I'd left my work phone at home and I had to drive home on my lunch to get it.

    She insisted that she come with me. I met her in a parking lot and off we went. She looked at me and could tell something wasn't right. I told her everything; I told her I didn't want her anywhere near me because of this thing. She reminded me that the angels would keep us both safe. I ran into the house, grabbed my phone, and then we went to a drive-thru to get something to eat. I dropped her off at her car. She gave me a big hug and a kiss and told me that she was praying for me.

    Needless to say, it seemed as if this was the longest day of my life. As I drove home, I called Tina. She told me that thing in my space was none other than the demon who used to be in her space, the one we thought was killed five weeks before when I gave her that healing. She told me that the demon was immensely powerful, and I should just stay away from it. It had done the same thing to her as it was doing to me. She told me that she would have to call her clairvoyant friend in Hawaii to see when the three of us could get together to remove it. She told me to be patient. She told me God was with me and the angels around me would keep me safe.

I told Tina what happened that night with Shelly. I asked her to call Shelly and tell her that it wasn't me who did those things to her and also to tell her how sorry I was that all of it had happened. Tina told me to be strong and she would call Shelly and explain everything to her. That evening, I shared everything with Peter. I lit a number of candles and tried to get some sleep. The thing kept talking to me, but I tried my best to block him out.

The next day as I sat there at my desk at work, I heard another quiet voice say, "We are surrounding you. No harm will come to you." I felt a peace fill my heart. I kept working to the best of my ability under the circumstance. To look at me, you would have never known what was going on inside of me. The thing just wouldn't let up. It continued to taunt me. I sat at my desk, fighting it as much as I could. I then was reminded of the conversation I had with Michael just before I'd left for Chicago. I heard Michael's voice say, "Remember, nothing can harm you." I got up from my desk and went to the bathroom. I decided I'd had enough. Once in the bathroom, I leaned against the vanity and closed my eyes and concentrated on my heart chakra.

I slowly found myself walking through a tunnel again, until I came upon a room. I walked in the room and in the center was a bricked-up section of wall with slits, so I could see inside it. There he was, just like I remembered him. He was immense and hairy with claws. He was snarling at me. I felt a rage fill me like I have never felt before. I opened the door to the bricked-up wall and walked inside. He immediately lunged at me. I grabbed him by the throat with my left hand and squeezed as hard as I could. His face filled with sheer terror as he realized I had a hold of him. He began to gasp for air. I clenched my right hand into a fist and said, "You picked the wrong human to screw with!" And with that, I began to beat the living hell out him. With every blow to his face, blood streamed down from where I punched him.

For five minutes, I beat him into a bloody pulp. And then I pulled my sword out and said, "Remember this? I don't have a sword, right!" I took my sword and plunged it under his collarbone and jammed it up towards his shoulder. He let out a scream of pain like I have never heard anything make before. I said, "But I don't have a sword! Why are you screaming?" I began to twist it and shove it in further. I threw him to the ground and said, "Wait, I'm not done with you yet! Here's something you forgot about. I have the life of God in me; the Holy Spirit!" I grabbed him by the throat again and dragged him into the light that was shining down in the center of my heart. As I pulled him into the light, he began to burn and scream out, begging me to stop.

As I held him there, I began to beat the crap out of him again. I picked him up with one arm and threw him across the room into the corner. I walked over to where he was huddling in fear. I grabbed him by the throat and slammed him up against the wall, lifting him off the floor and said, "Let's get something straight right now. I don't know why I shouldn't just kill you, but for some reason, I won't. So while you are here you will keep quiet and leave me alone until Tina and her friend figure out how to get you out of me. So help me God, if you make one sound, I will be back in here so fast you will wish you were dead! Do you understand me?" He nodded his head at me. Blood was flowing down from everywhere. He was covered in it. I took him and walled him up in the center of my heart near the Holy Spirit's light. I told him if he moved an inch he would get burned.

I quietly walked back to my desk and began to work again. I sent Tina an email informing her that I'd found where he was and that we now had an agreement. She told me to be careful. A few hours later, he started up again. I went back to the bathroom and meditated again.

As I walked into the walled-up room in my heart, I grabbed him by the top of his head and dragged him into the light. He screamed out. I asked, "What don't you get? Are you an idiot or something? I'm not joking about this!" I then made myself ten stories tall. I picked my foot up off the ground and smashed it on top of him. I then dragged my foot across the floor as if I had a piece of chewing gum stuck on the bottom of my shoe. With every step, I could hear him scream in agony. I picked him up with my thumb and index finger and held him in front of my face. He was so tiny now. I said, "Do we have a truce or should I keep going? The way I feel right now, which, by the way, is complete rage, I wouldn't have a problem coming in here every few hours and beating the living crap out of you! Do you think I'm being serious?" He nodded his head yes. I threw him back into the room and left.

That evening after work, I went to get my haircut. I spoke with the hairstylist about life in general and told her how uneventful my life was.

No, really, I did. I honestly don't think there's an appropriate time to tell someone that you are just totally exhausted from work, and that you were beating the crap out of a demon all day, do you?

It was now Easter weekend. Two weeks had passed, and I still had the demon inside of me. I called Tina to find out what was going on with her and her friend. She told me that it was hard to get hold of her friend because of the time difference. Also, they both had families. It was now a holiday weekend, and I should just be patient.

I exploded and said, "Be patient? Be patient? I have had this demon in me for well over two months! The only reason I'm in this situation was because I tried to help you when I gave you a healing! Give me a break! You, above all people, should understand what I'm going through!" She said she was sorry and would try harder to get in touch with her friend and help me.

Two weeks after Easter, I was still possessed, but life goes on. My cell phone rang. It was Tina. She said, "I tried calling you last night. Didn't you hear your phone ring?" I said, "No, I must have turned it off, which I never do." She said, "I had my friend Jenny from Hawaii on a conference call. We were ready to help you. I called four times, Jim." I told her I was sorry and that I would make sure I leave my phone on. She told me that there must have been a reason they couldn't get hold of me. Maybe it just wasn't time yet. She told me to be patient and that she would get hold of Jenny and find out when we could do it again. Needless to say, I was extremely disappointed, angry and ticked off.

Peter and I scheduled a conference call with Billy to talk about our business plan. Here's something you need to know about Billy. He had so many stories about his life. All the celebrities he knew, all the financial successes he had. As he spoke, I had that strange feeling in my gut that he was just full of crap. I gave him the benefit of the doubt because he had been dating Tina for over a year, and why should I second-guess her? He told us that he was willing to give us half our yearly salaries upfront so that we could pay off all of our debts. Next, he would buy us a house, for which we would pay him rent for a two-year period. He would take that rent and put it toward the mortgage on a rent-to-own basis. After two years, we would get our own mortgage and pay him off. He then told us to pick out the vehicles of our dreams. He would buy them as a company expense and we should just consider them a gift from him.

Yes, everything sounded just perfect, and almost too good to be true. When we got off the phone with Billy, I told Peter that I would believe it when I saw it. Peter laughed at me and said, "You, Jim, are going to wait to believe something until after you see it? That's rich." I told him I just found it hard to believe that Billy was willing to do all of this and that I wasn't getting my hopes up. All I wanted was the money to back the business. I didn't need a large house or a fancy SUV to impress anyone. Peter said he understood.

One week later while I was sitting at my desk working, I felt something change all around me. I sent an email to Tina telling her this. She sent an email back telling me that she could see that the angels had just changed. The ones that had been with me for a while had left and there were now four new angels of light surrounding me. It was the changing of the guard. She told me that this was what we had been waiting for and that I should make sure my phone was on because she and Jenny would try to call me very soon.

That evening, Peter and I met with a contractor. We were interviewing construction companies for our business. As I sat there and listened to Peter talk with the general contractor, I could feel a warm light all around me. The demon inside started up again. I clairvoyantly told him to shut up, or I would come in there and hurt him in ways he had never known. He shut up quickly.

The very next Saturday, my phone rang at 3:10 am. I grabbed it and saw that it was Tina. She calmly said, "Jim, it's time. Jenny and I are ready. Go into the family room and get ready to meditate." I went into the family room and started to meditate. Jenny explained everything to me. Jenny said, "Jim, we are building a safe space for you. Your angels won't let any harm come to you. Before we can help you, we have to give this demon a chance to speak." I said, "Are you nuts? I don't give a crap what this thing has to say; just get it out of me!" She said, "We need to know why this happened and it is the only thing that knows why. You are going to have to let him speak through you." I said, "There is no way I'm going to give myself over to this thing again. Let him speak through you!" Jenny said, "We can't do that for you. We are holding space for you. You are in control of your space, Jim. He can't hurt you. Just listen to what he says and relay it to us, okay?"

For ten minutes, we went back and forth about this and I finally said OK. I spoke to the demon and said, "Let's just get one thing straight. If you try to pull anything with me, I will kill you. Do you understand?" I heard a small voice say, "Yes." Jenny began to ask the demon questions. She said, "Demon, what is your name?" I listened to what he said and then spoke it out loud. The demon said, "Your primitive minds couldn't possibly comprehend my name. Your tongues can't even pronounce my name!" As I sat there, I saw a name flash before my eyes. It had over twenty letters in it and most of them were consonants.

Jenny said to the demon, "Where are you from?" He said, "I am from the Babylonian time period. I have been doing this for a very long time." Jenny said, "Then we will call you 'Babylonian.' Is that okay?" He said, "Yes." She said, "Why are you here?" He said, "God has a special plan for Jim. I was sent to test him, to see how obedient he would be. To see if he would follow unconditionally, even if it went against everything he believed to be true. I was also sent to test his ability to control himself. He passed. I have never seen or fought a human as strong as Jim. He must have a particularly special place in God's heart. That is why I fear him. I am afraid that when I step out of him, he will kill me. I was only doing what I was told to do. Satan sent me to keep track of Jim and God allowed it. That is all I know."

Jenny said, "Jim, it sounds like he is done and is ready to leave. Babylonian, if you are ready, then step out of Jim." He said, "If I step out of him he will kill me. He must give me his word that he won't kill me." I spoke up and said, "For crying out loud, get the hell out of me right now. I won't kill you!" He said, "I don't believe him! Jenny, if you give me your word that Jim won't kill me, then I will come out!" Jenny said, "Jim, are you going to kill him?" I sat there for a few minutes and didn't say a word. I was still extremely angry about all of this. Jenny spoke up again, "Jim! Can I have your word that you won't kill him?" After about five minutes, I relented and said, "Fine!"

Jenny said, "Babylonian, you were lied to. Satan told you that if you followed him and did his bidding, you would be rewarded. There are two doorways in front of you. One is glowing orange and the other is glowing white. Satan is waiting for you behind the orange light and once you step through, he will destroy you. If you ask God for forgiveness and would like to switch back to His side, then He will allow you to walk through the white glowing doorway." Can you believe this folks? It's all true!

Babylonian spoke up and said, *"Jenny, I have your word that Jim won't kill me, right?"* She said, *"Yes, you are safe."* I could feel him as he stepped out of my heart chakra. He was almost all the way out when he stopped with one foot still in me. He turned and said to me, *"I can't leave until you forgive me."* I said, *"You have got to be kidding me! You're a freaking demon! Give me a break!"* He said, *"The rage you have for me is holding me in your heart. Unless you forgive me, I won't be released; therefore I can't leave!"* I sat there for a few moments fuming about all of this. Finally I said, *"Fine, I forgive you!"* He said, *"You have to mean it."* I said, *"Okay, I forgive you! But mark my words, if I ever see you again near me, my family, or any of my friends, I will kill you in the blink of an eye! Do I make myself clear?"* He said, *"Yes, very clear."*

He then stepped all the way out of me and walked toward the glowing white door. But before he walked through it, he said, *"I want you to know how very sorry I am for everything I did to you. You have no idea how much God loves you, Jim, and because of His love for you, He is going to give you so many nice things. I know how hard it must be for you to hear these things, especially coming from someone like me but it's all true."* I said, *"Whatever! Just remember what I said."* He thanked Jenny and Tina and then stepped through the door.

Folks, please let me point something out to you. If you remember, every time I would have a conversation with Michael or Anthony they always seemed out of focus and never got close enough so I could see them clearly. It was because it wasn't my angels talking to me. It was this demon pretending to be them.

Jenny told me that I should get a healing immediately from Marty and Amanda to remove any part of Babylonian from my space. I also thanked Jenny and Tina for their help, and once I hung up the phone I began to meditate. Marty and Amanda were running toward me. We all embraced. All of us were crying. Yes, even Marty! I asked them where they were while this was going on. They told me that they were told to stay away from me the whole time, and they couldn't help me in any way. They both said it was agonizing to stand by and watch me go through all of this. While they were giving me my healing, Anthony and the other three angels slowly appeared in front of me. I screamed at Anthony and asked, *"Where were you?"* He calmly said, *"We were told to stand down and let all of this happen. We were always close by. Michael will come and talk to you when you are finished."*

As soon as the dynamic clairvoyant duo were finished, Michael appeared right in front of me. I glared at him and said, *"I don't want to hear a word from you right now! I am beyond mad at God!"* Michael said, *"I know how angry you are right now, but the Lord wanted you to know that you were never in any danger."* I said, *"Never in any danger? Well, my impression of danger and the Lord's impression of danger must be two totally different ideas!"* Michael raised his voice and said, *"They are definitely two different ideas! At no time were you in any danger! He would never hurt you, Jim!"* I said, *"How could God do this to me? I gave him my heart and my freewill, and this is what he does to me?"* Michael said, *"The faithful will be tested, and you passed the test. You are not in any condition to speak with me, so I am going to leave now and after you settle down, we will talk later. The Lord told Satan that there is now a truce in place. He and his are to leave you alone."* Then Michael disappeared. I returned to my room and went to sleep. I was utterly exhausted.

Peter and I had plans to attend a convention that day for our business. We spent the whole day meeting with new vendors. We accomplished a lot that day and I appreciated the distraction. I was more than happy that my chest wasn't hurting anymore.

The next day was Sunday. It had been almost one month since Shelly and I had spoken to each other. Every time I tried to approach her, she would walk the other way. I didn't blame her. Any time I would look at her, I could feel the fear well up inside of her. I made it a point just to stay away from her, and from Lannie, too. On occasion, Peter would talk with her and tell her what was going on. Peter would always tell me to give her time. So I did.

On Wednesday, I wasn't feeling that great so I didn't sing in the choir at church. I just sat in the back. During the service, Andreus showed up and sat behind me. He began to mock me. After a few minutes, clairvoyantly I turned around, and told him to leave me alone. He just kept it up. I told him to leave or I would pray and ask the Lord to send a few angels to drag him out of the Lord's house. He got up laughing at me and left. I prayed and said, *"Lord! Can't I even get a moment of peace? Can't I just sit and hear the service? I thought there was a truce!"* Once the service ended, I got up and left without saying hi to anyone.

As I walked to my car, I could see Andreus standing on the hill behind the church. He was mocking me again. I tried to ignore him. I got in my car and started it. There he was, standing right next to my car looking in through my window, mocking me even more. I'd had enough! As I looked up at him, I glared and with a very controlled, quiet voice, I said, *"If you don't step away from my car and leave me alone, I will kill you where you are standing."* His whole disposition changed. He stopped laughing and took two steps back and left. I drove home. The moment I walked into the family room Peter looked at me and asked what had happened. Peter had to work late that night and couldn't make it to service. I was furious about what had happened with Andreus. Even Peter couldn't believe that Andreus would come into church to harass me.

Then I just snapped. I was screaming at the top of my lungs about everything that had happened to me with Babylonian and now Andreus. I told my brother that there was a truce in place and Andreus just broke it. My brother just sat there and listened to me rant on. I told him how pissed off I was at God. How dare He allow this to happen to me? I gave him everything and he lets this happen. What the hell was he thinking?

Why would he do this to me? I was so angry that I couldn't even cry. I told Peter that ever since Babylonian was in me, it was hard for me to cry. I was livid.

When I had said everything that I wanted to say, I just sat there fuming. Peter came over to me, put his hand on my shoulder, and said, "Jim, I have been waiting for you to do this. You have been acting as if nothing happened to you. You keep pretending as if everything is OK. You were violated. This demon had his way with you for months. You are finally accepting this and you are letting go of the pain. It's going to take a lot of time for you to learn how to deal with this. I don't know what to say to you, Jim, to make you feel better. All I know is that God does love you very much. Michael told you that He would never hurt you and I believe him. Now, you are going to have to believe him, too. You are mad because you feel like the Lord broke your trust in Him. He's not human. He doesn't think as we do. It's okay to be mad at him. He can take it. You know He has a plan for you, and I believe that all of this is preparing you for that plan. You need to take as much time as you need to work through this. I'm here for you. You're not alone."

As soon as he finished speaking, I broke down and began to cry. As I stood up, we embraced. My brother just stood there holding me as I cried. I don't believe I have ever cried as hard as I did during that moment. I could feel all the pain leaving my heart. It shook me to my soul as I kept crying. Peter just held me and kept encouraging me to let it go. To this day, my brother and I are very close friends. We were always good friends, but because of this, we now have a bond that goes beyond friendship or even brotherhood. He is more than my best friend.

The following day, Michael showed up. He said, *"I can see that you feel better. Do remember last night when you told Andreus that you would kill him where he was standing?"* I said, *"Yes."* Michael said, *"Do you know why his disposition changed when you said that to him? Could you feel the fear he had toward you?"* I nodded my head yes. *"Jim, the fear he had toward you was real, because you have the power to destroy him. Your armor, sword, and shield protect and defend your soul and spirit. You have the ability to inflict pain and even destroy the spirits and demons that get in your way. I will caution you to be particularly careful.*

It is not your responsibility to run around killing anything you feel like. You have the Lord's authority to defend yourself, but you will not provoke Andreus or any other demon or spirit. And you will not be provoked. Stay the course and be mindful of the task at hand. The Lord forgives you for the things you have said. He knows you were angry when you said them. He still loves you very much. Be patient, Jim. He will reveal His plan to you in time."

As Michael left, I sat there pondering everything he'd told me. Yes, I felt guilty about all the things I said to the Lord. I prayed and apologized for everything and still asked for his forgiveness again.

The next evening as I was at the sink getting a glass of water, I looked outside. Standing right in front of the window was Satan. I looked at him and said, *"I don't care about what you have to say."*

He said, *"I came here to apologize to you for Andreus breaking the truce."* I said, *"You have got to be kidding me! The deceiver of man! You are a liar! Why would I believe a word you have to say?"* With his voiced raised Satan said, *"There's one thing you need to know about me! When I give God my word, I keep it!"* I said, *"You just can't seem to control your cronies, can you? I don't care!"* I walked away and left him there. I went to my bedroom to go to sleep. And he was standing outside my window again. He said, *"For what it's worth, I'm sorry. I will deal with Andreus in my own way. And he will stay away from you!"* Once again I said, *"I don't care!"* Satan grunted and left.

I looked at Anthony and asked, *"Can you believe this? Give me a break! Satan is actually trying to apologize to me?"* Anthony said, *"He was trying to be sincere and honest with you."* I said, *"I'm sorry, but I really don't care!"*

It was now April 28, 2005. While I was meditating, Michael showed up out of the blue. He said, *"Jim, in time, you will learn to trust the Lord again. He knows that what He put you through was very hard for you to cope with. But He knows you better than you know yourself."* I broke down and cried, *"Michael, I don't think I can do this. I can't go through anything like this again!"* He grabbed me by my shoulders and picked me up off the ground and shook me while he screamed a little at me, *"You have been chosen by God himself to do this! You have to do this! You gave him your free will! There is no one else who can do this!"* He then put me back down. I have never seen him raise his voice like that or yell at me. I just stood there stunned.

I said, *"I'm sorry. I still feel as if He has the wrong guy for this. I just don't feel worthy enough to do all of this for Him!"* I then fell to my knees bowing in front of Michael and the other angels. With a quiet voice Michael said, *"Jim, you are a human. You are the crown of God's creation. You do not bow to us."* He grabbed me once more by the shoulders and stood me up. He then said, *"If you were not worthy to do this for the Lord, then we would not do this for you."* Michael and the other four angels surrounded me in a circle. Then, one by one, they all went down on one knee and bowed their heads to me.

As Michael bowed his head and was still looking at the ground, he said, *"The Lord picked you for this task because He knew you could do this. He has prepared you. He is teaching you. He is training you, and we will defend you. He never breaks his promises, Jim. He needs you to do this for Him. You gave Him your word."* Anthony spoke up and said, *"Jim, it is a privilege for us to serve and protect you. You have no idea how hard it was for us to stand down and watch you go through everything. The Lord's will is served first."*

I just stood there in the middle of these five mighty warriors of God. I have never felt so small in my life. The word humble can't even come close to the way I was felt. I spoke up and said, *"I do trust the Lord, and I will also serve His will first!"* All of them stood up and Michael said, *"The Lord will test you through seven phases. You have just started the fourth phase. None of the next phases will be as trying as the third one was for you. The next four phases will be a shorter period of time than the first three. All of them will teach you something, so pay particularly close attention.*

The Lord will restore to you everything He took from you, but you must be patient. Good things are coming. Be strong and stay focused on the task at hand. Anthony and the others will keep a close watch on you. You are never alone, Jim, always remember that."

Chapter 9

Phases 4 and 5

It was now the end of April. Our deadline to have our business plan complete and submitted to Billy was May 15. Over the past six months, Peter and I had been collecting information, finalizing costs with vendors, and choosing our products. Every evening and weekend was spent writing our business plan. Neither of us had ever done anything like this before, so everything was quite an adventure. We would take turns typing it out. One of us would talk and the other would type. Peter was a much better typist than I was, so when it was my turn to talk out my ideas, he was quite fast. When I would try to type faster, it seemed like the letters would start appearing backwards like I was spelling out something in Russian. We would have to stop at times because the things I spelled out wouldn't make any sense. We laughed a lot.

During the past few months, I had also been working extremely hard at the flooring company. My one-year review was coming up, and I was hoping for a large increase. Our plan was to give notice to both of our employers once we broke ground on our business. We had planned on that happening in August of the same year. I had been keeping track of all of the savings the company received when I would negotiate a better price for products. I wrote a small summary of all of my accomplishments over the past year. The biggest accomplishment was automating their inventory by creating spreadsheets. I had well over seventy-five spreadsheets that I maintained manually because the company was too cheap to buy a software program to help me manage it.

Would you like to know what drives me nuts about all of the small businesses I have worked for most of my career? Every company I have worked for will spend a fortune on accounting software and then try to add an inventory control module that barely interfaces with it. Would you care to guess what a manufacturing company's largest expense is? Physical inventory! They always seem to forget that. Okay, I'm done venting.

So the day came where I was sitting with the owner of the company as he poured over the information I had given him two weeks earlier. I was poised on the edge of my seat, waiting for a large raise to prove to me that they:

1) Actually know what it is that I do for the company
2) Appreciate what I do for the company
3) Know how hard I work to save them money

So he sat there for a moment, rubbed his face with his hands, and said, "Jim, you know how much we appreciate everything you do for us. Everyone loves working with you because you always follow through with what you say. You really are doing a great job.

I sit and listen to you negotiate with all of our vendors, and I marvel over how you get them to cut their prices for us."

Are you ready, folks? Then he said, "Jim, it's been a lean year, and we just don't have a lot of extra money to give you right now. I have looked at the reports you gave me and to be honest with you, you could have made all of this up, so it really means nothing to me." Can you believe this, people? I sat there and listened to him make excuse after excuse as to why there was not going to be as large of an increase as I may have hoped for. He then finished by saying, "I tell you what, why don't you take the next few days to think about how much you would like me to give you and on Monday, we will talk some more." It was Thursday afternoon, folks. I thought to myself, "I have to wait four days for this guy to come up with some more excuses as to why I'm not getting a raise?"

Needless to say, I was just elated to come to work the next day and kill myself for the company. Yes, I was angry, but I will always do my job. I was sitting at my desk when the owner came running into the office all excited about the new company/personal truck he'd just bought for himself. He told me and all the other employees to come outside so he could show it off. So I just sat at my desk and kept working. I thought to myself, *"I wonder if it's wrong for me to slap him on the back of his head with my sword."* Wouldn't you know it; Anthony just shook his head, no.

Yes, everyone was so excited for the owner. He was like a little kid with a new toy. He bought himself a brand-new, fully loaded truck with all the bells and whistles known to man. Well, of course I thought to myself, *"But it's been a lean year. However can the company afford such a wonderful company/personal vehicle?"* I sat there in a quiet rage. Remember what happens when I get into a quiet rage? Yep, pretty soon, I give up.

I went home that weekend and continued to work on our business plan. The deadline was coming at us extremely fast. The problem was that Peter and I both worked full-time. In the evenings, our brains were like mush by the time we would get home. It would take us longer to formulate a thought during the week. My only solace was as soon as Billy approved our business plan, he would give us the check and we would both start drawing salaries. So I told myself to hang on.

Monday came and went. No conversation about my raise. Oh, no, the owner and I talked about the truck as if it were his new child. I would just smile like a happy idiot as he would regale me with all of the features and how fast it went. Yeah! Tuesday came and went. No pay increase. I knew that the owner and his wife were planning to go on a Caribbean cruise. They were leaving Wednesday, May 4, in the afternoon. So I thought,

He's going to talk to me before they leave because they're going to be gone for ten days. Yes, folks, I'm an idiot! He just left without saying a word. Was I pissed! I calmly finished everything I was working on. I made sure that everything was in place for the schedule the next day. I packed up all of my personal belongings. Then I wrote a short note that said, "I quit. Jim." I left it on the owner's desk with my company phone. It was 1:00 PM as I walked to my car and drove home. No one even noticed I had left. They never even called me to see why.

You see, the owner's weasel of a son-in-law had overheard my conversation about my business while I was sharing it with a coworker. The owner knew I was planning on leaving in a few months and figured, "Why should I pay Jim one dime more?" When I got home, I called Billy to let him know what I had done. He was shocked and surprised but told me that as soon as we got the business plan to him, we could get started with our business. I had a few dollars in savings and was planning on getting my last check, so I would be OK for a while.

I spent all of my time finalizing our plan and meeting with vendors. It was exciting being able to have the freedom to do everything I needed to do to get it done. Peter kept working his full-time job and everything seemed to be going as planned. On May 26, I sent our plan to Billy. Peter and I anxiously waited to hear from him. That evening, Michael showed up to tell me that I had completed Phase 4, and Phase 5 had now started. I asked him what I was supposed to have learned in Phase 4 because apparently I wasn't actually paying as close attention as I thought I should be. He gave me no answer but told me to continue with our business plans.

The next day, Billy called and told us that he'd sent our business plan to his lawyer for his review. He would let us know in a week. After we had hung up the phone, I told Peter that something didn't feel right. Billy had never told us that he needed to get a lawyer involved. We had been talking with him for over nine months about this project and not once did this come up in our conversations. So many times when I would ask Billy a pointed question about something specific, he would dance around it and then pull a story out of his ass about some celebrity he knew or some woman he slept with. I always felt he was lying about everything he would tell us, but we didn't care as long as he was willing to help us start our business. It always seemed as if he was stalling for some reason. I could never put my finger on it, so we just waited.

It was now the middle of June. We were still getting excuses from Billy about our business plan. He kept telling us that his lawyer wasn't comfortable with our plan. He would keep telling us to change this and elaborate more on that point. It was terribly frustrating. Week after week, we would make the changes and forward them to him. And then we would just sit and wait.

Lana and I were celebrating our one-year anniversary. We still had to sneak around so no one would find out we were still seeing each other. Yes, I know. How high school of us. The two of us would spend as much time as we could during the day because she had to work in the evenings and weekends. Things were also getting financially tight for me. I had spent my savings and last paycheck. Peter and I kept praying that the Lord would help us in some way.

Out of the blue on Sunday after service, our friend Matthew asked us how things were going. So we told him everything. He said, "Come with me to my car." So we both walked over with him. He said, "For two weeks, I have had this envelope in my car. I keep forgetting to take it to the bank. I would like you two to take it, no strings attached. Consider it a gift, please."

I argued with him for a while, but he insisted so I took it. He asked if we were doing anything the following weekend. His wife was out of town on business so he invited us to go out and have dinner with him. We could then go back to his house, relax, and smoke some fine cigars. We said yes; that would be great. We thanked him and went back to our car. I gave the envelope to Peter. He opened it up and counted it twice while I was driving home. He said very quietly, "Jim, take a guess?" I guessed, "$200." He said, "Try $2,000!" We both just sat there and started to get a little emotional. I had so many bills that I couldn't pay and here the Lord once again provided for us. The Lord is truly amazing!

Something told me that this process with Billy was going to take more time than I thought. I had a gut feeling that maybe I should start looking for another job while we were waiting to hear from him. I contacted a number of head-hunters and got the ball rolling. I looked in the newspapers and on all the job Web sites I could find, but there was nothing. I continued to pray that the Lord would show us the way.

The following weekend came and we went out to dinner with Matt and then ended up back at his house. We all enjoy a fine cigar now and then, so we indulged ourselves a little. As we were smoking, Matt and Peter were sipping scotch while I drank a glass of water. (I don't really drink alcohol. I'll have a beer now and then, but I never acquired a taste for any kind of hard alcohol. I tell people that I don't drink because if I got drunk, who would carry me, or I might start seeing strange things and talking crazily. We sat outside on Matt's porch. His house was on a hill overlooking the city and the bay area. As we were talking about church, Matt asked what had happened when I was accused of practicing esotericism by the church. I shared the whole Shelly story with him and even shared a little of the Michael story, too. He shook his head and said once again that he never believed that I would be involved with anything that had to do with Satan.

After a while, I needed to run in the house to go to the bathroom. As I walked in, there was an uncomfortable feeling in my heart. I tried to ignore it as best as I could. I looked around the living room and dining room areas but saw nothing. After the bathroom, I sat back down outside and joined the conversation. Matt said, "Can I ask you a question, Jim?" I said, "Sure." He said, "I don't know if you can feel anything in my house. Ever since we bought this house some strange things have been going on here." I said, "Like what?" He said, "So many times the stereo and TV will turn on all by themselves. Some of the other electronics will, too. Do you have any idea what may be causing it?"

I sat and thought for a minute. Then I said, "When I went inside a few minutes ago I could feel something. I don't get the impression that it's evil in any way. I think they are souls; two of them. Let me call my friend Tina in the morning, and I'll get back to you. Okay?" We spent a few more hours just talking about life, and then we went home. It was around 2:00 am when we left.

Saturday morning, I called Tina and spoke with her about what I felt was in the house. Tina said, "Jim, the two people in your friend's house are the original owners. They are husband and wife. The house is close to eighty years old. They both get a kick out of manipulating electronics. They both were fascinated by them, because as you know, they weren't invented when they were alive. They don't mean your friends any harm, and I get the impression that they are happy staying in the house. I don't think they WANT to move on to eternity." I said, "Thank you, Tina, for your insight. I had the same impression about them being happy where they are. I will pray that they find joy and when they are ready to move on, that they find grace."

I called Matt and shared Tina's thoughts with him. He said, "You know, Jim, I never was really frightened when all of this started to happen to us. I will pray for them the same way you are."

On Sunday morning before the service, I sat and started to survey the congregation clairvoyantly. As I looked around, I saw there were souls there from different wars, people from both sides of the wars sitting together. I had been praying for these kinds of souls for some time now. I also saw a number of slaves. There were a number of my family members there, too. To see all of these souls warmed my heart and in some way, I felt closer to God because He allowed me to have this gift. Never in a million years would I have ever thought this could happen to me.

It was now Monday. Week after week, we would get one excuse after another from Billy. He would tear apart the exact part of the business plan he'd told us to rewrite a few weeks before. He would criticize certain aspects that the three of us agreed upon months ago and then exclaim that he never approved any of it. One day, he told me that he was planning on flying me out to Chicago to do some side work for him and that he would pay me $1,000 for my time. Once again when I would ask Billy directly when he was planning on flying me out, I would receive more excuses. It was getting extremely frustrating for Peter and me.

It was now the end of June. Billy had our business plan for almost a month. My heart kept telling me that something wasn't right. I called Billy and told him I needed a time frame. He became unusually quiet and then started with another one of his bull-crap stories trying to change the subject. When he finished, I asked again. He grew a little angry and went out of his way to explain to me again for the thousandth time how much he was helping Peter and me and that he was taking an enormous risk giving us this money. I thought to myself, *"What money?"* I could tell that this was getting me nowhere so we both said goodbye.

When Peter came home from work, I said, "I just got off of the phone with Billy. I think he's running out of excuses. He seemed nervous and even a little angry when I kept insisting on a commitment date from him. I think we both need to fly to Chicago and confront him face-to-face." Perhaps you're thinking to yourselves, "Um, Jim? You don't have a job. How are the two of you going to pay to fly to Chicago? You can't use your good looks to get tickets!"

Every time I would ask my dad for some money he would always say, "Why don't you use your good looks? See what that can get you?" Yes, my dad is priceless.

Now to answer your question of how will we pay for it, I respond to you, Ahhhh, faithful readers, the Lord has provided free airline tickets for the two of us! The past year during the Christmas season, Peter let himself get bumped off four flights home. The airline gave him four stand-by tickets. Pretty sweet. Can you see how the Lord works? I asked Peter if he thought he could get a few weeks off from work. He said, "Yes, Jim, I can. I was laid off today. How long should we go for?" I looked amazed at him and said, "I hope you're kidding, right?" He said, "Nope, it's the truth!"

We called the airline to check flights for the following Monday. Everything was good to go. We called the family and told them we were coming home for three weeks because we both actually had nothing better to do. And then I called Billy. Yes, I wish you could have heard the surprise in his voice when I shared the wonderful news with him. Shocked, surprised, and unbelieving don't even come close to what I think he was feeling. So I told him with great exuberance how much I couldn't wait to sit down with him and finalize all of this. He didn't seem as if he was filled with great exuberance at all. Go figure.

The Friday before we left, Michael showed up. He said, *"I know that you are aware that this weekend is the Preparatory Service for the Departed. It is not a coincidence that you will be in Chicago for both services. The Lord and your family here on earth and in the departed need you to be in Chicago. Pay very close attention to everything around you. Listen to your heart. It will lead you to the truth. When you come back from Chicago, Phase 6 will begin. Anthony and the others will keep a very close watch on you. Remember, God is with you, and you are never alone!"* He then turned and left.

I kept running through everything that I had been through the past few months trying to figure out what I was supposed to have learned through each phase. I just couldn't narrow it down to anything. I would ask Marty for help. All he would say was, *"You have to figure it out yourself."* I would then ask him, *"Well, then, what am I paying you for?"* To which he would respond, *"You don't sign my paychecks. It's a guy with a beard."* What a goof! Whatever!

We landed in Chicago on June 27, 2005. We spent the first week just relaxing and spending time with our family. We were staying with Ellen and her family. One evening, after the kids went to bed, I was standing in the kitchen with Ellen. She said, "I need to ask you something. For a while now, Sydney has been talking to an imaginary friend who she calls Telly. You know, Sydney's only four years old, so I don't think this is out of the ordinary for a girl her age to have an imaginary friend. I was wondering if Telly was just imaginary or if there was something more behind this. Sydney tells me that Telly's mommy died in a car accident and she can't seem to find her. She also tells me that Telly is a little girl with blond hair and blue eyes and that she's just a little older than she is. Can you see now why I'm asking you? Imaginary friends don't usually come with this kind of baggage, do they?"

While Ellen was talking to me, a small blond-haired, blue-eyed girl wearing a dress was standing by the stairs that led to the basement. She was smiling at me the whole time Ellen was telling me this. As I pointed to the stairs, I said, "Well, Telly is standing right there. She is a soul. She looks just like you told me and she is six years old. I think Telly knows that Sydney might be able to help her by praying for her." Telly nodded her head yes. I continued, "And now that we know about Telly, we can all pray for her, too." I turned to Telly and said, *"I don't know where your mommy is but my whole family is going to pray that God helps you and then helps you find your mommy."* Telly seemed uncommonly shy. She just smiled, waved, and then left. Ellen said, "I'm scared that Sydney is going to have the same experience that James had when he was close to this age."

    Folks, please allow me to explain what happened to my nephew when he was barely three years old. One night around two o'clock in the morning, my sister and her husband awoke suddenly because James was screaming. They both ran to his room and found James cowering in the corner of his bed. He was scrunched up against the wall sobbing. His eyes were filled with terror. James kept pointing at the foot of his bed, screaming in terror. Now, being that James was barely three years old he had a very limited vocabulary at the time and couldn't actually tell his parents what he saw. My sister and her husband kept looking at the foot of his bed telling James that there was nothing there. He kept screaming and crying in fear and then said, "That man! That man!" This actually happened several times to James.

    My brother-in-law then realized that when he was James's age, he had souls that would come to him, too. But because he was so young, they would scare him. All they had wanted was some help. My brother-in-law has a gift on his side of the family, too. But he prayed to the Lord and asked Him to take it away because it was just too much for him to handle. Fred immediately pulled the family together and started to pray. He asked God to send this soul to someone else so that he would get the help he needed. He also asked the Lord to send more angels to protect James and them, too, while they slept. After a short time, James calmed down and they all went back to sleep. Ellen also prayed privately, asking the Lord to send the soul to Ann so that it would leave James alone.

    The following day, Ellen called Ann to tell her what had happened to James the past night. Ann said, "Last night, a huge man dressed in a hospital orderly's uniform came to me and woke me up. He was covered in blood from head to toe and was crying out asking me to help him. After about ten minutes, I got him to calm down and I promised him that I would pray for him. An angel came and led him away. So please pray for him." Ellen then knew why James had been so afraid. After Ellen had called all of us, Peter told us that he was scared that same night, too, because the same man came to him. Peter said, "He kept putting his face right in my face asking if I could help him. I probably was just as afraid as James was. I have never been so frightened in my life. He had to be over six feet tall. He was as big as a football player. No wonder James was so scared." We all continued to pray for this soul. To this day, Ann sees him in our services for the departed. He makes a point of letting her know that he is there and how thankful he is for her help by praying for him.

I told Ellen that I didn't think the Lord would put Sydney through that but that we should just pray that the Lord uses us to all of our best abilities, and we should just trust Him. He would never do anything to hurt us.

The next day was the Service for the Departed. As I clairvoyantly looked around, I saw both of my parents' sides of the family. I had no idea who a number of them were. All I knew was that they were all related to us. My girls sat with me. Emily sat with my brother. The church was filled with souls from all walks of life. I could see soldiers from World Wars I and II, the Civil War, the Revolutionary War, and every other war you could think of. The most surprising thing about all of this was that the soldiers from both sides of these wars were sitting together. They would have had to forgive each other for this to take place.

I saw small children and babies. Some of the souls were from the groups I had continued to pray for; those from witch hunts, those persecuted for their faith, those who felt they were forgotten and those from the deepest darkest realms where light barely even shines. It was quite a sight to see. Many of the souls became very emotional during the service. A lot of them were crying and couldn't believe they were there to receive grace. When it came time for the souls to be directed to the district apostle's service so that they could have the sacraments they wanted, my girls gave me a giant hug, and I watched as all of these souls left. I once again thanked the Lord that He allowed me to see all of this.

We all celebrated the Fourth of July with a parade and picnic with the family. We ended up at my parents' condo that evening because they lived on the fourth floor and we could watch two different cities' fireworks shows. It was amazing.

The next day, I sat and had coffee with Ellen. I shared with her my frustrations with Billy. She told me that he had promised to help them, too.

All they had to do was to give him $1,500 and he would invest it for them. You see, folks, Billy was a stockbroker, or so he said. He would regale us with stories about some of his biggest clients and how he made them all rich.

Billy would take all of his clients' money, pool it together, and make a large investment that he could turn around in a small amount of time and deliver a huge payout. Ellen gave him an additional $250 for him to invest. He told them that he would need $10,000 on a specific date. Once he had that money he would pool that together with his other clients' money and after two years, he would take that $10,000 and turn it into three million dollars. Yes, you heard me! Three million dollars!

Perhaps you're asking yourself why we would believe Billy. He was in a relationship with our good friend Tina, who is clairvoyant. She'd told us that he was a decent guy and we could trust him. That's why we all took him at face value. Ellen told me that he sent them out house hunting. They got a real estate agent to take them around to all of these huge houses. He would email them information on houses that he thought they would like. He told Fred and Ellen that he would help them put our parents in a very upscale retirement community that would cost around $200,000 a year.

Also, he would help them buy Fred's parents a house that they could retire in. Plus the kids' college funds would be taken care of.

All they had to do was to give him the $1,500 as a down payment and then within a few months come up with the $10,000 and then, BAM, everything would be as he said. So they set a date, June 10, two years from the time he started them on this fantastic journey. June 10 was going to be the day that their lives would change forever.

Billy told them that he would get a private jet and fly the whole family out to wherever they wanted for two weeks while the contractor made all of the changes to their current house. He built their hopes up every chance he had. Ellen would tell him that they didn't have the $10,000. He told her that he would just cover it for her and after the investment grew, he would just take the $10,000 out of that.

Everything seemed as it was going as planned. Ellen told me that Billy called her one day and said that they could move the date up to one year because the investment was growing faster than he had expected. They were very excited. Well, wouldn't you know it, Billy showed up on their doorstep the day before the deadline. He told them that because they couldn't come up with the $10,000, he couldn't really cover it for them because if his other clients found out that he had cut them a deal, it would look bad for business.

I sat there in awe as she told me all of this. Everything he promised to do for them, he promised to do for Peter and me. We were told by him that we would be financially sound. He asked Peter and me to go look at expensive houses, too. We got a real estate agent, too. Our real estate agent was a priest in our church. I can't begin to tell you how many evenings and weekends we spent looking at houses.

The only difference between Ellen and us was that we never gave him one dime. I could tell she was very disappointed. I shared more with her about how he would call Peter and me. We would all agree to do things a certain way for the business and then a few days later, it was as if he had amnesia or something. He would exclaim that he never agreed to that.

Ellen told me that, on numerous occasions, Billy would tell her and Fred that Peter and I were spending too much money and that he thought we were out of control on our budget. We started with $250,000 and, by the time we finalized everything with Billy, it was now $1.2 million. I told her that, over the past few months, Billy had told us that we needed to think bigger. We need to get the best quality we can get. If we had to spend more money, he was okay with that. Billy would tell her that Peter and I would tell him that we wanted this and that and that if it cost more he would just have to cover it.

He made Peter and I sound like a bunch of money-hungry bastards. I was furious! I told Ellen that I was always arguing with him about costs. I told him I didn't want to spend that much, that I could do it for a lot less, but he would always insist that we should spend more money.

There were also many times when all of us would catch him in a lie, but he always had an answer for why he did what he did. And it was always a great answer.

We always heard how rich he was, but he dressed like a slob all the time. He would tell us that he wanted to be just like everyone else, never sticking out in the crowd, so he would always dress down. We were all too trusting of him because he was in a relationship with our dear friend Tina.

When I met Billy for the first time, almost two years prior, Tina called me later that evening and said, "I need you to use your gift and tell me what your impression is of Billy." After I had thought about it for one-tenth of a second I said, "He seems to be a good person. He's easy to talk, too; very likable. The only thing I feel is that there is something not right about his financial situation. He's hiding something." She agreed that she had that same feeling. As time progressed, Billy told us that he was under investigation by Homeland Security because one of his clients was from Iran. While they were investigating him, they froze all of his assets and he couldn't touch them. It sounded pretty honest to me.

Okay, back to present day. The more I spoke with Ellen, the more I could understand. All of this time I'd had that sinking feeling that he was lying to us, but I shirked it off because Tina said he was okay. I called Billy and told him we would like to meet with him as soon as possible. He told us he was busy during the day but that we could meet with him that evening around 9:00 pm. It was Tuesday, July. He asked us to meet him at Tina's house and then the three of us would go somewhere to talk.

As we pulled up to Tina's house, Billy was walking out to the car. He yelled for us to follow him. We drove around for about thirty minutes. I told Peter that Billy was an idiot if he thought he was going to take us on a wild goose chase. You see, Billy didn't know that I had lived in this area he was driving around for almost seven years. I knew exactly where we were the whole time. He kept driving around in circles, trying to make us think that we were actually going somewhere important. We finally pulled into a driveway. I had an uneasy feeling about all of it. Billy got out of his car and said we could talk inside. I asked, "Whose apartment is this?" Billy said, "Oh, I own this property and building. The woman that manages it for me is out of town, so I told her I would keep an eye on her apartment while she was gone." I turned to Peter and said, "Something isn't right about this."

As we walked into the apartment, I had a very uneasy feeling about it. I thought to myself, *He's lying to us, but I can't prove it yet!* As I walked around this person's home, I looked at the pictures she had. She was a single mom raising one child. I had the feeling we were violating this woman's space by being there. I could feel that Billy was uncomfortable about being here and had a wall up about talking with us. Billy fed the lady's cat. He looked up at us as he filled the cat's dish with food and said, "Do you see what I do for people?" Then he puttered around the apartment trying to look as if he was doing something. I finally asked if we could talk because I didn't feel comfortable being in someone's apartment without her permission.

Billy spoke up and said, "Guys, it's okay! This woman works for me. She collects my monthly rent from all of my tenants and looks after the building for me. In exchange, I let her live here at a much-reduced renter's fee. As a matter of fact, I am planning on selling this property. Would you guys be interested in buying it from me? It's a great deal."

I looked him square in the eye and said, "Billy, if we could afford to buy an apartment building, why would we come to you for a loan? Can we get started about our business? It's after 10:00 pm." He laughed and said,

"Oh, yeah. You're right. What was I thinking?" He asked us to go over our entire plan with him again. So we did. He asked us to justify every expense to him. So we did. He talked us in circles, like he always did, when I would ask him a direct question. But I didn't let up. Round and round we went for two and a half hours. It was now 12:30 in the morning and I didn't let up for one minute.

When he would express a concern about our plan, I would ask him why. I forced him to give us answers, because the Lord knows that after we had poured our hearts into this business plan for over ten months, he owed us an answer! I was pissed off by this time. He never had a smart-enough answer that would appease me. Numerous times, he would pull the, "Well, if I'm going to hand the two of you $1.2 million, I have to be sure about this!" And I would respond time and again with, "Well, Billy, then tell me what you're uneasy about and I'll clarify it for you." It would be at these moments when he would jump into one of his bull-crap stories. Peter and I would sit there for fifteen to thirty minutes and let him pontificate until I just couldn't take it anymore. I would say, "You keep skirting the questions! Are you going to help us or not? We've been sitting here now for hours!" Yes, faithful readers it was now 2:30 am.

Billy took a deep breath and said…are you ready for this? He said, "I'm hungry! You guys hungry? Let's get some breakfast! We can talk more about this over the next few days. I just have to get my head around all of this before I can completely commit to you two and hand you over the check." Can you believe this guy? So we went to IHOP and had breakfast. As we sat there waiting for the waitress to come, I just couldn't let it go by without saying something about the wild-goose chase he took us on before we got to the apartment. So I spoke up and said, "Hey, Billy, you probably don't know this, but I used to live in this area for seven years, so I know this area pretty well." Oh, folks, you should have seen his face. He then proceeded to tell us that he had forgotten how to get to the apartment.

Maybe you're thinking what I was thinking at this time, Hmmm? So I said, "Really? I'm pretty sure that if I owned a property like that one, I don't think I would have forgotten how to get to it!" Wouldn't you know it, the waitress walked up and saved him! We sat and ate and listened to Billy tell his stories again except this time, I would speak up and say; "You told us this one!" or "We've heard it!" I was fed up beyond words with this guy! When the check came, to our surprise, Billy paid for us. We finally got to bed around 4:30 am. I prayed to God that he would help us figure this whole thing out.

The next morning, I sat with Ellen and told her everything that had happened. When I told her where we met and how Billy owned the building, she almost spit her coffee out. She wiped her mouth and said, "You have got to be kidding me! He doesn't own that building! Tina told me that her friend was on vacation and she had asked her to watch her apartment and feed her cat!" Yes, you heard it too! He was lying, and we finally caught him! I asked Ellen to get Tina on the phone for me so I could confirm all of this. I tried my best not to sound as if I was accusing Billy of anything because I knew that Tina was in love with the guy. Do you folks remember my phrase about love? Love is blind and stupid!

I asked Tina if she was house sitting for a friend who has an apartment in the area I used to live in. She told me she did. Then she asked me why. So I told her everything. She didn't believe me. I asked her why I would make the entire thing up and why Billy would go to such a great length to lie to us. All he had to do was tell us the truth. I wouldn't have cared. But you know that saying, "Once a liar, always a liar!" She told me that she had to call Billy to see what he would say. I told her to go right ahead and then please call me back. After twenty minutes, she called me back and told me that he never said any of that to me. I must have misunderstood him. I took a deep breath and said, "Tina, you're my good friend. I want you to know that Billy has been lying to all of us for a very long time. I am going to end all of this the instant we get off the phone. I am not mad at you for any of this, but I am going to warn you that Billy had better stay away from my entire family and me. You and your daughter are welcome anytime, but don't bring him around at all. I will just leave it at that!" I called Billy and left him a voicemail to call me.

Here's something else you should know about Billy. For the past two years, he had been living off of Tina. He would continually make excuses as to why he had no money at all! And they were very good excuses. Once again, his funds were tied up with Homeland Security. He couldn't touch his investments or he would suffer a substantial loss. Any day now, his funds would be released. He had excellent answers every time.

Once in a while, Tina would ask him to provide proof of his investments. And wouldn't you know it, he would. I seriously doubt much that they were his funds. You can go onto any Web site and pull up a stock portfolio. He would tell Tina that these were the stocks he had made investments in and that all of his stock certificates were in a safety deposit box in California. That's where he used to live before he moved to Chicago. He was a cancer on my friend's life. He played her, my sister Ellen, my brother, my parents, and me.

I guess what upset me the most about Billy was that he had openly told me numerous times that he had a spirit in his space that helped him in his business dealings. Yes, you heard me. Billy served a spirit. I never put two and two together to figure it out until now. Yes, I feel like a moron!

I let this piece of crap manipulate all of us. I need to tell you something about spirits once more, just in case you missed it before. Spirits play on our hopes, desires, dreams, and fears. Can you see how this thing did its work on all of us?

Billy finally called me back about an hour later. He started by telling me that he never said he owned that building. I had enough! I calmly said, "Billy, I just wanted to let you know that Peter and I have decided NOT to do business with you any longer. It is very evident to us that you are not comfortable with our business plan. So we will seek funding elsewhere. We have no hard feelings towards you and I wish you all the best." Folks, did you see what I did there? I didn't accuse him of anything. I didn't call him a liar. I didn't want to give him or that spirit a chance to defend their selves. By the grace of God and a brief moment where I was struck with wisdom, this whole situation was defused. Billy did start up with the, "Look at all of the time and money I invested in this." I calmly said, "Well, I guess you will just have to write this off as a cost of doing business and a loss. I'm sure you know how to do that!" And then I hung up. I immediately formed a company with my brother and filed for a business license in the state where we lived. I then sent Billy an email outlining everything I had told him on the phone. I informed him that if he tried to steal our business plan to start his own business, I would take legal action, and he would truly regret the day he met the Rybak brothers!

As we continued to enjoy our vacation, Tina would call Ellen and tell her that Billy was completely surprised that I called everything off. He couldn't understand what went wrong. He couldn't understand why he wasn't allowed to have any contact with our family anymore. No, I'm not kidding! He actually did! I told Tina to have him talk to the spirit in his space because I was pretty sure he could explain everything to him.

One evening, Tina came to the house to apologize to us. I stopped her cold. I told her she had nothing to apologize for and if anyone should be offering an apology, it should be Billy. We all sat and tried to piece together all of Billy's lies for the past two years. It was truly remarkable how he did it. He always tried his best to inform all of us that we should just keep our conversations with him to ourselves. That's why none of us ever knew he was lying to our siblings. If Ellen and I had never had that one conversation over a cup of coffee, we would have never figured it out.

Do you remember what Michael had said to me before we left to come to Chicago? *"Pay very close attention to everything around you. Listen to your heart. It will lead you to the truth."* God sure was with us. We made our plans to fly back to the west coast. We had been in Chicago for three weeks. The day we flew back just happened to be Lana's birthday. After she had picked Peter and me up from the airport, Lana and I went out to dinner to celebrate. I shared everything with her. It was good to be home and in the arms of the girl I loved. I would be lying to you if I didn't tell you that I was just a little curious about what Phase 6 would hold for me.

Of course, you may be asking yourselves, but Jim. Wait a minute. What were you suppose to learn in Phases 4 and 5? Well, readers, I'm glad you have been paying attention and have asked this question. In Phase 4, I learned perseverance and trust. No matter how busy or tired Peter and I were, we always found the time to work on our business. Every spare moment of time during the week or on the weekend was spent planning our business. We worked full-time jobs, went to church two times a week, had a small social life, financial struggles, and spiritual enlightening, and still had time to work on the business. If you trust the Lord with your whole heart, it will always work out. He will always provide. It may not be the way you expected it to be, but rest assured; it is the way He wants it to be.

In Phase 5, I learned to trust myself, to have patience, and never to give up. I always had that sinking feeling in my heart that everything Billy told us was too good to be true. My gut feeling was also telling me that something wasn't right. I didn't listen to myself.

Now, class? Where is the third chakra located, and what is it used for? It is located in our solar plexus or stomach. It is that gut feeling we get. "Honor thyself." Remember? Through the whole process, I exercised patience. No matter how many times Billy tore our business plan apart; we would go back to the drawing board and make the changes. No matter how many times he put us down, we wouldn't give up. No matter how lousy things seemed to get through that whole phase, we pushed forward. And through it all, we waited patiently for the Lord's help.

Folks, I don't care how miserable you may think things are in your life. If you keep fighting, the Lord will continue to fight alongside you. The moment you give up, He can't do much for you anymore. There is a saying that I know you all have heard before: "The Lord helps those who help themselves." It's not "The Lord helps those who are helpless." Have you ever felt like a candle in the rain? No matter how hard you fight, it seems as if you're getting nowhere? All I can tell you is when those moments hit you head on and you feel like stopping, the Lord will take His hand and cover you. You are never alone. Never quit. Never give up. Never give in. And always trust in the Lord.

Chapter 10

Phase 6

As Peter and I landed at the airport on the west coast, Anthony turned to me and said, "Andreus knows you are back! Stay sharp! We are surrounding you and Peter." As we sat there waiting to deplane, Peter leaned to me and whispered very quietly, "Jim, I am having a difficult time breathing. It feels as if someone is sitting on my chest. What is happening?" I said, "The angels are closing in around us to protect us. Andreus knows we're back. Because there are so many people standing around us on the plane, the angels are standing in our space. That's why you feel uncomfortable. Just take deep breaths and once we get off the plane the angels will spread out. For now just hang on and breathe." Peter said, "This is the weirdest feeling I have ever felt." Once we got off the plane and were away from everyone I watched as the angels formed a protective defense. Four angels formed a diamond shape surrounding Peter and me. Four more angels formed a square defense around the diamond, and then six more angels formed a rectangle around the square defense. I don't think I have ever felt so safe in my life.

As we walked through the airport Peter started to breathe easier and said, "Does this happen to you often?" I said, "Only on a few occasions, when the angels feel the level of danger is greater than normal will they close in around me with their shields out and swords drawn. That's a good sign that things are usually not going to be that great for a while." Peter said, "Well, if I had any doubts about what you have been telling me over the past few years, they are now all gone. I don't believe two people can share a psychotic episode, can they?" I told him, "No, they can't, and welcome to my interesting life, brother."

When we got home that evening Michael paid me a visit and said, *"You have done very well in Chicago. You are now in Phase 6. You must remain aware of everything. The Lord would like you to accept the task He has assigned to you and have no more doubts."* I said, *"Michael, I still have no idea what the task is that He has assigned me."* Michael said, *"Just trust in Him and in time He will reveal to you everything you will need to know. I am to tell you that you are not allowed to provoke Andreus in any way. You will ignore him. Remember, the Lord will not be provoked; you are His representative. Anthony and the others will protect you. Have no fear; the Lord is always with you."*

The next day I had an appointment with a headhunter. We sat for a while and talked about the career path for which I was looking, whether I should stay in purchasing or go back into the warehouse management field. As I walked to my car, I had this sinking feeling that I'd just wasted two hours of my life that I would never get back. The moment I got home I started looking on many job Web sites again. I found a few jobs, so I sent my resume and hoped for the best.

A week later I filed with the state and chose our business names. Then Peter and I called all of our would-be vendors and told them that we'd recently found out that our backer was a fraud and that we were trying to find other means of funding. All of them were saddened by the news and told us to keep in touch with them.

That afternoon I received three phone calls about three different job opportunities. (Yes, honestly I did.) One interview was with a family-owned hardware store chain; one was with a distribution center, and the other one was with a custom motorcycle company. I scheduled two interviews on Thursday: one interview in the morning; and one in the afternoon. The third one was a phone interview on Friday morning. The Friday morning interview was through my headhunter. I nailed all three of the interviews and was felt particularly confident about how I presented myself to them. The phone interview turned into an actual face-to-face interview on Monday, with the motorcycle company.

On Monday, after my interview, I called my headhunter to tell him that I thought it had gone exceptionally well. He then told me that he had set up another interview for me on Wednesday with a specialty cement company, the largest cement company in the area. They were looking for an inside sales person. When I got off of the phone, it immediately rang. It was the hardware store company asking me to come in for a second interview on Thursday. Yes, it was very exciting.

Wednesday afternoon was here. As I sat in the waiting room of the cement company, I thanked the Lord for all of the opportunities He had presented me over the past few days. The manager came and got me and took me to a conference room. I sat there for a while making small talk with him and one by one other people came in and sat down. So there I was on one side of the table, and on the other side of the table were four other people. I thought to myself, "This is going to be fun!"

One by one they all took turns asking me about my past work experience, how I would solve problems, how I would handle certain things that may arise on the job. As the interview progressed, one of the interviewers, Stan, always had an attitude about him. Some of his questions were to the bone. A few times I thought to myself, Man, this guy is a raging jerk! I took everything in stride. I answered all of their questions for over an hour to the best of my ability. All of a sudden, the guy with the attitude leaned across the table and with a smirk on his face said, "Why don't you tell us something about you?" So I started to share some of my past work experience that we hadn't discussed. Stan cut me off, and with a raised voice said, "No, I want to know about you!" I said, "Do you mean something personal about me?" He said, "Yes!"

I took a deep breath and leaned back in my chair and said, "Do you mean like, I'm a Pisces, I like quiet walks on the beach, I'm not afraid to cry, and I like to be held?" All of them, including Stan the jerk, started to laugh out loud. I told them about Lana and that I was planning on marrying her in the distant future. They told me they would be in touch.

I called my headhunter and shared my experience with him. I told him about how Stan was a jerk to me the whole time. He asked how I handled him. I told him I stayed calm and answered his questions.

He said, "Well, if I hear anything I will call you." Later that afternoon, I received a phone call from my headhunter telling me to call the manager of the cement company, because he would like to talk to me.

I called the manager, He said, "Jim, we are very impressed with you. Stan is very impressed with you. We have never seen anyone handle Stan as well as you did. We bring Stan into the interviewing process because he can be rude and calloused at times. We believe if you can handle Stan; then you can handle our customers because, at times, they act the same way. I have watched applicants fall apart time and again as Stan would tear into them. But you just sat there and methodically handled every question he threw at you. We also love your sense of humor and I would like you to come in tomorrow to take a personality test. Based on this information we will decide if you are a good fit for our company."

As I hung up the phone, I got that sinking feeling in my stomach. Folks, every time I take a personality test for a potential job, I never get hired. No joke. Never! What also irritates me is they rarely tell me why. One company told me it was because I showed too much independence and drive. I was applying for a sales position at the time. I was always under the impression that those were the two greatest qualities you would want to have in a salesman. But no. The next morning I met with the hardware store folks; I thought the second interview went well. I then drove over to the cement company and took their test.

That afternoon I had Marty and Amanda give me a healing. When the healing was almost through he said, "I have a gift for you from Jesus. He has restored your virtue." As I sat there I could feel the energy engulfing my space, it was warm, and it caused my skin to freckle up with goose pimples.

What is the definition of virtue? Let's see what Merriam-Webster Online says.

VIRTUE

1: moral excellence; goodness; righteousness
2: conformity of one's life and conduct to moral and ethical principles; uprightness; rectitude
3: a beneficial quality or power of a thing
4: manly strength or courage: VALOR
5: a commendable quality or trait: MERIT
6: a capacity to act: POTENCY

Yes, I had to look it up too, to see what it meant. Marty wasn't giving me any answers. I was wondering why he still got paid! Marty said, "Take a deep breath." As I was breathing Jesus appeared to me and said, "I would like to show you something." Marty bowed in front of Jesus and stepped back. Right in front of my eyes there appeared a huge Christmas tree with lights on it. In the middle of the tree, there was a light that shone brighter than the rest.

Jesus asked, *"Do you understand what you are seeing?"* I said, *"Not really, Lord. Are you the brightest light in the middle of the tree?"* Jesus said, *"Do you remember your chief apostle's wish that 30,000 new members would be added to the United States?"* I said, *"Yes."* Jesus continued, *"Your chief apostle spoke of a Christmas tree with 30,000 lights on it. You, Jim, are the brightest light in the center of this tree."* I started to cry. He continued, *"Do you remember when your friend Tina told you that the plan my Father had for you was to sweep across the United States first, and then the world?"* I said, *"Yes."* Jesus said, *"In time, my Father and I will reveal our entire plan for you as well as how all of this will come into being. Because of you, Jim, all of these souls will be added to the United States. We are very proud of you and love you very much. Stay the course. I am always with you."*

Then Jesus faded away. I sat there totally overwhelmed. My mind was racing; trying to figure out how would all this come into being. Marty said, *"Jim, relax. They will tell you everything in time. Just be patient."* You see folks; patience is a virtue that I seem to lack most of the time. But I took to heart what Marty said. I silently prayed, thanking God and Jesus for allowing me to be a part of their plan. I also asked for patience and a lot of wisdom. Oh yeah, I also asked them to make sure I didn't mess this up for them.

The following night Peter and I had dinner with our friend Matt. Once again, we ended up back at Matt's house smoking cigars and talking. As we talk, an Asian male soul appeared and stood off to the side of us about ten feet away from me. I could tell that this soul knew I could see him, but he said nothing. He just stood there looking very sad. I said nothing as Matt spoke about how his wife and her family came to this county. As he spoke, hundreds of souls started to walk up and stand in front of Matt's house. I could see that a number of them had come from the bay area, which we were overlooking as we sat there. These souls looked as if they were soaked to the bone. Matt continued to tell us that things were tough for his wife's family. Matt's father-in-law had an extremely hard time fitting himself into our culture. He was never happy. He always felt that he had failed as a father. Matt told us that one day his wife came home and found a note from her father telling her that he was going to the bay to drown himself. He said that he couldn't take it anymore. By the time they got down to the bay, it was too late.

Matt stood up and pointed out to the bay area and said, "Do you see the area right over there? It is at that point that my father-in-law and hundreds of others have killed themselves." The soul that was next to me then stepped forward towards me and pointed at Matt. I said, "Hey, Matt? There's an Asian soul here that I believe is your father-in-law." I then described him to Matt. He said, "That sounds like him. Why is he here?" I said, "I get the feeling that your wife blames herself for her father's death. That because of this, he is bound here and can't move on." The soul nodded his head, yes.

I said, "I would also like to point out that there are hundreds of souls now standing in front of your house. I watched them as they walked from the place that you pointed to, all the way up to your front lawn. They know we can pray for them." As I spoke the souls stepped towards us and then stopped. Anthony and many angels formed a barrier between us and them. They were all so sad-looking that my heart ached as I felt their sorrow and pain. I asked Matt if he could share any of this with his wife. He said, "Jim, I wish I could. You know she's doesn't go to our church. She doesn't have the same faith as we do. She would think I'm crazy if I tell her any of this. Maybe in time, but I can't tell her anything now. What should we do?" I said, "All we can do is pray for your father-in-law and all of these souls. Pray that they are able to forgive themselves and then ask God to forgive them. I will also start praying for your wife that the Lord opens her heart so that you can share this with her. In the meantime, that's all we can do."

Clairvoyantly I stood up and promised all of the souls that the three of us would pray and offer for all of them. In a few months, we would have a special service for them, and by God's grace they all may be invited to come. They all seemed a little happier as they started to walk back to the bay. Matt's father-in-law stayed and listened to our conversation. Once again, it was very late by the time we left. I have to tell you that I have always enjoyed talking about my faith and sharing what I have seen.

On Friday morning, I received two phone calls. The first call was from my headhunter with an offer from the cement company. The second call was from the hardware store company. Both were offering the same money. I'll be honest with you people. I hate sales. I have been in sales a lot during my career and never actually enjoyed it. The hardware store was looking for a buyer. I love being a buyer. I loved negotiating prices and saving the company money. So I chose the hardware store. They asked me to start the following Tuesday. Needless to say, I was excited. I called Lana first, and then my entire family.

That evening, Lana, had called me crying hysterically. She told me that her mom found out that we were seeing each other again and kicked her out of the house. I was angry that her mom would do this to her. I always felt that her mom was trying to hurt me; in the process she was always hurting her daughter more. I asked Lana what her choices were. She told me that she was going to move in with her dad, but he wouldn't let me see her either. I told her she needed to do what was best for her. I felt completely helpless, and that I couldn't help her in any way. We talked for another fifteen minutes. She told me that she wasn't allowed to call me after Sunday night. My heart was broken, once again. When I hung up the phone, I lost it. I broke down and asked the Lord why this was happening, and if He would please give us both the strength to get through this.

Sunday afternoon, I met Lana at a park. We sat on the bench and just held each other. I felt like I would never see her again. She told me her mom was forcing her to go to another congregation. I said, "Your mom can't tell you where to go to church. You are an adult in our church, and you're not living with her anymore. She kicked you out, screw her!" Yes, folks, I was mad. I told her I was going to call her uncle to see if he could intervene on our behalf. At least there was a little gleam of hope.

I called Lana's uncle and explained everything to him. He said, "Jim, there isn't anything I can do. You broke your promise, and that is all they are thinking about." I said, "I'll have you know that after we had been caught the first time, I told Lana's mom that I would not keep my promise and that I had retracted it! It was foolish for me to try to make them happy, while, in the process, the two of us were miserable.

So, as far as I'm concerned, there is no promise that I have broken!" He told me there was nothing he could do except to pray that things would work out for the two of us.

The best thing I could do for Lana was to stay away from her. Can you see a pattern here, folks? Whenever I turned to Lana's family for help, I got nothing!

It was Tuesday morning, the first day at my new job. It was tough getting up at 6:30 in the morning. I had to be at work at 8:00 am for employee orientation. As I sat there in orientation, listening to all of the wonders and pure excitement of the organization, they pointed out to each of us what our work hours would be. They told me that my hours were 6:00 am to 4:00 pm, with an hour lunch. I thought, *"Whoa, whoa, wait a minute! I'm not working forty hours; I'm working forty-five hours a week?"* You see, folks, I negotiated my salary on forty hours. I was now making less than I had five years before. I was ticked off. I felt as if they had lied to me. Never through this whole process did they say that salaried employees worked forty-five hours a week. I decided to talk to the vice president when I had a chance.

The next morning, I woke up at 4:45 am. I started work at 6:00 am. I had forgotten there was a six in the morning too! They paired me up with the person I was replacing. We had a great time as she told me everything I was going to be doing. After seven days, I was on my own. The woman I replaced was moving away, so she left me her cell phone if I had any questions. When I had a chance, I sat down with the vice president and explained how I felt. He told me that he would fix this and apologized for the misunderstanding. Two weeks later, he approached me while I was in the warehouse checking on inventory. He pulled me aside and informed me that he increased my salary by $6,000. I thanked him and was now very happy.

So I should probably tell you that Lana and I still stayed in contact. She would call me on pay phones so her parents wouldn't know. They always checked her cell phone bill. Yes, I thought we were being extremely dishonest, and I even told Lana many times how uncomfortable I felt about it. But we still talked every day. As the weeks passed, I still saw her in church. We just didn't talk to each other at all. One day I finally got tired of the whole pay phone thing, so I got Lana her own cell phone, which I paid for. It made her life a little better. We finally broke down and started seeing each other again. I know what you're thinking. I'm sorry, folks, I was in love with her.

It was the end of September when all of a sudden, Michael showed up. He said, *"Jim, things are moving along as the Lord has planned. You need to stay the course. Satan is even more aware of you and the Lord's plan for you. He will do everything he can to try and stop you. I am assigning more angels to watch over you. Anthony will guide you and continue to protect you. Please kneel down. The Lord has a blessing for you."* As I knelt down he placed his hand on my head and said, *"It is now the hand of God that rests on your head. Receive the strength and wisdom from the Creator. It is by God's hand that He opens your understanding to the future. He renews your armor, sword, and shield. He quickens your spirit with speed and agility. Through this blessing, you are spiritually now nine feet tall. He gives you the strength of ten angels. Satan will now fear you for all that you now hold in your possession. The Lord gives you patience. He increases your faith. In time, all will be revealed to you. The Son of God restores upon you His mantle of peace and renews His covenant with you that you are never alone.*

Please stand up." Clairvoyantly I stood up. I noticed that I was no longer looking up at Michael. Now we were eye to eye. Michael said, *"I know you have questions, the Lord will answer them in time. He has asked me to tell you that He would like you to refrain from seeing Lana for the next two weeks. You may talk to her on the phone, but you are not allowed to have any physical contact with her for a two-week period. Do you understand?"* I said, *"Yes."* He said, *"Stay strong, Jim. Stay the course."* Then he left.

I called Lana and explained to her that I wasn't allowed to see her for the next two weeks. She asked why God was punishing us. I told her that the Lord wasn't punishing us; He was testing us. We could do this. She said, *"I don't understand why He would do this to us."* I said, *"Lana, there is so much going on around us that you are not aware of. I feel that this two-week period is for your own good, as well as mine. You need to trust the Lord; He will bring us through this."* She cried for a while and then accepted it in faith, as I did. We saw each other in church that week. We spoke on the phone, and we both stayed away from each other. Oh, yes, it was exceedingly hard to stay away from Lana, but there was no way I was going to let the Lord down.

The following Friday while having a healing, Marty said, *"The Lord wanted me to warn you that Andreus and Markus will stop at nothing to mislead you. Keep alert and keep a watchful eye out for anything unusual."* I know you folks remember who Andreus is. If you have forgotten who Markus is, he is Satan's number-one general. He's huge and has the face of a pig. Remember? Marty continued, *"Phase six will be over soon. You will know that Phase seven has started when Michael comes to you. Through this healing, the Lord has now changed the color of your armor to gold. You now symbolize the truth in the Lord's plan. You are now bigger than Markus. Stand your ground, Jim, but do not let them provoke you in any way. Anthony and the others are still watching you very closely. Be patient and all will be told to you in time."*

Let's see what Merriam-Webster says about truth.

Truth

1: a *archaic:* fidelity , constancy b: sincerity in action, character, and
   utterance
2a: (1) the state of being the case: fact (2): the body of real things,
   events, and facts: actuality (3): often capitalized : a
   transcendent fundamental or spiritual reality
 b: a judgment, proposition, or idea that is true or accepted as
   true <truths of thermodynamics> c: the body of true
   statements and propositions
3a: the property (as of a statement) of being in accord with fact
   or reality b *chiefly British* : true 2c: fidelity to an original or to a
   standard
4: capitalized Christian Science: god

It was now the end of the two-week period. I had asked my boss if I could take half a day off to take care of some personal business. I told Lana that I would come pick her up at her house on my lunch hour. You should have seen her face when I told her I had taken the afternoon off from work. We spent the whole afternoon together until she had to go to work. It was amazing when we kissed again for the first time after not being together for two weeks.

The following Friday, Shelly invited me over for a cup of coffee so we could talk. It had been months since we had spoken to each other, so I gladly accepted her invitation. I don't actually know how we got on the subject, but Shelly started talking about her childhood and growing up in the South. She described her father and his decision to move the whole family to Montana. At that time when she was a little girl, there was such a prejudice against black people where she lived. She went on to say that she remembered when there was one time when they hung a young black man from the tree in her front yard. I was horrified.

As she shared this story with me, suddenly her living room started to fill up with black people, well over fifty of them. The men and boys were all dressed in blue jeans and coveralls. The women and young girls were wearing dresses. As I watched, they all started to sit all around Shelly. Some sat on her furniture others sat on the floor by her. Others sat by the fireplace. They said nothing to me. They just sat listening to Shelly as she told me how these people had such a special place in her heart, and how she always prays and remembers them for the Service for the Departed. Almost all of them were smiling.

I tried my best to pay attention to what Shelly was saying when three young men got up from where they were sitting. They walk down her hallway towards the bedrooms. As I watched, they tied ropes from her ceiling and proceeded to hang themselves. It was very graphic for me to watch. At that moment, I couldn't help but close my eyes and turn away. Shelly had stopped talking while this was happening, but I didn't notice. When I opened my eyes, Shelly asked me what was going on. I asked her to give me a minute. Clairvoyantly, I motioned to Anthony and asked him to help those young men down. I then asked him to clear the room.

With one motion from Anthony's hand, everyone stood up and walked down the stairs to Shelly's basement. I sat there for a moment as these souls walked past me. An elderly woman put her hand on my knee as she walked by, and said, *"Please, tell Shelly how much we appreciate her prayers; if you don't mind?"* I smiled and told her I would.

Once all the souls had left, I told Shelly what had happened. I also shared with her what the elderly woman had asked me to tell her. She began to cry and said, "We really have no idea how much our prayer's impact these souls, do we? They have suffered so much. I am glad you told me what you saw. Is there anything else I can do for them, Jim?" I told her that all they need from us is our prayers and offerings. She told me that she would pray even harder for them and offer more. I told her I would do the same.

The next morning Michael came to me. He reached up and touched my shoulder and said, *"Phase 7 has just started. The color of your armor is now silver. It represents God's righteousness."* Let's see what Merriam-Webster says.

RIGHTEOUSNESS

1: acting in accord with divine or moral law: free from guilt or sin
2a: morally right or justifiable <a righteous decision> b: arising from an
outraged sense of justice or morality <righteous indignation>
3: slang: GENUINE, EXCELLENT

Michael continued, *"This phase is for you to prove yourself to God. I need to tell you that you can now wound and inflict pain ten times greater than before on any spirit or demon that crosses your path. You must control yourself, be patient, and as always; God is with you."*

Now, perhaps you are wondering what I learned in phase 6? I learned self-control and not to give into my physical desires, but to keep them in check. I learned a small part of God's plan for me, the 30,000 new souls. I also learned to trust what I see, and always know that the Lord is near. And most important, I learned that God will always be there to help me through anything that comes my way.

Chapter 11

Phase 7

It was now Sunday, October 23. Our preparatory Service for the Departed was one week away, and there were two weeks before the service for the departed. It was during the week between both services that we would all prepare our hearts by praying for ourselves so that we, by example, would show the souls that we have forgiven those who have harmed us and also that we hold no grudges against anyone. We try even harder to forgive those who have wronged us. We read our Bibles more, watch TV less, and try to talk about our faith with our family and friends. We seek peace, as much as we possibly can get.

In church before the preparatory service started, I sat clairvoyantly with my two little girls, Amanda and Carrie Ann. Amanda said, *"Papa, someone wants to meet you."* I said, *"Who?"* She said, *"Shamus."* I said, *"Who's Shamus?"* With that, a little black boy walked over and stood at the end of our aisle. He had to be only six years old. He proudly stuck his hand out to me and said, *"I'm Shamus."* I took his little hand and while I shook it. I said, *"Shamus, it's a pleasure to meet you."* He said, *"I've been waiting to meet you for some time now. You see, Jim, I've been watching you."* I asked him, *"Why?"* He said, *"I watched you while you were being persecuted and while all of those bad things were being said about you. And, after everything that they did to you, you were able to forgive them. I know that wasn't easy for you to do."* He grabbed my hand and said, *"This is what happened to me."*

Right in front of my eyes, I saw a group of slaves standing across from a white man. He was yelling at them. He seemed to be drunk at the time. I could feel the rage he had as he yelled at them. He stopped speaking, took one step forward toward a woman holding a baby, and grabbed the small child by the feet; ripping him right out of his mother's arms. He then took the baby and smashed his head against the rocks on the ground, and then threw his lifeless body back in front of the mother. He then walked away. I was crying the whole time as I watched this happen. I could feel my girls squeezing my arms as they held me.

Shamus clasped my hand with both of his and said, *"I figured if you could forgive them for what they did to you, then I should be able to forgive what happened to me."* He turned and looked behind us and smiled. I turned and looked to see what he was looking at. There on the bench, five rows behind us on the left side of the church were his mother, his father, and the white man who had done this to him. They were all sitting together. As I looked at the white man, he hung his head in shame and began to sob. Shamus said, *"It is okay, Jim. I forgive him, and so do my parents. Please, tell Shelly thanks for her prayers. We love her very much, and we love you, too. Never forget, we are watching you. You are such a great example of faith for us, and we pray for you, too!"*

Shamus asked if he could sit with me and my girls during the service. I said of course. So the four of us sat together, arms entwined holding each other's hands as we listened to the service. As the service ended, we all hugged and said good-bye. After the service, I walked up to Shelly and said, *"You have a little admirer."* She looked puzzled at me. I told her what had happened. She told me that she had noticed that I was crying and was going to talk with me after the service. Once more, she spoke of how we actually have no idea how much our prayers impact the departed.

Okay, I should probably tell you that during the past few months, while I was seeing Lana, we would sneak around. I feared that she would be caught again, and punished. Six times I broke up with her. Yep, six times. Then, we would get back together again. What irritated me the most about our relationship was that no one knew we were seeing each other except my friends and family. I would speak of Lana and tell everyone how much I loved her. I got nothing in return from her family. I always felt that when Lana had time, she would fit me into her life. I was getting tired of being her secret.

One day, in the middle of November, I'd had enough. I told Lana that if we couldn't date out in the open like a normal couple, then I was officially done with her. She argued with me about it, telling me that we had a good thing. I told her a good thing? No way. So often through the past year when she'd needed me, I was always there for her. She would call me at all hours of the night. Even at work, while I was in the middle of something, I would drop my life to be there to support her and help her. But when I needed her, she was never around. So many times, while I was suffering through a test from God, I would have liked it if she had supported me in some way. But no! Her family always came first. Her job always came before me. And her friends, they also came before me. I told her that she didn't really have any positive role models in her life to show her how you should be when you're in a relationship. I also reminded her that her parents were never married. Then I pointed out that I felt she was a very selfish, self-centered person like her mom and her aunts. I asked her if she wanted to end up like them. All three of them were in their late forties. Two had never been married. The other one had been divorced. All three of these women were angry, crabby, negative, and "mad at the world" kind of people. They blamed their lives on everyone else. I told her that she and her family had a lot of growing up to do. I was tired of the way they treated me. I told her at the rate she was treating me, I could see her turning out exactly like her family: angry, sad, and very alone.

    Yes, folks, I know that all of this was hurtful and mean. What you don't understand is the crap her family put me through in my own church. And never at any time did Lana stand up for me. They spread rumors and lies about me. I didn't even come close to telling you what all of them actually did to me. On one instance, Lana's grandmother confronted me in church and told me to leave Lana alone. I told her that this was none of her business. She became outraged and said, "Who the hell do you think you are? None of my business? She's my granddaughter! You really are an asshole!" Yes, right in the middle of the main aisle, in front of God's holy altar, she called me that.

    I leaned in towards her and got extremely close to her face and said, "Woman, you had better be careful how you talk to me. I have had it with you and your ignorant family!" She grunted at me like a goat and stormed off. Maybe now you can figure out why I was so frustrated, tired, and fed up with them.

    About a year earlier, my sister Ann came to visit Peter and me. It was around Easter. Lana's family, including her grandmother, went out of their way to invite the three of us over to spend the holiday with all of them. They acted like Jesus himself had come to visit them. They told Ann that we were the nicest family: so loving, so kind, and so friendly. They told us how excited they were that we decided to spend the day with them. We had two other invitations that day, but we decided to go spend the day with them. Now a little over one year later; I'm the jerk? Can you now see why this all seemed so psychotic to me?

    Basically I told Lana that I was done sneaking around. If she wanted to be with me, then it would have to be out in the open. No exceptions anymore. If she couldn't do that for me, than I was done. She was crying the whole time. I was furious and had to get back to work. All of this happened on my lunch hour. I can't even remember what set me off that day. It actually doesn't matter now. I told her to let me know what she decided.

    That evening she called me to tell me that she broke down and told her dad that she couldn't stand being away from me, and that she still had strong feelings for me. He had told her before she did anything that she might want to call me to see if I still felt the same way about her. Her dad didn't know that we were still seeing each other. To Lana's surprise, yes, I did still have the same feelings for her.

Lana and her dad called her mom to tell her that Lana wanted to start seeing me again. Yes, you guessed it. Claire had a thermal meltdown! If Claire's not happy, no one is happy! So we decided to start dating out in the open. You would think that all would be well now. Nope. I went out of my way in church fellowships to spend time with Lana so that everyone would see us together. She would walk away from me like she didn't even know me. I was fed up again. I confronted her and asked if she was embarrassed to be seen with me in church. She told me, "My friends wouldn't understand." I told her, "Then they are not your true friends. If this is how it is going to be, then I am truly done! I will no longer be your little secret." If you are in love with someone, then you go out of your way to tell everyone how you feel and why you feel that way about this person. Yes, I took her age into account, but give me a break. She was nineteen years old and knew how she should treat me. She apologized and told me to give her time. Good thing for her that I am a patient man.

The next day, when I was driving to work, it was cold outside. I turned my heater on, and nothing but ice cold air was blowing out at me. I took it to the local dealership near work and dropped it off. For two days, all I heard them say was that they were still trying to diagnose the problem. Finally, after three days, they told me that the heater door assembly was broken and that it was going to cost me over $800 to have it fixed.

Now would probably be a good place for me to tell you that, for over ten years, I worked on and off in the automotive industry as a parts counterman. So I know the racket. Keep the car for a few extra days to make it look like there is a huge problem when there actually isn't. Charge the customer through the nose, because, as you know, we are all idiots when it comes to our automobiles. We just fork out the money and go on our happy way, never knowing that we just got screwed over. Please don't take this wrong. I am not saying that all automobile repair shops and dealerships are crooks. There are lots of reputable places out there. You just have to find them.

Remember the gut feeling? Mine was going crazy. I knew that they were lying to me. My problem was; I couldn't prove it. And the Academy Award for the best liars in a real-life drama goes to, yes, the service writer guy. He told me it would be another day because they had to order the part. Bull-crap! But there was nothing I could do. I complained that they were keeping my car too long, so they offered me a loaner car at their expense. I hope you folks know that when a dealership does this they have already factored in that cost into your repair and you end up paying for it anyway. No? You didn't know that? Well in most cases that's how it works. You can pay me later for this information.

Do you know that mechanics only get paid a certain amount of money for each repair? It's called "book price." If the book says he only gets paid three hours to do a certain repair, and it takes him one hour to do it, well, he gets paid for three hours and you pay for it. But, if the job takes him six hours he only gets paid for the three hours. Now he has to come up with some other repair to make up for his losses. Ah, the automobile industry. It is so wonderful. That's why I got out of it.

So, I said, "Fine, give me a rental car." Wouldn't you know it; the car they offered me at no cost was about as big as my shoe. Seeing that I am six feet five inches tall, there was no way I could fit into that car. So I had to pay for the upgrade into a car that would fit a full-figured man such as myself. I was thrilled. And one day turned into two days. The service guy called me to tell me that he could save me a few bucks by not replacing the part but by having the mechanic fix the door. Now the repair was only going to cost me $750.

When I finally picked up my car I was a little ticked off. I stood there in front of this little man as he continued to lie to me. At one point, I told him that I knew this repair wasn't as serious as he had told me. You should have seen his face. He started stepping all over his story as I picked it apart. He was quite an arrogant little guy. I ended up paying them what they wanted. There actually wasn't anything I could do, although something was telling me that my problem wasn't fixed.

I picked up Peter at the house because Matt had invited us to his place for dinner that night. As Peter got in the passenger side of the car and tried to put his seat belt on, he couldn't find the female end of the buckle to attach it to. The mechanic in his rush to move onto his next victim put my center console over my seat belt assembly.

Now I had to bring it in again. I immediately called the service guy. He told me to bring it in the very next day, a Saturday, and they would fix it. Peter and I picked up Matt and went out for dinner. During dinner, Matt explained to us how frustrated his wife was with her small business. Her sales manager was quitting, and she didn't know what to do about increasing her business. I told Matt that I had been the general manager of sales and marketing for a small business back in Chicago. I had helped that owner turn his business around within the first year I worked for him. I shared with Matt what I had done, and pointed out a few places where he should tell his wife to concentrate her efforts. He thanked me, and I never gave it another thought. We had a very enjoyable time that evening.

The next morning, I called my bank and put a stop payment on the check that I wrote to the dealership. I figured I would let it ride for a few days and wait to see if the repair actually had been fixed. Then when they called me, I would pay them. I brought my car in; two hours later, I had my seat belt back.

One week later, it was still cold outside. I was driving to work and I turned my heater on, and no heat once again. Big surprise! I called another dealership in the area and made an appointment. I brought my car in but I didn't tell them that I had just had it fixed seven days before. I wanted to see what they would find. Later that afternoon I get a call from the service guy. He asked me if I'd had my car in for a repair lately. I told him, yes, for the same reason that he had it. He asked me to tell him what they had fixed, so I faxed my repair invoice over to him. He called me back to inform me that the cost to replace the broken heater door assembly would cost me $230, with parts. I was beyond words. He told me that he didn't know what they had fixed except they did a superb job of screwing up the assembly door even more. I asked if he would be willing to write me a letter stating these facts, but no he couldn't do that. These guys stick together.

I paid the $230. The service guy asked why I hadn't just brought it back to the first shop so they could fix it again. I told him it was because it wouldn't have been covered under the warranty. I also told him that they'd lied to me and I knew it. Why would I go back, so they could lie to me more? He shrugged his shoulders and told me that they were an honest dealership. I told him I knew that. As I left, he pointed out to me that this repair has a ninety-day warranty, and if I had any problem to please give him a call, because they stood behind all of their repairs. I told him thanks.

The following Sunday after service, Matt asked Peter and me if he could join us for lunch. We said sure. During lunch, Matt told me that he had spoken to his wife about what I had suggested and how happy she was. Without taking a breath, he offered me the sales manager job. I was stunned. I told him I would have to think about it. He said, "That's fine. The sooner the better though." There's another rule I try to live by; I don't go into business with church members. I have watched close friendships fall apart because feelings would get hurt in businesses they shared in. Some people don't know how to separate business from personal life. I have always been able to keep them separate. My concern was if Matt could.

His wife wasn't part of our faith. I didn't want to lose Matt's friendship if something went wrong. So I decided to sleep on it. Never make a rash decision. It is always better to sleep on it, because while you sleep, your spirit will gather information on the subject for you. When you awake in the morning, you will be better informed. No, really. It's true.

The following day, I called Matt, and told him I would like to meet with him and his wife to discuss the position. Later that evening, I met them at her company. She told me everything she expected, and we discussed a salary. I made a particularly strong point that no matter what happened, business was business and church was church and friendship was friendship. If either of them had a problem with that, then I would have to pass on their offer. They both reassured me that they understood. I gladly accepted the position. After a two-week notice to my current employer, I would be able to start. They were both very excited.

It was now the Saturday before I was to start my new job. As I was meditating Michael showed up. He said, *"I have something for you. Please meet me in the center of your head."* As I stepped into the center of my head, I could see that he was holding something. I walked over to him as he spoke, *"Jim, I have this red cloak for you. Please turn around, so that I may place it on your shoulders. It is a gift from Jesus. This cloak signifies the commission he has given you. In time, all will be explained to you in detail. For now, the color red represents his sacrifice for man and the new covenant he makes with you. From this time forward when anyone opposes God and his Son, Jesus, they will know that you have been sent by them. This cloak represents the authority that has been placed in you, by them. I am also to tell you, that you are not allowed to provoke Satan or any of his forces. It is also not your place to correct the leaders of your church."*

As Michael spoke to me, I turned my back to him as he fastened the cloak to the armor covering my shoulders. The cloak was a royal deep red with gold fringes on the bottom. It was quite beautiful. He continued to speak to me, *"Many things have been revealed to you. These things are to strengthen your faith. It is not your place to tell your leaders what you know. They wouldn't believe anything that you would tell them at this time. You must, be patient; in time, they will come to understand the role you will play for the Lord. Phase 7 will end soon. The trials will begin shortly. Through all of this, trust in the Lord, He will always be there for you. Stay strong, Supplanter!"*

As I watched Michael leave, I would be lying to you if I didn't tell you I was a bit concerned about what the trials meant. As always, all I could do was to take everything in faith and just trust the Lord. God had never let me down in the past and I knew whatever He would decide to put me through, I could handle it. Otherwise, he wouldn't have me go through it. Folks, when you find yourself feeling lost, or you have no idea what to do, all any of us ever need to do is to trust in the Lord.

He has never let you down. He will never do anything to you to hurt you. Even when your faith is not as strong as it could be, He will always answer you when the time is right. I know this to be particularly true in my life. So many times when I felt that I wasn't worthy of His attention or my faith was weak, He still answered me and has always proven to me that he was always there.

So my first day on the new job with Matt's wife was spent getting myself acquainted with the product catalog. I familiarized myself with the current customer base and made a number of phone calls introducing myself to a few of our largest clients. The one thing that probably surprised me the most is that there wasn't much training at all. I was shown my desk and how to work the database, and that was pretty much it. Often, I would find that I had many questions, but when I would ask Matt's wife, Cindy, she would be extremely belligerent and condescending. I have never worked for someone like that before. I shook it off and told myself that she must be exceedingly busy.

And, so went my first week. Anytime I needed some information; Cindy would go out of her way to belittle me in front of the people I was supervising. She would undermine my decisions when I made some changes to improve the way we did business. I felt as if I was fighting with her every moment. She criticized everything I did, even the way I signed my emails. I started to see how she treated her other employees. She even did it in front Matt when he would come to the office. I was stunned that she was like this. I spoke with one of the other employees after she cut him down because he had made a shipping error. I asked him if she always treated everyone like this. He hesitated and said, "Why do you think the last sales manager had quit? He couldn't take it anymore. Most of us just put up with her because she pays better than most jobs; we are kind of used to it." I couldn't believe what I was hearing.

On Friday, I had finally had enough. At the end of that day, I walked into her office and confronted her on everything. She was surprised that I talked to her about the way she had been treating the others and me. She told me I needed to grow a thicker skin and not take things so personally. I explained to her that there is a difference between constructive criticism and abuse. She apologized for the way she had been treating me, and then in the same breath told me she didn't appreciate the changes I was making. I asked her why she hired me then. I told her if she wanted her business to fail then she should just keep doing what she was doing. At the rate she was going, she had already lost thirty percent of the market share because of the way she did business. I again told her what I was planning on doing, and if she didn't want my help then I would step aside. She told me to tell her in detail what my plan was. So I did. When I left, I felt much better. I was now looking forward to coming in to work on Monday, unlike the previous few days where I was dreading every day.

The following Monday arrived. It was one week before Christmas. As the day progressed, it was as if I had never even had a conversation with Cindy three days before. Only this time, she was even more condescending and abusive. One of the employees walked over to me and asked why she was treating me this way.

I shared with the employee that Cindy and I'd had a talk on Friday. I thought everything would be OK now. The employee told me that she felt sorry for me and hoped that Cindy and I could work it out. She then told me that so many times she had been treated that way, too. She had just always just put up with it. I told her no one had the right to treat another human being like that. I don't care how miserable your day may be. It is wrong, and I don't have to take it.

I tried twice to talk with Cindy, but she always had an excuse. I never got a chance to talk with her. That night, as I drove home, my gut was killing me. I hadn't been sleeping particularly well ever since I'd started working for Cindy. I prayed to Lord that He would help me make the right decision.

The next day, after being at my desk for only ten minutes, she started in on me again. I sat there and let her do what she did best: to make a fool of herself. When she left to go an appointment, I composed a short email and copied Matt on it. I explained how surprised I was that Cindy felt it was okay to treat not only me, but her other employees as she did and for the sake of our friendship, I regretfully resigned as sales manager. This was effective immediately. Then, I packed up my belongings, walked to my car, and left.

Later that afternoon, Matt called me completely surprised and asked what had happened. I told him what I felt. I even said that if Cindy, wasn't his wife, I would have used a few other choice words. Since he was my friend, and I respected him, I controlled myself. He didn't argue with me at all. All he told me was that he thoroughly understood and was sorry I had to quit. He asked me what I was going to do for work now. I told him I had already left my previous boss a voice mail asking for my old job back. Matt told me that he would pray that everything worked out. I thanked him and asked if we could still be friends. He laughed and said of course.

It had been a little over a week. I still hadn't heard anything from my former boss. I got on my hands and knees and prayed out loud, "Dear Lord, I get the feeling that I don't need to be in this area anymore. I get the feeling that I belong back in Chicago. I have contacted my previous boss but haven't heard anything from him. If he doesn't call me before the end of this year, then I will know that you want me to move back to Chicago. I pray all of this is in accordance with Your will, and in your Son's name, please hear me, Amen."

The Friday after Christmas, Lana came over to see me before she went to work. I could feel that something wasn't right. We sat on the couch and talked. Lana said, "Jim, I don't feel right, something is wrong and I can't put my finger on it. I feel so scared and I don't know why. For weeks now I have had this feeling of dread and I can't explain it." She started to cry. She said, "Can you see anything, or feel anything?" I took her face in my hands and looked into her eyes. As I looked deeper into her being, she began to pull away from me and started crying harder. My heart was killing me. That is always a warning sign for me that evil is extremely close. I grabbed her and pulled her closer to me.

I told her, "We need to pray, now!" I asked God to help us, to open my eyes to see what was happening to Lana, and if I could help her; to please allow me. I asked for added angels' protection and for peace. As I prayed, Lana seemed to calm down a little. I finished my prayer with Thy will be done. When I finished, I pulled her close to me and just held her.

Clairvoyantly, I began to peer into Lana's space. As I looked in, all of a sudden a demon jumped out of her space, and started laughing at me. I continued to hold Lana; she had no idea what was going on. The demon said, *"I'm Antonius. Brother to Andreus! For weeks, I've been playing with her, waiting to get close to you!"* In an instant, I drew my sword, sprung to my feet, and without even thinking, I cut Antonius's head clean off. He didn't even have a chance to draw his sword. As I stood there, I was utterly surprised at what had just happened. Clairvoyantly, I watched his head hit the floor, and then watched his body slump to the ground. In a matter of seconds, his head and torso fizzled away and then disappeared.

I stepped back into my body, which was still holding Lana. Two seconds later, Andreus appeared and screamed at me, *"Supplanter, who do you think you are? You don't have the authority to kill any of us!"* Before I could say anything, Michael appeared and said, *"Andreus, you will leave now!"* Andreus kept yelling at me. As he left, he told me, *"This isn't over!"* Michael said, *"Jim, it will be fine. You do have the Lord's authority. Andreus will try to seek revenge on you. He knows that he cannot touch you, if he did, God himself would step in and destroy him. This is all part of God's plan for you. In time, you will understand."*

As Michael left, I kept holding Lana. She looked up at me and asked what had happened because she didn't feel the same way anymore. So I told her. You would think she would have been scared, but she wasn't. She took it all in stride. We thanked the Lord for His help, and I asked for His protection for Lana and my family. I didn't want any of this to come back on my family. I knew, in my heart, that the Lord would preserve my loved ones.

Monday, January 2, 2006, arrived. Happy New Year! I still hadn't heard a word from my previous boss until that afternoon. In the morning, I sent an email explaining to him that I had decided to move back to Chicago and asking him if I could use his name as a reference. He responded back telling me that he had been on vacation for the past few weeks, and just got my voice mail, and now my email. He wished me the best and told me I could use him as a reference. Can you see how the Lord works?

I told Peter what my plans were. He looked at me surprised, and then told me that he was planning on staying because his boss had just told him he was getting a hefty raise and a promotion. I told him it was his decision. The main reason why I wanted to move back to Chicago was because I was tired of being persecuted by Lana's family and the leaders in my church. There was nothing I could do to change their opinion of me. I have never run from a fight in my life, but I have always taken my grandma's advice. Whenever my sister's kids would act up, my grandma would say to my sisters, pick your battles.

I knew in my heart that God wanted me back home in Chicago. I called my two sisters back in Chicago to tell them my plans. They were very excited. They both offered Peter and me a room in each of their homes until we got back on our feet. I told them that Peter, Lana, and I had already made plans to come for a visit the third week of January. I wanted my family to meet Lana. My intentions were to move back to Chicago the first week of February.

I started searching the job Web sites for positions in the Chicago area. I contacted a few headhunters, too. I found a number of jobs, and in my cover letter, I explained that I would be in town for a few weeks near the end of January to interview. I included that I would be ready to start work the second week of February.

I called Shelly to let her know that I was planning on moving back home. She was not surprised. She told me that she fully understood why I had to leave. I told her, no matter what, I would always cherish our friendship and would keep in touch with her. She was very happy to hear that. Then I called a number of members from my congregation to let them know of my plans. Some of them took it extremely hard. I promised that I would stay in touch with them, too.

On January 19, 2006, I landed in Chicago. I had been planning on being in Chicago for a convention for Cindy and Matt's company. In my resignation letter, I told Cindy to deduct the airfare to Chicago from my last paycheck. Peter and Lana had a flight they took the next day. Our plan was to stay over the weekend and then fly out together on Monday. I spent time with my whole family. Lana met everyone. They loved her, too. As Monday approached, I had the feeling that I should stay a little longer. So I decided to stay until the following Tuesday. Later that afternoon, I received a phone call asking me to come in for an interview on Thursday. It was with a hospital in the northwest suburbs. I had faxed my resume to them only one week before. I had a good feeling about this place.

Over the weekend, as we all spent time together, my father asked my brother to move back with me now. He didn't want me to be driving through the mountains by myself during the winter months. You see, folks, my father's health wasn't that great. He was eighty-two years old. He's an extremely proud man, and would never admit to us that he actually missed us. My mom, on the other hand, pulled us both aside and told us how much dad missed having his boys around. We made our plans to have my car fit with a trailer hitch so we could move all of Peter's belongings back with us. Almost everything I owned could fit into my car.

Lana and Peter flew out Monday evening. Lana was very sad that we would be apart for a week. Then, two days after I got back, I was leaving again for Chicago.

I went on my interview at the hospital and felt that it went very well. When they asked me what I could tell them about myself that would stand out from every other person that they had interview, I told them, "I don't scare very easily and I thrive in chaos!" The two people interviewing me smiled.

On Saturday, I decided to have Marty and Amanda give me a healing, so I could start getting used to the energy in the area. You may think this is a little weird, but there is totally different energy from one city to another. For instance, the energy in Chicago is highly chaotic compared to the west coast area where I had been living for the past two years. It can take you almost one year to acclimate to the new energies after you move. That is why in some cases, people find it hard to move away from home. They just don't feel as comfortable in their new surroundings.

When I was getting my healing, I could see off in the distance what appeared to be Michael. As he walked towards me, I couldn't see his face clearly. All I know is that my heart was hurting. We all know what that means. As he started to talk to me, the tonality of his voice wasn't right. Even the way he was forming sentences didn't sound like Michael. Clairvoyantly, I stood up, and drew my sword, and pointed it at his throat. Immediately, he changed into who I thought it was. It was Satan.

He began to laugh at me and said, *"Well done, Supplanter. It looks as if I am going to have to try even harder in the future to try to deceive you. I just thought I would stop by to let you know that no matter where you live, I can find you. And don't think that I have forgotten what you did to Antonius!"* I didn't lower my sword the whole time he was talking. When he finished, I said, *"If you are finished, you can leave now! In the name of Jesus Christ, I command you to leave!"* Suddenly the real Michael showed up, and made a hand motion for Satan to leave. As Satan turned to leave, he smiled at me and then left.

Michael told me to meet him in the center of my head when I was done with my healing. As I met him in the center of my head, he told me to kneel in front of him. As I knelt, he put his hands on my head and said, *"Receive the blessing of God the Father. This is a reward for your faith. For gold is tried in the fire, and acceptable men in the furnace of adversity."* He told me to stand up. Then he said, *"Do you recall one of your favorite Bible verses? You are aware of the last line of the Lord's blessing over you, are you not?"* I said, *"Yes, it's from the Apocrypha. Ecclesiasticus, the Son of Sirach, Chapter 2."* He said, *"Can you now see the truth in this scripture, Jim? The Lord has tried you and you have passed. He is very proud of you. He wanted me to tell you that you will find work very soon. Just be patient. He is with you."*

Folks, the first time that I gave up my free will, when I was done praying, I flipped open the Bible to this verse:

Sirach (Apocrypha), chapter 2 (KJV)

1: My son, if thou come to serve the Lord, prepares thy soul for temptation.
2: Set thy heart aright, and constantly endure, and make not haste in time of trouble.
3: Cleave unto him, and depart not away, that thou mayest be increased at thy last end.
4: Whatsoever is brought upon thee take cheerfully, and be patient when thou art changed to a low estate.
5: For gold is tried in the fire, and acceptable men in the furnace of adversity.
6: Believe in him, and he will help thee, order thy way aright, and trust in him.
7: Ye that fear the Lord, wait for his mercy, and go not aside, lest ye fall.
8: Ye that fear the Lord believe him, and your reward shall not fail.
9: Ye that fear the Lord, hope for good, and for everlasting joy and mercy.
10: Look at the generations of old, and see, did any trust in the Lord, and was confounded? Or did any abide in his fear, and was forsaken? Or whom did he ever despise, that called upon him?
11: For the Lord is full of compassion and mercy, longsuffering, and very pitiful, and forgiveth sins, and saveth in time of affliction.
12: Woe be to fearful hearts, and faint hands, and the sinner that goeth two ways!
13: Woe unto him that is fainthearted! For he believeth not, therefore shall he not be defended.
14: Woe unto you that have lost patience! And what will ye do when the Lord shall visit you?
15: They that fear the Lord will not disobey his Word, and they that love Him will keep his ways.
16: They that fear the Lord will seek that which is well, pleasing unto Him, and they that love him shall be filled with the law.
17: They that fear the Lord will prepare their hearts, and humble their souls in his sight,

18: Saying, We will fall into the hands of the Lord, and not into the hands of men: for as his majesty is, so is his mercy.

Can you truly see how great and wonderful the Lord is? He will never cease to amaze me. I can recall when I read this for the first time, I was a little nervous, but there was no way I wasn't going to trust Him. Looking back, over these years, I can honestly say that I tried my very best to hold to all of these principles. Folks, never doubt what you can do with the Lord's help.

Now what did I learn through Phase 7? I learned something that one of our chief apostles said many years ago: "Injustice is the best teacher!" Even though the dealership cheated me, the Lord taught me tolerance. And everything happens for a reason. If I had not worked for Cindy for seven days, I would have never thought to move back to Chicago. Sometimes we may not see what the Lord's plan is for us at the beginning. But, if we trust Him, He will show us what his plan is when we come out on the other end. All we have to do is stay true to Him.

Chapter 12

The Journey Home

It was now Tuesday, January 31, 2006. Lana, picked me up at the airport, and we went out for dinner. The next day, I got up early, because I had to be at the trailer place to get the hitch installed. When I called to confirm, they told me that the hitch they ordered for me wasn't going to be in until the next day. We were planning on leaving on Thursday morning. Now, we had to make our plans to leave Friday morning instead.

Michael showed up out the blue and told me that he had something for me. As we greeted each other, we shook hands like Roman Centurions. This was done by grasping each other's forearms with our right hand, then shaking them. He said, *"Jesus wanted me to give you a new mantle of peace."* I bent my head forward as he draped it over my head and shoulders. Immediately, I felt peace pour over my heart and soul. Then he said, as he put his hand on my shoulder, *"The Lord God blesses you with strength and wisdom. He gives you insight and takes away from you all fear. Anthony and the other angels will be with you on your journey home. Pay close attention to what he tells you. You and Peter will be safe."* We shook hands again, and then he left.

Peter and I spent the next two days packing everything we had. I got my hitch and picked up the trailer. By Thursday evening, we were ready to go. Lana spent the night with me. It was very early Friday morning, and under a veil of many tears, she tried to say goodbye. At one point, she was crying so hard and wailing that the neighbors turned on their light to see what was going on. I told her I would call her once we got on the road and she could call me at any time. Together, we prayed one more time, and then Peter and I drove off.

Six hours after we left, my heater stopped working. Yes, it was forty degrees out and I had no heat. We decided to stop in Boise, Idaho, to see if they could fix it. I called the last dealership that worked on my car. I was informed that it was still covered under a warranty and that they would pay for whatever it cost to fix it. After many phone calls, we found a dealership that was open on Saturday. I dropped it off for the night. I called my sister Ann to see if she could find us a hotel for the night, which she did. We settled in for the evening. I called Lana to tell her what had happened and then we watched TV and ordered a pizza.

In the morning, around 11:30 am, I called the dealership; only to be told that they still couldn't find the problem. His plan was to tear apart the dashboard on Monday and try to get a better look. There was no way I was going to spend my weekend sitting around in Idaho. I wanted to get home. Heat or no, heat. I asked him to put my car back together and that I would be over to pick it up. He told me to give him a few hours. Peter suggested that I should get one of those heaters that you plug into your car lighter. I told him he was brilliant!

 We went to a store, and wouldn't you know it, they had nothing. The only thing I could find was those packs that hunters use to keep their feet warm. You squeeze them and stick them into your socks. Yes, they worked pretty well for my feet, but what about the rest of me?

 It was now 3:00 pm, and the sun was fading fast. It was 35 degrees outside. Yes, I was cold. I was wearing two sweatshirts, my thick leather jacket, and two pairs of gloves. Yet, I was still cold. I decided to pull off at a truck stop for gas, even though my tank wasn't that low. My hopes were that maybe they had something I could use to keep myself warm. Oh, I should also probably share with you that because of the weight of the trailer I was pulling, I was only getting 6 to 8 miles per gallon. Pulling that beast up the hills through the mountains was quite a joy; I have to tell you. My car has a six-cylinder engine. Peters has a four-cylinder engine, so I chose to pull the trailer. I filled my car up, and then we looked for anything that would get to give me heat. Yeah! We found a heated seat cushion that plugs into the cigarette lighter. I was kind of thrilled. At least my butt would be warm, now.

 As we drove on for the next few hours, I looked out onto the horizon only to see two weather systems on the verge of colliding with each other. They were directly in front of us. As I watched; the outside temperature gauge dropped. I prayed out loud and said, "Dear Father, please protect us!" The traffic started to slow. The next thing I knew we were all at a standstill. Peter got out of his car to tell me what he knew. Peter had a CB radio, so he was talking to truckers to find out why we had stopped. Peter told me that a semi trailer had slid, and was blocking one lane of traffic. They were waiting for a tow truck to come and move it.

 The sky grew even darker, until it was pitch black. The only lights you could see were from the headlights behind us. We were out in the middle of nowhere, and it began to snow. We were sitting at the bottom of this hill that led into the mountains. The road was a sheet of ice. For almost thirty minutes we just sat there. As the traffic slowly crept up the hill, my tires began to spin. My biggest fear was that I would have gotten stuck towing this trailer, and we would be stranded out in this weather all night.

I glanced up at my thermometer, which read only twenty-eight degrees as the outside temperature. I could see that my windshield was starting to fog up. The only way to defog a windshield is to turn on the defroster, right? But I had no heat. Do you know what that meant? I had to turn on the thing that blew even colder air into my car now. I had no choice. Unless I decided to hold my breath for a while and if I passed out, I'm pretty sure I would have killed myself. So, that wasn't actually an option.

I turned on my defroster, and immediately I was hit in the face with an arctic blast. How invigorating! I kept it on only for a minute or two, and then I turned it off. Still, my tires kept spinning. I decided to hug the side of the road as I drove. Here's a bit of family trivia for you. When I was growing up, my family would go on road trips. If my dad were in a playful mood, he would steer the car to the shoulder so that the tires would roll over what we kids at the time referred to as the "runta-runta strip." That was kind of what it sounded like as the tires rolled over the bumps.

Of course, what I am referring to are the grooves that are on the side of the road that warn you that you are about to drive off the road. This is so you don't kill yourself if you don't start waking up to get back onto the road. Some of you college kids may know what I talking about. It's not just when you're tired, either? Hmmm? Maybe it's when you close one eye that you discover your vision becomes a little sharper. Dare I say perhaps after a night of beverage consumption? Hmmm? Oh, you know what I'm talking about!

Anyway, I decided to drive over the "runta-runta'" strips to see if my tires would grip them. Surprise! They did! I had to be extremely careful. If I gave it too much gas, the tires would spin. I found if I gently pumped the gas pedal, the car gripped the road better. We continued to crawl slowly up the hill. At one point, we all stopped. I hated to stop. It would take me a while to get my car moving again. I looked as far as I could see through the blowing snow to see the emergency lights flashing. We reached the point where the semi truck slid of the road. The police directed us around the accident. The whole area was an enormous mess.

As we kept driving on, the storm picked up and started to drop even more snow. The wind was blowing even harder now. Okay, I have a question for all of you wonderful readers. What do you get when you combine 28 degrees with wind and snow? I'll give you a minute. Think hard? Did any of you guess ice? Yes, ice. How wonderful for me. Please, let me sum up my situation for you. It's pitch black out, I'm in the middle of nowhere, I have no heat, it's 28 degrees, snowing, my windshield is now getting covered with ice, and oh, yes, and the windshield started to fog up, again. Can you say, sudden death is just around the corner?

I took a deep breath, and prayed out loud, "Lord, I thank you for your angel's protection." As I looked at Anthony, "And for always being there for me. I do seem to be having a problem right now. As you can plainly see, my windshield is now getting covered with snow and ice, which makes it kind of hard for me to see. I don't have any heat to melt the ice, and I'm pretty sure if I kill myself right now by driving off of the road, it would really ruin my evening. I don't know what to ask you for, so, I'm just going to ask for your help!"

As soon as I finished praying my thermometer caught my attention. I stared at it, and watched it start to go up. Twenty-eight, twenty-nine, thirty-two, forty and then it stopped at forty-five degrees. I looked at my windshield as the snow and ice began to melt. I couldn't believe my eyes! No, honestly I couldn't. Slowly, the windshield became as clear as it would have been on a sunny day. When all the ice and snow had melted away, I looked back up at my thermometer as I watched it drop back down to twenty-eight degrees. I glanced over to Anthony and said, *"Wow!"* Anthony said, *"The Lord is kind to those who trust Him."* I said, *"Well, if the Lord can make the outside of my car forty-five degrees, can't he make the inside of my car a balmy seventy degrees?"* Anthony paused for a moment and then said, *"He chooses not to."* I said, "Okay, Lord, I'm okay with that. Thank you so much, Lord. Love Ya."

The storm was now blowing out of control. I could feel the trailer fishtailing behind me as the wind slammed into it time and again. Sometimes, I had to slow down, just to keep the car on the road. The whole time, I kept my eyes on Peter's taillights, only to watch my windshield once again start to freeze over. Before I said anything, I watched my thermometer once more as it rose again from thirty degrees up to forty-five degrees. I felt a wave of emotion sweep over my heart, and my eyes began to tear up as I thanked my Heavenly Father for his watchful eye and loving help. Once again, it dipped back down to twenty-eight degrees.

As we made our way down the hill to the gas station, Anthony spoke up and said, *"The Lord would like me to share a few things with you. The Lord caused your heater to break so that the two of you would stay in Boise for a while. Do you recall stopping at the store looking for a heater, but you did not find one there? He kept you in Boise because the two storm fronts you drove through were the tail end of the storms. He had you stay at the hotel and go to this store to delay your departure. If you had left even one hour earlier, you would have been stranded. Look at your gas gauge right now."* I looked at it, and it was almost on empty. *"Do you recall stopping at the truck stop to get your seat cushion? While you were there you decided at the last minute to fill your tank, even thought you did not think you needed gas at the time? If, you had not filled up when you did, you would have run out of gas in the middle of the mountain pass. Jim, the Lord loves you very much. He promised you, that He would protect you. Look around your car, clairvoyantly. Can you see Him?"* Clairvoyantly, as I looked beneath my car, I saw that my car was sitting in the Lord's hand. Anthony said, *"He is always with you. After you get gas, and continue on your trip, the Lord would like you to stay overnight in Salt Lake City. You will find that the temperature will stay at forty degrees and you will have clear skies all the way there."*

Sure enough, as I pulled into the gas station my thermometer read forty degrees. I shared everything with Peter. He stood there with his mouth open. Peter said, "The most amazing thing that I saw was while you were pulling the trailer, it always stayed directly behind your car; no matter how hard the wind blew, or how fast you were driving."

I said, "Every time I looked in my rearview mirror, I saw an angel sitting on the tow hitch. That's probably why it always stayed directly behind me." Yes, the Lord God is truly amazing. I finally had cell phone service, so I called Lana. I wanted to tell her what had happened. Then, I called Shelly. Shelly told me that she had been praying extremely hard for us that afternoon, and now she knew why.

Peter called our sister Ann to see is she could find us a hotel in Salt Lake City. My brother-in-law, Gary, offered his hotel reward points to us so we could stay there for free. Peter and I had miscalculated how much it was going to cost us in gas to get home. We had also figured it would only take us three days. Boy, were we wrong. We dropped off our things in the room. We were starving! The only thing open at 11:30 pm was fast-food places. So we drove through one and went back to the hotel to settle in for the night. Two days down, and we weren't even halfway home yet. As I went to sleep, I thanked the Lord, once more, for His protection.

It was now, day three of our journey home. Sunday, February 5, Super Bowl Sunday! I'll be honest with you; I'm certainly not much of a sports fan, although I do like football. Peter wanted to make sure that wherever we decided to stay that night, we would have a chance to watch the game. I told him OK! We had breakfast at the hotel. I wasn't really in any hurry to freeze my appendages off again, but I didn't have any choice. Peter offered to drive my car, but I told him I'd be OK. Besides, if we hit another storm, I would feel more comfortable driving my own car.

I layered myself up again and climbed into my mobile icebox, ready for another adventure. Yes, faithful readers, there is nothing quite as majestic as watching your own breath as it wafts out of your mouth in your car. Even after an hour, I could still see my breath. As I looked ahead, I could see another storm front approaching. I smiled, because I knew the Lord was with us. Slowly, the sky grew darker, and it began to snow. My cell phone rang; it was Peter. He told me that overnight there had been a huge storm, and a truck driver lost his life. We both decided to pray for him. Peter was listening to the CB radio as a number of drivers were talking about it. Peter then told me that we would be driving through some exceptionally severe weather and that I should watch his taillight for when he slowed down. I, of course said, *"Duh!"* He didn't think that was very funny.

We drove on. As we made our way up the next mountain pass, the wind picked up again. I could feel my car shaking back and forth. It was snowing pretty hard, and the roads were covered with freezing ice and slush. The plow trucks had been salting, which I was thankful for until my windshield washers stopped working. Here's another question for you. What happens to a windshield that gets splashed with freezing water and salt, and you have no washers to clean it off? Yep, you can't see anything!

I yelled out loud, "Come on Lord! Give me a break!" I sat there quietly waiting to hear anything that would make me feel better about this situation. Waiting. Waiting. Nothing! I got nothing! So, there I was, freezing my butt off, and now I couldn't see where I was going. I hit the gas and drove up to the back end of Peter's car. His tires kicked up the "road goo" that we were driving on. As it hit my windshield, I turned my wipers on, and then backed off again. Yeah! It was just enough moisture to clean it off. That is how it went; back and forth for the next two hours. I could tell that Peter was trying to figure out what the heck I was doing. The problem was we were in the middle of nowhere and our cell phones didn't work. So he couldn't call me.

Finally he slowed down in the lane next to me, and rolled his window down. I yelled to him, "I need gas now, and my windshield washers are broken!" We pulled off at the next exit. You would have thought we were in the middle of the Arctic Circle with the way the storm was raging around us. It had to be twenty degrees outside. I pulled out my car owner's manual to see which fuse controlled the washers. I found it. It looked OK. Yes, the realization that I would have to drive the rest of the way home without windshield washers was hard to take at first. Then, a sarcastic joy filled my heart as I remember that I didn't have any heat, either.

We went into the station to buy supplies for our long journey ahead in the hopes that we would not be attacked along the trail by marauding thieves and left for dead! I'm sorry. I was felt like I was back in the old west. No, really, we did buy some snacks. "Snacks" just doesn't sound as exciting as "supplies" does. Hey, I'm trying to build a level of suspense here. Can you tell?

Peter has always had a knack for striking up a conversation with a perfect stranger. After talking to these two truck drivers, he found out that we weren't even halfway through this storm yet. It didn't look as if it would subside for hours. That's why the truck drivers decided to stay put for a while. But Peter and I had something that these truck drivers didn't have. We were stupid! Well, actually, we had God watching over us, and Anthony also told me to keep going. Still, keeping the faith!

So I climbed back into my ice road chariot. What an adventure we were on! I'm being a little sarcastic here. Can you blame me? And off we went. There were moments where the storm was so strong; I could barely see Peter's taillights. It was at those times that I slowed down to eighty miles an hour. I'm kidding. Most of the time, we had to slow down to around twenty miles per hour, for fear of sliding off the road. It was horrible out there. Freezing rain, mixed with snow and ice. Forty-mile-an-hour winds blowing. Yes, a true winter wonderland.

After three hours of driving, I motioned to Peter that I needed gas again. We pulled off while the storm seemed to have subsided. I can tell you; we were truly thankful. After we both had filled up, we went into the store for some beef jerky and a soda. As any guy can tell you, that is the standard staple for any road trip. As we paid, in true Peter fashion, he struck up a conversation with the guy behind the counter. Within 5.6 seconds, my joy was turned into a small voice in my head that said, *"Aw, crap!"* The attendant wanted to make sure that we knew we were currently sitting in the eye of the storm. As we drove to the east, it was only going to get worse. Yay! I love a challenge!

I would be lying to you if I said I wasn't a little tired of all of this, but we drove on. I looked over at Anthony, my copilot. He was always quietly just sitting there. He's not much of a talker. None of the angels that surround me ever are. I asked Anthony, *"How much longer should we keep driving?"* He said, *"Drive till you reach a larger city in Nebraska. Once the sun goes down, the roads will freeze. The Lord doesn't want you to be driving when that happens. I believe you are cold enough during the day. It will only get colder as the sun disappears. Soon, you will be out of this storm. The skies will clear, and you will have no more challenges. The*

Lord is still with you."

I called Peter to tell him we should drive to Lincoln, Nebraska, and stay the night. With the way we were making time, now that we were out of the storm, we would arrive around the time that the Super Bowl would start. He was very happy. I called my sister Ann next to see if she could find us a hotel once more. She was happy to help us. It was twenty-five degrees outside as we pulled up to our hotel. We were both exhausted and hungry.

We found a steak restaurant and spent the next few hours eating and watching the game. I finally thawed out by halftime. I called Lana later that evening and shared the highlights of the day with her and then I went to bed.

Day four was upon us. We looked at the weather forecast for the day. I was pretty disappointed when I learned that the temperatures would be in the mid thirties with bright sunny skies and no storms in sight. It looked as if it was going to be another uneventful day. I was ecstatic! We had breakfast and then planned our trip. It was still twenty degrees out as we pulled out of Lincoln, Nebraska. I was used to the cold by now, and being numb can have a few advantages.

As we drove through the day, I realized that we were making excellent time. Our three-day trip home had now turned into a five-day trip. Good thing it was anything but boring. At the rate we were driving, I felt we could make it to my old stomping grounds; Des Moines, Iowa, before it got too late. As I drove, I pondered my life. I looked at how far I had come in the past few years since my divorce. I found myself getting a little emotional. Out of the blue, I looked at my passenger side seat and I realized that my grandma, my mom's mom, was now sitting there. She had passed away many years before. It was February 6, my grandma's birthday.

She put her hand on my arm and said, *"Jimmy, you have no idea how proud I am of you. The Lord loves you very much; that's why He picked you for this task. I know you have many questions. All I can tell you is to stay the course and the Lord will bless you. In time, you will truly see how much He loves you. The family asked me to give you their love. Your girls love you too and are fine. There are so many wonderful things coming for you. I know how hard it is for you to wait and be patient. We are all praying for you. You will not fail. We all support you, Jimmy. I love you very much."* As Grandma finished talking with me, she leaned over and gave me a hug, and then kissed me on the cheek. Then she was gone. Tears were streaming down my face. I thanked the Lord for the wonderful gift of sight He had given me, and for His kindness in letting me see my Grandma on her birthday.

I called Ann to see if she could, for the last time, find us a hotel for the night. When she told us which hotel she'd reserved, I knew right where it was. We pulled into the hotel around 7:00 pm. We had dinner. I took a long, hot shower. I called Lana and then went to bed. It was hard to fall asleep right away. I was excited about being home tomorrow. Luckily for me, I was totally exhausted, and fell asleep sooner than I thought I would.

It was now Tuesday, February 7, 2006, the final day of our journey home. We were only five hours away from home. I wished I could fly. The day was to be in the upper thirties, with bright and sunny skies. Yay! We were almost home. Around 2:30 pm, we pulled into my sister Ann's driveway. We were finally home. Five days, 2,300 miles later, home, sweet home!

Peter and I were starving; so we drove to find a restaurant to get something to eat. My cell phone rang; it was Lana. She was crying and screaming. I had a hard time understanding what she was saying. All I knew was there was panic and fear in her voice. Finally, she said, "I don't know what's wrong; I am so scared! There is something in my house." She began to scream as she said, "Something is pulling me up the stairs; I can't stop it!" The next thing I heard was Lana screaming as she was falling down the stairs. I said, "What are you doing, are you trying to hurt yourself?" She said, "I'm not doing it! I can't stop myself!"

I listened as I heard her screaming and crying as she was dragged up the stairs, and then thrown down them again. I prayed out loud, "Dear God send an angel to protect Lana!" I knew Andreus was behind this! Again, I prayed out loud, "Please Lord, help her!" I closed my eyes and took a deep breath. I concentrated on Lana. The next thing I saw was Andreus grabbing Lana by the back of the neck. He was pulling her up the stairs again. Two angels appeared and grabbed Andreus and threw him across the room. Lana stopped on the stairs where she was.

Andreus looked right at me and said, *"I want you to know; now that you are not here anymore, I will take great delight in tormenting the woman that you love."* He started to laugh as he pointed at her. I could see and hear Lana. I stared at him and said, *"In the name of Jesus Christ, I command you to leave NOW! You had better back off! I have had enough of your crap! You are such a coward! You pick on my girlfriend, now, after I leave? You, spineless jerk!"* The two angels grabbed him by the arms. He was yelling at me, the whole time they dragged him out of

Lana's house. He said that he would be back.

    I asked Lana if she was okay. She said, "What happened? I really couldn't stop myself from doing that." I told her it was Andreus, and that there were two angels with her now to protect her. I told her she would be safe. We talked for another half hour until I knew she would be all right. I told her to call me if anything else happens. I prayed with her, and thanked the Lord that she didn't get hurt and that He would now protect her from Andreus.

Chapter 13

Home At Last!

Now, maybe you're wondering, "Jim, whatever happened to your car?" Well, once again I'm glad you asked. I called the local dealership and after I had shared the horror story of my numerous repairs, car failures, and my trek across the frozen tundra without any heat, I gave the service writer my keys. He assured me that they would find the problem and fix it. As if I have never heard those words before. I was very excited, to say the least. (I am of course being sarcastic.)

The following afternoon I got a call from the service writer. He told me that there was a recall on my car. A tiny little relay that controls the heater failed. They replaced the relay at no charge, as well as the twenty-five-cent fuse that controlled my windshield washers. Yes, I asked the same question that maybe you're thinking right about now. Why the heck didn't the other two dealerships know about this? He couldn't answer that question for me. Here's what I think. If my heater had worked, then the Lord wouldn't have had the opportunity to show me miracle after miracle. If I had to live through it again, I wouldn't change a thing.

Peter and I tried our best to settle in now that we were back in Chicago. I decided to stay with Ellen and her family, because they lived north of Chicago, and I had a feeling that the hospital that I'd interviewed with might hire me. If that were the case, then I would only be three miles away from work. Pretty sweet! Peter then would stay with Ann and her family. They lived about forty-five minutes south of Ellen. Both of us kept sending out resumes in hopes to secure employment. I had a number of interviews, but no offers.

It was the end of February. I was getting a little discouraged about finding a job. I had recalled what Michael had said to me before we left the west coast. He told me that I would find a job right away, and I shouldn't concern myself. But yet, I was still unemployed. I fervently prayed every day asking the Lord for help, but nothing changed. One evening, I broke down and pleaded for God to help me.

The next day, I decided to have Marty and Amanda give me a healing, because I was seriously down. As I sat there, taking deep breaths and trying to let go of my frustration, the two of them said words of encouragement, trying to console me. Marty said, *"Jim, buddy, you are just going to have to be patient. Michael will be by when we are done to tell you something. Just wait and see what he tells you."* As I looked around my space, I saw Michael standing a little way off. He waved and motioned that we would talk when Marty and Amanda were through. As the two of them finished, Michael walked towards me and stopped. He said, *"Jim, you need to understand that the Lord is moving the powers of Heaven for you. He is dealing with people's free will. He cannot force someone to hire you. You know this. Even though you seem to think nothing is happening, the Lord is helping you more than you will ever know."*

I said, *"But Michael, you told me I would have a job right away once I moved back. It's been almost a month."* Michael said, *"Your definition of 'right away' and the Lord's definition of 'right away' are two different things. You are looking for a certain salary. The Lord is trying to get that for you, but it will take some time. You just need to trust Him. He was touched by your prayer last night and told me to come and speak with you. Just trust in Him. Everything will work out according to His will."*

As Michael left, Marty and Amanda both gave me big hugs and told me to cheer up. I did feel better. I decided to call the human resources lady that I'd interviewed with at the hospital over a month before. I wanted to let her know that I was still interested in the position. Actually, for the past three weeks, I had called her to see if she had any information only to find on her voice mail that she would be on vacation that week.

I decided to call the director of material management directly. When I called him, I got his voice mail. I left him a message. Later that afternoon, the director himself called me back. I was a little surprised. The director said, "Jim, I wanted to let you know that you are in the top running for this position. I can't make you an offer right now. I want to be honest with you though. The salary you are asking for is a little higher than some of the employee salaries that have been working here for over fifteen years. I am in the process of trying to raise their salaries. I guess I'm asking you to be patient. I would still encourage you to keep looking for work elsewhere, but if something changes I will be in contact with you. And thanks for calling."

As I hung up the phone, I smiled. What do you know? Michael tells me the Lord is trying to get me the salary I need, and the director is trying to get me the salary I requested. Folks, it's not every day that we get a confirmation of our faith. I got on my hands and knees and thanked the Lord for His help. I also apologized for losing faith, not trusting in Him, and not being patient. Sometimes I can be such a moron.

It was now the first week in March. Lana called me to let me know that she was planning on coming to Chicago to visit me for my birthday, which is on the eighteenth. She told me that she had a break in her college schedule for two weeks and who better to spend time with than me. I was excited, to say the least. She told me the only problem was that she couldn't come in till the twentieth, but she would make it up to me for missing my actual birthday. I told her I didn't care if she was there on my birthday, only that she was coming in. I wanted to make her second visit to Chicago particularly special. So I booked a hotel, dinner, and theater package for the two of us, but I wouldn't tell her until that night. You see ladies; romance is not dead.

On March 10, I was working out when my phone rang. It was a number I didn't recognize. I answered it anyway. To my surprise it was the hospital making me an offer.

They asked if I could start in ten days. I, of course, said, "Yes." And wouldn't you know it, the salary they offered me was only a few hundred bucks less than what I asked for. I immediately prayed and thanked the Lord for His kindness and His patience with me.

Those ten days went by fast. March 20 was one of the happiest days of my life. I started a new job and the love of my life was coming in that evening. Life was good. I spent most of my day in that wonderful nonstop roller coaster ride of adventure and employee orientation. Yes, quite exciting. I was glad to have an income again. Later that evening, I picked Lana up at the airport. If you were standing in the baggage claim area, you would have thought someone was shooting some romantic movie of sorts. It was almost like slow motion as our eyes met each other's. We walked toward each other. I just held her for what seemed like an eternity. Then we finally kissed. It was good to have Lana back in my arms again.

We went back to Ellen's house, and stayed up late talking about everything that had been going on in church, back on the west coast. I was very disappointed that nothing had changed, but it wasn't my place to say anything. She told me how her family felt about her coming to see me. I guess all I'll say is that they were not particularly happy. They thought that when I left they would be rid of me. So sorry to disappoint them, but I honestly didn't care what they thought.

Every day I went to work, and then in the evening Lana, and I spent time together. On Friday, I can home and told Lana to pack a bag. She of course asked, why. So, I told her. She was thoroughly surprised. My plan was to spend the evening at the hotel and then on Saturday take her into Chicago to go sightseeing.

The dinner was superb, and so was the show. The room was even great. They gave us a suite. It had a bedroom, living room, and a small kitchen. As the evening was winding down, we decided to hang out in the room and just watch TV. All of a sudden, Lana started to cry. I asked her why, but all she would say was that she was frightened. For the next five minutes, she kept crying. As I pulled her close to me, and held her, I said, "Please tell me why you are so frightened." She finally said, "I feel the same way I did when you left to come back to Chicago. Do you remember that day that Andreus was in my house?" I said, "Yes, I do." She said, "That is exactly how I feel. I am so afraid right now, and I don't know why."

As I held her, I prayed quietly to myself, *"Dear Father, Lana is having a difficult time. She is frightened, and I don't know why. Please help me to figure this out. Amen."* As soon as I finished my prayer, I heard someone laughing; the voice was very familiar to me. I looked all around the room, but I couldn't see anyone. Anthony and the other angels surrounded the bed. Lana was crying the whole time. I closed my eyes and surveyed the room. There he was, standing in the doorway between the bedroom and the living room.

It was Andreus. Clairvoyantly, I sat up in bed. Andreus said, *"Are the two of you having a nice time?"* As he stepped towards the bed, Anthony and the other angels drew their swords and shields. He continued, *"Did you think that I would not stop by to say hello to you? I know where you are at all times and if I had the chance I would destroy you, Supplanter."* I just sat there holding Lana. I wasn't frightened. I was concerned about Lana. I closed my eyes and looked into Lana's space.

I could see Andreus had his hand in her space. That's why she was so scared. I looked directly at him and said, *"In the name of Jesus Christ, I order you to leave now!"* Two more angels grabbed him by each arm and forced him to leave our room. The whole time he kept yelling, *"I will be back! This is not over yet, Supplanter. I will see you very soon!"*

Once he left the room, Lana stopped crying. She asked me what had happened. I told her. She asked, "Why won't he leave us alone?" I said, "He knows he can't touch me, so he will go after you and my family. I pray every day that the Lord protects all of you from Satan and all of his evil friends. I'm sorry you have to go through this. I did warn you that being with me will be anything but a normal relationship. He won't be back for a while." As we fell asleep, I quietly thanked our Heavenly Father for His help.

The week went by quickly, and we found ourselves at the airport again. We said our tearful goodbyes and Lana flew back home. As the months went by, my heart would ache every time I realized just how far away Lana was. Many times, I would ask Lana when she was planning on moving to Chicago. She would give me excuse after excuse as to why she couldn't move yet.

In June, I had finally had enough with Lana's excuses. I told her that if she had no intentions to move, then why should we stay together? She finally told me that when she finished school at the end of that year, she would pick a date. I told her OK. Deep in my heart I felt as though she would never move here. A couple of days later, while I was meditating, Michael paid me a visit. We spoke once more about the task at hand, and how I shouldn't provoke Andreus. I spoke up and said, *"Give me a break Michael. If anyone is provoking, it's him! I swear, the next time I see him, I may just destroy him!"* Michael said with an unusually stern voice, *"Jim, under no circumstances will you engage, attack, or destroy Andreus, or anyone else! It is not your place to do as you wish with the power the Lord has given you! You will exercise patience and control yourself at all times! This is not your work. It is the Lord's. He has asked you to be a part of it. Do you understand?"*

I said, *"Yes, Michael, I understand. I just don't understand why the Lord allows Andreus to terrorize Lana. She is very young, and I don't think she should be exposed to this."* Michael quietly stepped towards me and said, *"There are lots of things that you will not understand. In time, you will see why the Lord allows certain things to happen. Perhaps the Lord is trying to increase her faith too."* I said, *"A while ago, the Lord had shown me a picture of me standing on a hill. Next to me was this beautiful young woman. I am assuming that she is my wife. My problem is that this woman doesn't look exactly like Lana. Is Lana this woman?"*

Michael said, *"Jim, there are a few things you need to understand. Every person has their own free will. Lana can be this woman for you if she so chooses to be. This woman will have to have a very strong faith. She will have to trust God, and also accept the fact that the Lord has chosen you for a special task. This woman will be very special. Lana is very much aware of all of this, but she may choose not to be the woman of your dreams. Continue to pray that the Lord will help her make the right decision that is best for the both of you. In time, everything will be made clear to you. Just trust in the Lord."*

As the months went by at work, I befriended a few women I worked closely with. All of them were married. There were a lot of times when they needed help with a few work problems, and I would jump in and lend a hand. Tory had just been made the supervisor of the chemistry department. She had numerous questions about how things worked in regard to placing orders with my department. Over the course of many weeks, we worked together to help reorganize the way she placed her orders, and how we would streamline the process.

On one occasion, Tory asked me to join her and one of her friends to take a break with them. I have no idea how the subject came up, but there I was talking about the situation in Shelly's house. I even spoke of how Michael talked to me. They both sat there awestruck. At one point, I said, "I'm pretty sure you think I'm doing drugs. I can assure you I'm not." Both ladies smiled and told me that they knew I wasn't doing drugs. They were just fascinated by what I had told them.

While I was walking back to my office, I was kind of regretting what I had told them. I mean, come on. Who sees dead people and talks to angels? Man did I feel like a nutcase. Later that afternoon, I had to go back to the lab for another problem. I asked Tory if I had scared her. She told me, "No. You just have a fascinating life. I'd love to hear more sometime." I was totally shocked. We shared a few more break times together, and I would share more of what had happened to me. Yet she was never scared off or even thought I was delusional. It was pretty wild, if you ask me. Over time, I heard all about her husband and three kids. To me, she sounded as if she had a great family.

A few days later, one afternoon, Ellen called me at work while she was driving home with a concerned tone in her voice. She told me that Telly was back. Folks, do you remember the little blonde girl, or soul I should say, whom Sydney was playing with? Ellen said, "I just don't have a comfortable feeling about this, Jim. There are times when Sydney is whispering to herself, and I can hear her talking just as if she was talking to someone. She says, 'If I do, then my Mommy isn't going to like it.' Do you feel anything?" I sat at my desk for a few seconds. I was taking deep breaths the whole time Ellen was talking to me, because my chest was hurting. What does it mean when my chest is hurting? Evil is usually close by.

I said, "Ellen, is Sydney in the car with you now?" Ellen said, "Yes." I said, "Do me a favor. Ask Sydney if Telly has eyes." I listened as Ellen asked Sydney my question. Ellen said, "Jim, Sydney says she has no eyes and doesn't even have a face. She looks just like a little girl with blonde hair wearing a flowered dress." I took a deep breath and said, "It's not Telly. It's an evil spirit pretending to be Telly so it can get close to Sydney. Somehow, you are going to have to tell Sydney that this is not Telly. She should tell this thing to leave her alone." My little niece was only five years old at this time.

As I kept working at my desk, I listened to Ellen explain to Sydney how this was not Telly, and that it was a bad spirit that was trying to get her in trouble. She should tell it to leave her alone. It was so cute listening to Sydney while she told the thing that she couldn't play with her anymore. She told it that she didn't want to get into trouble so she should just leave now. After a few minutes, Ellen told me that Sydney said she was gone. I warned Ellen that this thing would probably be back, and it would bring a few friends with it too. Ellen then asked Sydney to tell her if Telly comes back.

Folks, when we stand up to spirits, they don't take no for an answer. They will always try to come back, and when they do, they bring more spirits with them. That's why it is so hard to get rid of them. But, if you have faith in God, pray for protection, and stand up to them, they have to leave. And, eventually they will leave you alone. Just don't give up or give in.

Over the next couple of days, I waited to see if the thing would come back or not. Yep, it did. I got a call from Ellen one afternoon, telling me that she had prayed after Sydney told her Telly was back. Ellen had heard Sydney in the basement talking to someone, but she looked as if she was alone. Ellen stood at the top of the stairs and listened to Sydney's conversation. It seemed as if Sydney was talking to more than one person. She was arguing with them about things they wanted her to do. Sydney kept saying, "If I do that, then my Mommy isn't going to like it."

When Ellen asked Sydney to come upstairs, she asked her whom she was talking to. Sydney said quietly as she looked down at the floor, "I'm playing with Telly and her friends, Mommy. But I told them I didn't want to do the things they told me to do." Ellen asked Sydney what they had told her. Sydney said, "They told me that I don't have to listen to you or Daddy anymore and that I should just listen to them. I told them no." Ellen asked her how many friends Telly had. Sydney said, "Three Mommy. One of the little girls is Telly's sister. She kept telling Telly not to be so mean to me. The other little girl has a scary face."

Ellen told Sydney to tell the three of them that she can't play with them. Tell them that they are not allowed in the house anymore and that they should leave right now. Once Sydney told Ellen that they were outside, Ellen prayed that the Lord would send angels to keep these spirits out of the house. Ellen told me that she could actually hear the spirits telling Sydney that she should come outside to play with them. She told me that she yelled out loud at them telling them that they had better leave her daughter alone. After a few minutes, Sydney told Ellen that they went into the forest behind the house.

Ellen asked me why the Lord would allow this to happen. I said, "Ellen, you know that you, Fred, and your kids all have gifts, but you are in denial about it. Who better to use to get your attention than your own kids! God will not let anything happen to her." Ellen said, "But Jim, she's just a baby." I said, "You need to trust the Lord and see what happens. Maybe the Lord needs your help to. You have to decide if you are going to help Him or not."

As the days progressed, Telly and her friends would return time and again. But they never came in the house. Instead, they would jump in the car with Sydney, and Ellen would tell them to leave. One day, while I was driving Ellen and Sydney to the store, I heard Sydney say, "I told you, I can't play with you anymore. Now leave me alone!" As I looked in my rearview mirror, there she was, a faceless spirit that looked just like a little girl. I heard Sydney say, "If you don't leave now, my Uncle Jimmy is going to kill you!" I chuckled to myself. Kids say the darndest things… don't they?

The spirit spoke up and said, *"I would love to see that, Supplanter!"* I said, *"I'm going to give you ten seconds to leave or I will kill you!"* As the seconds ticked away, she just sat there laughing at me. Without even thinking, I drew my sword, swung around behind myself, and took the spirit's head clean off. I spoke up, "Ladies; I would like to inform you that Telly's imposter will no longer be a problem. She's dead! Sydney, honey, if any of the others come and bother you, please let me know." To this day they haven't been back.

The summer was going by quickly, and July was upon us. My sister Ellen and her family decided they wanted to move to a different city where there were better schools. Besides, they were currently living in a condo and wanted a house of their own. So, they found a very nice house in one of the best school districts in the area. It was located forty-five minutes from where I was working. A great rejoicing filled the hearts of the entire family, except me. I thought to myself; I would have to drive forty-five minutes in the morning to work and than sixty minutes on the way home. Rejoicing was not what I was feeling in my heart. But, because of my lengthy unemployment periods and my divorce, I had a lot of debts that I was still paying off. So, I had no other choice but to continue living with my sister. Please, don't get me wrong. I was happy I had a place to live.

Now, if you live in Chicago, you already know that July is one of the hottest months we have. I believe the day we moved in was at least ninety-five degrees with 400 percent humidity. Yes, I believe those statistics are correct. I was sweating from places I didn't even know I had sweat glands. And, to make the day even more of a delight, there was absolutely no wind that day. Yes, it was quite a little paradise. At one point, I was completely soaking wet. I asked my sister for a bar of soap, because I didn't think I would need to be in the shower with the amount of water that I had streaming out of me. I could just soap up and then let nature take its course. So, just to make my point even clearer, with all of the sweat I was expelling, you would have thought I lost twenty-five pounds. But that just didn't happen. Yes, very sad.

We started to settle in by trying to find everything we packed. Isn't moving fun? Every day, I would leave a little earlier in the morning, trying to find the best way to get to work. No matter which way I went, there was construction. Ah, yes, we have a saying here in Chicago. There are two seasons: winter and construction. No joke. I went five different ways there and back. No matter which way I went, it was an hour both ways. Like I've said before, it's a good thing I like me and enjoy spending time with me, or I may have gone crazy.

The months went by. Lana and I would still have that conversation about when she was moving to Chicago. It would never go well. She would get mad at me for asking. I would get ticked off because she would never give me a straight answer. On top of everything else, her family was still giving her a hard time about seeing me. She would tell me what they would say. I finally told her that I didn't care about what her family thought and that she should just keep it to herself. They were always acting like a bunch of three-year-olds who couldn't have their way. I just thought to myself, "Grow up!"

On Monday, October 16, 2006, while I was meditating, Michael appeared to me and asked me to meet him on the raft in the center of my mind. As I greeted Michael, I could see that he was holding a long golden staff. On the top of the staff was a glass ball that looked as if it had a little sun burning in the center of it. It was so bright I could barely look at it. Michael said, *"The Lord God, has asked me to give you this. It is the Staff of God. From this point forward, if anyone looks at you, they will know that you have been given this power and authority by God Himself. They will also know that there is something different about you. You will use this power for the task He has chosen you for."* I said, *"I don't really know what He has chosen me for, Michael."*

As Michael handed me the staff, I could feel a rush of energy filling my being. Michael asked me to kneel down because he had a blessing from God to give to me. As he spoke, he put his hands on my head and said, *"In the name of God, the Creator, I bestow upon you the wisdom of the ages. He unlocks your understanding and opens your mind. He grants you strength and courage for the task at hand. The color of your armor is now turquoise blue. You are now the symbol of hope for the Lord's plan. It is God, Himself, who gives you all of these gifts today."*

As I stood up, I looked at my armor. Yes, it was turquoise blue. It was radiant and breath-taking. Michael said, *"The Lord would like you to know that Lana is well protected now. Nothing can harm her. He would also like me to share with you what His plan is for you."* I couldn't believe what I had heard; for so long I had often wondered what I was going to be asked to do or what He needed me for.

Michael continued, *"When the final battle ensues, you will lead a portion of God's army against Satan and his forces. With one word, you will use the power of God to destroy everything in your path. In time, I will teach you this word. For now, you must remain patient. Do not provoke Satan or Andreus in any way. You are still a representative of God, and you will control yourself. The Lord God is not provoked."*

As Michael shared with me God's plan, I flashed back to the time when I was back in Chicago visiting with my sister Ann over a year earlier. It was in July when Peter and I had come to confront Billy about our business dealings. Ann and I were sitting in her back yard sipping coffee. She told me she had a vision about God's plan for me. She said, "I saw you and Michael together kneeling in front of Jesus. Both of you were clad in the most amazing armor I have ever seen. Jesus put His hands on both of you as He gave the two of you His blessing. Behind the three of you, were millions of angels clad in armor too. In front of you, I could see Satan's forces. Behind them, I saw Satan standing there so defiant and confident. But, I felt that Satan was underestimating the strength of God's army."

I sat there hanging on to every word she said. She continued, "I see you at the Head of God's army. You will lead the first attack, and what Satan underestimates, is that when he thinks he's about to win the battle, Michael will sweep in with a force even greater than the one you will be leading. The two of you will completely surround Satan and his forces, and you will crush them! The whole time that this is happening, Jesus will be standing on the hill, watching this entire battle take place." As she shared this with me, I became a little emotional. It wasn't that I didn't believe her. I was once again totally overwhelmed.

Michael continued, *"Jim, can you see the irony in all of this?"* I said, *"No, I don't understand what you're telling me."* He said, *"Ever since the fall of man, Satan has gone out of his way to try to destroy mankind, because he has always been jealous of man. When the final battle takes place, you, Jim, Supplanter, a man, a human, will defeat Satan and all his forces. The one thing Satan has tried to destroy will end up destroying him. Can you now see the irony and how the Lord's plan will work?"*

I said, *"Michael, I have read the book of Revelation in the Bible, and I don't recall anything like what you are telling me."* Michael said, *"It is not written anywhere in the Bible. What man would not aspire to hold the power you currently have in your hand? You hold a power that no man has ever been given in all of God's work. If it were written down, someone would be seeking after it. He picked you for this task because you have always remained humble. Do you recall when Babylonian was in you? You had your sword and, at any time, you could have destroyed him. Yet, you controlled yourself and proved to God that you could handle this responsibility and power."*

I said, *"But Michael, we have a chief apostle in our church. He is the one who will lead us to God's kingdom."* Michael said, *"Your chief apostle has his responsibilities, and you have your responsibilities. It is God's will that these things will take place. In time, He will reveal more to you. He loves you more than you will ever know. Be strong, Supplanter. For the Lord, God has chosen you for the task at hand, and you will not fail Him."*

As Michael left, I sat there pondering everything that was now in my heart. I told God, that I would not fail Him. I didn't thoroughly understand everything. I also asked Him if he really had the right guy for this. I can honestly tell you that I don't think I could feel more privileged than I do right now. I am nobody, really. I'm just some guy who gave up his free will and worked through all the things the Lord saw fit to test me with. And, I know that if I hadn't God's help, I would have surely failed. This whole process is truly a humbling experience.

Okay, so maybe you're asking yourself, "Do I still stay in contact with Shelly? Yes, we still call each other every month and talk for over an hour each time. Things were still kind of the same there as far as church went. But yet, Shelly and her daughter Lannie still remained faithful and kept going. So many times I had found that Shelly was very down, but by the time we were finished talking, she was feeling better and filled with hope. I always tell her that it's God who uplifts her. What I found so startling was that after I was finished talking with her, I felt better too. I got just as much out of our conversations as she did. I am thankful the Lord uses all of us at times when He knows we can help others. I'm glad Shelly's such a treasured friend and I hope we will always be close.

Chapter 14
Life, Loss…and Wonder!

As the weeks went by, every so often Andreus would stop by to give me his best. He would always start with a wonderful threat of some kind, like, "I'm going to kill you," or "If I had the chance, I would kill you," or my favorite, "Soon I will destroy you." Yes, it was truly a pleasure to see him. Every time he showed up, I would pray, and angels would come and ask him nicely to leave. It wasn't easy for me to control myself every time he spouted off. You have no idea how many times I would pray and ask God if I could have permission to kill Andreus. But, every time I would speak with Marty, which would be almost every day, he would shake his head no or just tell me I can't. Andreus is such a jerk. I have always hoped that someday the Lord would say yes.

It was now the last week in October, the week for the Preparatory Service for the Departed, when I received a call from Shelly. This was unusual, because she was calling me during the week. We usually called each other on the weekends. We talked for a few minutes and then Shelly said, "The reason why I'm calling you is because of Lannie. She lost a very close friend to a motorcycle accident recently. It is just tearing her up. She was very much in love with him." She told me that Lannie had come to her asking how my gift worked and if I would be able to help her. I told Shelly that my gift was not for seeking out souls and that I didn't have all of the answers. I would of course be more than happy to talk with Lannie and see if there is anything I could do. Shelly thanked me and told me she'd give Lannie my number.

A few days later Lannie called me and said, "Jim, I'm sorry to be bothering you but, I don't really have anyone to talk to about this. I know you have a gift. I talked with my mom about it and asked her if it would be okay to call you. A very close friend of mine was killed in a motorcycle accident. I was wondering if you can help me at all by telling me if you know anything about how he's doing." I said, "Lannie, my gift doesn't work like that. I don't have the ability to focus and find someone in the realms of the departed. If the soul chooses to seek me out, and is permitted by God to do so, then I may have the privilege to help. I'm not the answer man. I just want to tell you that up front." Lannie said, "I understand. I just feel so lost. I can't talk to the ministers out here because they just wouldn't understand. He moved away recently with his family. I was in love with him and I still am. I really cared for him. I know deep in my heart that he loved me too. I'm just looking for some closure."

I said, "Well, maybe you can tell me something about him. What is his name?" She said, "Tyler." I said, "My first impression of him is that he was a very caring person. He would always go out of his way to help others, a very selfless person." Lannie said, while she was crying, "Yes, he was all of that and more." I continued to say, "I also believe that he had a good sense of humor, was kind-hearted and even-tempered."

Lannie said, "Yes. That's why I loved him so much." I asked, "How did the two of you meet?" She said, "We worked together at the hotel. He would always help me along with everyone else. My biggest problem was that I didn't get the chance to tell him how much I really cared about him. He was planning on moving back a year from now, and was going to come in for a visit in a few months. Now I will never have the chance to tell him how much I loved him." I said, "Lannie, I'm pretty sure Tyler knows how you feel. Love is not bound by flesh or time. Sometimes the Lord permits a soul to stay around until they are sure that their family and friends are okay." Lannie said, "It's funny that you say that. I have gotten the impression that he is near me at times. I've even had the thought that he was standing in my bedroom a few times while I was crying and praying for him."

I said, "He may still be here. If the two of you shared a love, as you say, then I'm pretty sure he knows exactly how you feel. If you feel his presence, then he's been listening to your prayers and knows. He will be close to you and his family until he's comfortable enough to know that all of you are ready to move forward with your lives. I tell people that the first impression you have is always the correct one, and that impression comes from God. The second thought that comes is usually one that doubts or discourages the impression, and that comes from Satan. Always go with your first impression." Lannie said, "How will I know if he's doing okay?" I said, "Lannie, I don't know the answer to that question. All I know is that if we both keep praying for him that the Lord grants him grace, I'm sure that he will be fine. Bring a special offering for him at the next service and I will too." She said, "What is it exactly that our offerings do for the departed?"

I said, "I'm not really sure. All I know is that they don't have the ability to offer for themselves, so we bring something on their behalf. We plead with our Heavenly Father and ask Him to bless our offering for these souls. Every service, I put an offering in for my two girls and all the groups and individuals I'm praying for. I will now add Tyler to my list, and then I leave it up to God to decide how He wants to use my offerings for them. The most important thing is that we do offer for them. It's not the size of the offering that counts; it's the heart's attitude that counts when we place it in the offertory for them. I think it shows our Lord that we are making a special effort for them, and would He be so kind as to pay a little more attention to their needs. If you were to ask your mom to do something for Tyler, wouldn't she go out of her way to do it? Of course, she would, because you're her daughter and you asked her."

Lannie said, "Yes, I know she would." I said, "It is the same way with our Heavenly Father. We pray and touch His heart. We ask Him to help us, and because He loves us, He will." Lannie said, "I have been placing offerings for Tyler. I pray for him every day. I just wish my heart would stop hurting; it's killing me. Why would God take him now? He was so young!"

I said, "I don't know. Sometimes, we don't understand the big picture. God sees everything. When I was a priest, I would tell this story when this subject would come up." There was a young man in one of our congregation's who always gave his priest a hard time about how he was handling things. If the priest would ask him to do something, this man would question the priest. Then, he would tell him how he thought the situation should be handled. Many times, the priest would go home frustrated. He prayed often, and would ask God to open this man's heart. One night as the young man slept an angel came to him in a dream. The angel told him to get dressed and pack some things, because they were going on a journey. The angel said, "Do not ask any questions. Do as you are told, and pack. We are leaving now!" After they had been walking for a few hours, they came upon a house. The angel knocked on the door and the homeowner answered the door. The angel said, "We have been on a journey for a while. Would it be possible to get something to eat and drink? We would greatly appreciate it. We won't stay very long." The homeowner let them in and ushered them toward the kitchen. As the angel walked past a small table in the hallway, he grabbed a golden goblet that was sitting there. He put it in his bag. The man saw him do this and grabbed the angel by the arm. The angel pulled away from the man, and held his finger to his own mouth and said, "Shhh, you will say nothing!" The man was angry, but did as he was told. The family sat around the table. As they ate, they listened to the man (angel) speak of the past journeys he had been on. They had no idea he was an angel.

After they had eaten dinner, the angel thanked the family as they stepped out the front door. After the family had closed the door, the angel ran around to the back of the house and started it on fire. He grabbed the young man by the arm and told him to run! The man stood there angry and in shock. The angel grabbed the man and forced him to run. The man said, "First, you steal from the family. Then you start their house on fire! What is the matter with you?" The angel said, "It is not your place to know everything. Just do as you are told!" The man was extremely angry, but kept walking.

After a few more hours, they came upon a small shack in the middle of a forest. The angel knocked on the door. A very old crabby man answered the door and said, "What do you want?" The angel said, "We are on a journey, and were wondering if it would be at all possible to have a drink of water?" The old man said, "No! Go away!" and slammed the door. The angel said, "I would be willing to trade you something for the water." The old man opened the door. The angel pulled the golden goblet out of his bag and handed it to the old man. The old man grabbed the goblet and slammed the door, laughing at the two of them. The angel turned to the young man and said, "Let's go." The young man said, "You're just going to let him take that from you? You're crazy! Did you forget that you're an angel? Do something!" The angel said, "It is not your place to question everything. We are leaving now."

The two of them continued on their journey for a while longer. They came upon another house. There were two boys playing outside. The angel asked if he could speak with the boys' parents. After they had talked for a while, the parents invited the angel and the young man to stay for dinner. During dinner, the angel told the family where they were headed. One of the boys told the angel that he knew a shortcut that would save the two of them a few hours. If they would like, he said, he would show them the way. The angel agreed. He thanked the family. The angel, the young man, and the boy left.

As they walked, the little boy talked to the angel telling him all of his dreams and what he was planning on doing when grew up. After a while, the three of them came upon a bridge that crossed a large river. The boy told them that all they had to do was cross this bridge and that was the shortcut. The angel asked the boy to accompany them to the other side and he would reward him for his efforts. As they came to the middle of the bridge, the angel grabbed the little boy and threw him off the bridge, drowning him. The young man stood there in total shock.

The young man said, "That's it! What are you doing?" The angel calmly walked back towards the young man, and said, "God has told me to share everything with you. You only know what you see. God sees everything. The first house we went to, I set the house on fire because when they clear away the old house, they will find a treasure under it. I took the golden goblet from that family, because it was laced with poison.

If any of them would have drunk from it, they would have died. I gave the golden goblet to that old man because he will drink from it. The Lord has decided to end his life, because he is a selfish, self-centered man. I killed this little boy because when he would have grown to be a man, he would have been a murderer. The Lord took him now to save him, and his family from the pain this boy would have caused them in the future. It is not your place to question God!"

All of a sudden, the young man woke up from his dream crying. He thanked God for opening his eyes. From that day forward, he didn't question anything that was asked of him.

I continued, "Lannie, maybe, God is doing your friend a favor. I really don't know. *All we can do is pray and trust in the Lord.* Did Tyler ever come to church with you?" She said, "No." I said, *"Well, maybe this is the Lord's way of getting him to come now. I should tell you that when a soul passes away they are exactly the same way they were when they were alive. In most cases, death doesn't change them. They still have their own free will and can decide that they don't want help or even want to change. As long as we pray that the Lord softens Tyler's heart, and opens it, then maybe we will find out how he is doing."*

As we spoke, I could feel a presence just around the corner from my bedroom. I couldn't see anyone, but I could feel that someone was listening to our conversation. Just then, I heard a very small, timid voice say, *"Thanks for your help, Jim."* I told Lannie what I just heard and how it sounded. She said, "I get the feeling that it could have been Tyler thanking you for talking with me, and helping him." I said, "I had the same feeling."

Lannie said, "Would you like me to send you a picture of Tyler?" I said, "Yes. That would be great. There are times when souls come up to me and tell me their names. Then there are times when they say nothing to me, but I know their names. If I see Tyler, I will let you know. I'll be honest with you; please don't get your hopes up. You need to take as much time as you need to heal your heart. There is no set time for something like this. I can guarantee that time heals everything. God will help you and Tyler, to move forward when you are ready." She said, "Jim, I really appreciate you taking the time to talk with me." I said, "Lannie, it's an honor and a privilege for me. If there is some way I can help, and in the process repay God for everything He has done for me, then I'm more than happy to help you. Please, feel free to call me whenever you want. I know how hard this is for you and I'm here for you. Okay?" She said, "Yes. I know. Thanks again for all of your help." I said, "You are welcome. Let's give thanks to our Heavenly Father for all of His help." She agreed, so we prayed together.

The following evening, while I walked into the auditorium at church to take my seat, I noticed the soul of a young man sitting on the end of the bench that my family was sitting on. He sat leaning forward with his elbows on his thighs looking forward. He looked up at me and just smiled. I took my place as my girls ran up to me to greet me. I gave them both big hugs. I didn't ask who the young man was because, in my heart, I knew. It was Tyler. Amanda said, *"Papa, we are working in a new realm. It is called the realm of the unredeemed."* I said, *"Sweetie, I thought everyone in the realms were unredeemed."* Amanda said, *"Oh Papa. We refer to it by that name because you wouldn't be able to understand what really goes on there. All the souls that had ever persecuted Christians are held in this realm. Please, pray for them, Papa."* I told Amanda that I would. During the service, I would glance over to where this young man was, to see what his reaction was. He listened very intently. As soon as the service was over, he was gone with the other souls.

The next day was Thursday. When I got home, I checked my email and found that Lannie had sent me some pictures. I opened the pictures and to my surprise, well not actually, there he was, the young man I saw sitting in service. It was Tyler. I sent a response back to Lannie telling her that I had seen Tyler in service and also that he listened very closely to what was being said. I told her that I would continue to pray for him, as well as for her too.

On Saturday afternoon, I decided to meditate so I would be ready for Sunday. As Marty and Amanda finished giving me my healing, Michael came to me. He said, *"Lana is the one. I know you have been looking at this picture in the center of your mind for some time now and wondering if this woman is Lana. Yes, she is. You have to be patient, Jim. She is very young, and you cannot pressure her into moving out here to Chicago. She has her own free will and if she decides to be with you then it will happen. Trust in the Lord, and take heart!"* And then he left.

I looked at Amanda and Marty; they just shrugged their shoulders and kept working on me. I thanked Marty and Amanda for their help. As they began to leave, I heard a quiet voice behind me say, *"You were wondering what your offerings do for those in the realms of the departed?"* As I sat there, I saw a large pit appear in front of my eyes. There was a darkness that surrounded it. Within this pit, I could see thousands of souls trying to climb out of it. Right in the front I saw Tyler.

The voice said, *"This is what your offerings do for these souls."* All of a sudden I saw golden ropes coming down from the sky; every soul held onto a rope and they began to pull themselves out of the pit. The voice said, *"Prayers build bridges and your offerings help the souls pull themselves out of the mess they have created for themselves. The chief apostle unlocks the way from eternity to the Lord's altar here on earth."* I watched every soul pull themself out of the pit. The voice said, *"Be watchful tomorrow. Pay close attention to what you see. The Lord's blessing is with you."*

I sat there for a few moments sobbing. I couldn't believe what I saw. I tried to figure out whose voice that was. But I had no idea who it was. I had never heard his voice before. I thanked God for opening my eyes and showing me these things.

On Sunday morning, I could feel the excitement as I walked into church. Clairvoyantly, everywhere I looked at the church, it was packed. Inside the church and outside the church, thousands of souls were waiting for the service to start. Once again, I could see souls from all walks of life. I saw numerous service men and women from all kinds of wars. I saw slaves, those from witch-hunts, small children, and infants. And, yes, I saw a lot of my family. Once again, sitting on the end of the bench with my family was Tyler. Clairvoyantly, I walked over to him and shook his hand. He smiled as he stood up and said, *"Thanks, Jim. Would you please do me a favor and tell Lannie how much I love her, and appreciate her prayers. It is because of her that I am here today. Please tell her."* I assured him that I would.

As the service came to an end, all of the souls that were interested in receiving our three sacraments started walking towards the altar. I looked at Tyler and motioned to him and asked if he was going to go. He said, *"Jim, this is all very new to me. I don't completely understand everything yet. It is going to take me a while before I am comfortable with all of this. Thanks again for all of your prayers. Please let Lannie know I love her, and don't forget about me."* Tyler and many others began walking the other way and soon everyone was gone.

Later that afternoon, I called Lannie and left her a voice mail asking her to call me. A few hours later, she called. She said, "You may not believe this, but I know Tyler was in our service. I had this feeling that he was. I can't explain it Jim I just know he was." Folks, maybe you're asking yourself how is it that Tyler can be in two services on the same morning. Well that's easy. The west coast is two hours behind Chicago. As our service was ending at 11:30 in the morning, it was only 9:30 over there. That's how Tyler was able to be in two services. Lannie continued, "I would have called you sooner but the priest who held the service came to our house. He told us that he had been driving around for a while trying to figure out how to talk to us about this morning's service. He just showed up on our doorstep." She said this is what the priest said, as he had tears in his eyes, "As I held the service, I had this strong feeling that your friend Tyler was there. I can't explain why I felt this. I'll be honest I have never felt these kinds of emotions before. I hope you don't think I'm crazy, but I just had to come and tell you that I know Tyler was there this morning!" She told me that he stayed for almost an hour, and never thought that this man even cared for them at all. From this day forward, they looked at him a lot differently.

    I shared everything with Lannie. I told her that Tyler was in our service too. I told her what I had seen yesterday about how our offerings affect the souls. Then I told her everything Tyler asked me to tell her. She broke down and started to cry very hard. How often do we go through life with enormous regrets because we never took a chance? And here she was getting an answer to something she had a huge regret about. Yes, Tyler knew how much she loved him, and now she learned just how much he loved her.

    Folks, now is the time to tell your friends and family you love them. Never hesitate to open your heart. When that feeling sweeps over your heart you have a split second to act on it, or it fades away forever. And then all you are left with is regret. Love should never be bottled up and ignored!

    I said, "Lannie, I need to tell you something else. It has been my experience that on the day of the service for the departed, the souls are allowed to go to only one service that day. And the moment the service is over they are ushered back into their respective realms. Because of your prayers touching God's heart, He permitted Tyler to go to both services. Do you have any idea how huge that is? You must have a very special place in God's heart. Because of your faith, God is showing special favor for your friend. If you ever wondered if God hears your prayers, I think this should be a good confirmation of your faith." We talked for almost an hour. I love talking about our faith and sharing the experiences that go with it.

    A few weeks later, Lannie called me again. She said she needed to share a dream she had. She said, "It was so surreal. Tyler, one of my coworkers, and I were just hanging out in my kitchen talking. We all knew that Tyler was dead. My co-worker was telling him how much she missed him. The whole time I sat there listening to Tyler telling her how much he missed her too, and how much he cared about her. I started to get a little angry and jealous. It was because he kept talking about her and not telling me anything. As I sat and listened, I kept screaming in my mind, *"I'm the one who loves you! I'm the one who misses you more than you will ever know!"* I could feel that his time with us was short, and he'd have to be leaving. My coworker just kept on talking and he kept looking right at her. He never once looked at me. The entire time they talked he looked only at her. It was seriously pissing me off! I could feel the moments ticking away, and soon he'd be gone. He began to tell my coworker that he had to go, and suddenly he looked me in the eyes and said, 'Lannie, you know how much I love you. She didn't know how I felt about her, but now she does. You will always have a very special place in my heart. Never forget that. I appreciate everything you have done for me. Please, don't stop praying for me. I love you very much!' And then he was gone. Do you think this was real or did I just imagine all of this happening?"

I said, "Lannie, this was not a dream; it was a vision. Dreams come and go and we remember very little. You felt real emotions and were able to describe in detail everything that happened. Once again the Lord is being very kind to you and Tyler. How wonderful that He would let the two of you share in these few moments together. The Lord really loves you, Lannie." We talked for a few more minutes and then said our good-byes. Over the next weeks and months, I saw Tyler in every service. He was always there.

It was now the middle of November. Many times Lana and I would talk about our future. I would always ask her when she was planning on moving. Once again, I would get excuse after excuse. I tried to explain to her that we needed to make plans for a place for her to live, and a job so she could support herself. I could feel the fear welling up inside of her every time we talked about this subject. For almost a year we would argue about it. I would get so upset because she would never give me a solid answer. I kept feeling in my heart that she would never move here. But Michael said that she was "the one."

It was a Saturday afternoon, when we were talking about this, that I had enough. I just came out and told her that if she couldn't commit to me, then it would be better if she just lets me go. I couldn't handle being apart from her as long as we had been. We wouldn't see each other for over three months at a time. Wow, I sound just like a woman. I can't help that I'm an emotional guy who's not afraid to express how he feels about the love of his life. I hate long-distance relationships! I had told Lana how hard it was going to be when I left almost a year ago.

We went around and around for over an hour, and finally she told me that she would move out to Chicago at the end of July, the next year. She wanted to go with her youth group to Estes Park, Colorado, where our chief apostle was planning on being. I told her that would be fine, but deep in my heart I still didn't believe it would actually happen. My heart was broken over all of this, and I was tired of this crap. Have you ever given everything you had to someone? And were always there for them when they needed you, and then felt you received very little in return! Well, that's how I felt most of the time. Yes, I know how young she was, but I was in love with her. I had always hoped she would have returned to me what I always had given her: unconditional love and support.

On Monday, as I drove home from work, I tried my best to let go of everything Lana and I had gone through on Saturday. It had been eating at me all weekend. My emotions were getting the best of me. As I drove, I went into the center of my mind. I took some deep breaths, and the next thing I knew I was in my heart chakra. Yes, I know I was driving a car too. I can multitask. I found myself kneeling in front of a big picture that looked like a shattered heart that was made out of glass. There were pieces of my heart all over the floor. Some were large pieces, and others were little pieces. There were hundreds scattered all around me. As I picked the pieces up off the floor and tried to put them back where they belonged, I started to cry. There were so many pieces. She broke my heart.

I continued to cry and I was still aware that I was driving home. It's kind of hard to see where you're going with tears in your eyes, but I did my best. I focused back on my heart and I fell to my hands and knees. I was utterly overwhelmed by the condition of my own heart. Suddenly, two female angels appeared next to me. I can tell you folks that this is the first time I had ever seen a female angel. They were both dressed in white flowing dresses, had wings, and they were quite beautiful. One of them knelt down in front of me and pulled me towards her. As she held me she spoke with a sweet, quiet voice, *"Jim, the Lord God knows how hard all of this is for you. He sent us to help you put your heart back together."*

As she held me, the other angel started picking up the pieces of my heart and put them back together. Whoa! Traffic was coming to a screeching halt! See, I can multitask. The three of us picked up all of the pieces off of the floor and put them back where they belonged. She said,

"Take a deep breath now." As I did, I watched all of the cracks in my heart slowly disappear until it was completely whole again. She said, *"Jim, be patient. In time, the Lord will reveal everything to you. Lana still has to make up her mind whether she wants to be with you or not. The responsibility that the Lord has given you is great. The woman that will spend the rest of her life with you must have a tremendous faith too. That is why the Lord tests Lana even now. Always remember that Lana still has her own free will. The Lord will not force her to be with you. Just trust in the Lord."*

And with that being said, they were both gone. I reached home and sat in the driveway for a while, thinking about everything she said to me. I thanked the Lord for His kindness in sending the two of them to help me. He never ceases to amaze me.

It was now the week after Thanksgiving. As I was meditating, Michael spoke to me. He said, *"Jim, you are doing well with the power the Lord has given you. Andreus cannot touch you or Lana. Both of you are well-protected. Anthony and the others will keep you safe. The Lord has placed two angels to keep watch over Lana. The pain in your feet will end soon. The Lord caused this pain to humble you and cause you to realize that you are not devoid of suffering and that you are still just like anyone else on this planet. Keep your eyes open and continue to be patient. The Lord is with you."*

So now, maybe, you're asking yourself, "What pain in my feet? I haven't mentioned it before. Here's what I will share with you. Before I lost the eighty pounds, I had been a Type II diabetic. And my blood sugar was pretty close to being under control. I'm still a diabetic the last time I checked. They still haven't come up with a cure for that, yet. I had high-blood pressure, high cholesterol, and my thyroid was all screwed up too. I would get migraines, and on occasions, a flare up of gout would happen. Yes, folks, I was quite a mess. Well, after losing all of that weight, I didn't have to be on any medications anymore. Thanks to meditation to this day, I don't have migraines either. I'm sure my weight loss has helped with that too.

Over the past year, I had gained back forty pounds. I found that my feet were killing me. They were not just always on fire; it felt as if someone was ramming a knife through them. I went to four different doctors who told me that I had diabetic neuropathy. One doctor said I had Reynaud Disease, in which either your feet or your hands are affected by the cold. The fourth doctor, after giving me a CAT scan felt I might be having circulation problems. He gave me something that opened up my blood vessels to increase circulation and a nerve medication to deal with the pain. It worked most of the time. I can tell you that there were days when I would be sitting, and all of a sudden I would scream out loud because the pain was that intense.

I would call my doctor constantly complaining. He would tell me to give the medication a chance to work. I would always crack jokes, and after a while my doctor learned how to handle my sense of humor. In time, I found that he had one too.

After I had shared with him my family history of cancer, high-blood pressure, cholesterol problems, heart attacks, thyroid problems, diabetes, gout, and bad back pain, I said to him, "I really haven't got a prayer do I?" The doc said, "Why sure you do, Jim. There are so many wonderful drugs on the market now. You'll just be on all of them." And so I am. For now, my feet pain has subsided. That's good news.

Christmas and New Year's Eve came, and went. There I was once again, all alone for the holidays. Did I mention to you how much I hate long-distance relationships? The New Year, 2007, was now upon us. I thought to myself this is going to be the best year! At least, that's what I was hoping for.

Chapter 15

A Prelude...

I would like to say, Happy New Year everyone! Welcome to 2007! It was January 11. Why does this day have such great significance? Well, could it be because the love of my life is coming for a visit? Yep that would be why. Lana came and stayed for almost two weeks. We had a fabulous time together. Although, at no time was I allowed to talk to her about moving to Chicago. Well that would just be crazy talk. Do I sound a little bitter...maybe?

January whipped by and soon February was close to an end. One Saturday afternoon, while I was meditating, Michael stopped by. He said, *"The Lord has given you permission to destroy Andreus. It will happen very soon."* I said, *"Wait a minute! You have been telling me I can't kill him. What's changed?"* He said, *"Andreus has defied the Lord for the last time. Satan is having trouble keeping him in line. So, you will destroy him. You have been talking to Lana about visiting her out on the west coast next month for your birthday."* I said, *"Yes. Michael, that's all we have been doing, talking. I am trying to figure out how I can financially afford to do it. Airfare is not cheap, plus I would have to stay in a hotel."* He said, *"Have faith, Jim. The Lord will arrange for it to happen."*

Over the next few weeks, I said nothing to Lana about my conversation with Michael. I did tell my family. They were all concerned for me. I told them that all I could do was trust in the Lord and keep my faith. If you forgot and feel the urge to send me a gift for my birthday, once again, my birthday is March 18.

One afternoon, as I was driving home from work, Lana called me. This was not out of the ordinary, because we always talked to each other during the day. She said, "Honey, I have a surprise for you. I bought you an airline ticket. Happy Birthday! Now we can spend your birthday together. Are you surprised or did you know I was going to do that?" I said, "Yes, dear, I'm very surprised! Awesome! Thank you so much!"

Ah yes folks, the Lord works in mysterious ways, doesn't He? I made my plans to fly out Tuesday night March 13 and then fly back the following Monday morning, the day after my birthday.

So it was March 13; the day that I flew out to see Lana. I was so excited once the plane landed. Lana picked me up at the airport. We drove to a restaurant to get something to eat. As we walked into the restaurant, I coughed a little bit. I could feel that my lungs were burning a little. I asked myself, *"Am I getting sick?"* As we ate dinner, I told Lana about my conversation with Michael, and why I was really here. She was completely surprised. We went to my hotel.

Later that evening, I started to cough even more. By the time Lana had left to go home, I had a fever. She told me she had to work in the morning, but we could spend the afternoon together. That was OK with me. I wasn't going anywhere. I had no car, and I felt like crap.

The next morning, Lana, called and woke me up. She just wanted to see how I felt and to tell me that she loved me. The next thing I knew there was a knock at my door. It was Lana; she had made me breakfast. She cooked me an omelet. Lana doesn't really know how to cook, but I can tell you this, the omelet was great. By this time, she was running late and had to leave. I thanked her for making me breakfast, while I was coughing up a lung. She gave me a loving hug, and off she went to work.

As I sat there eating, Michael showed up. Now here's what I find most intriguing, I wasn't meditating at the time. I could see Michael, plain as day, standing in my hotel room. My gift had advanced more than I could believe. I then remembered that the Lord had given me a blessing. He had opened up my understanding. Now it all made sense. I didn't need to meditate anymore to see what was going on around me. I said, *"What's the plan?"* He said, *"You are sick. Rest today. I will be back tomorrow."*

The next day, I was sicker than a dog. I was drowning in snot, coughing up lung butter, and I probably had a fever of 103 degrees. How did I know I had a fever? I am never cold, but now I was freezing. Our plan for the morning was for Lana to pick me up at the hotel, and then for me to drop her off at work. I needed a car to run some errands. Once I was done, I would have lunch where she worked, and then later that afternoon we would go see a movie. After we had breakfast, I dropped her off at work and drove back to the hotel. As I walked into the room, Michael was standing there. He said, *"It is time."* I said, *"What do you want me to do?"* He said, *"Meditate and go into the center of your mind."*

As I climbed into the center of my mind, the next thing I saw was Michael and five other angels. Michael said, *"Keep up. Stay close to us."* Clairvoyantly, we began to run. My body stayed in the chair I was sitting in, but in my mind, I could feel us running. We ran through dark tunnels, and up and down hills. The whole time we ran, Michael was by my side and the others were right behind me. It seemed so strange to me. I knew where I was supposed to be going. I had never been to this area, place, realm, or wherever we were going. All I knew was that soon we would find Andreus.

As we rounded a corner, at the end of the road, there he was. Andreus drew his sword and shield, and without even thinking I did the same. I engaged him without saying a word. He swung his sword at me and in an instant I blocked it with my shield. I swung my sword, and he blocked it. Back and forth we went, sword hitting sword. Our shields were smashing into each other. We fought for what seemed like two or three minutes. Andreus lunged at me with his sword.

I pulled back as he overextended his reach past me. With one single blow, I struck his sword as hard as I could and disarmed him. He stepped back abruptly and looked completely surprised as I plunged my sword into his throat, so he couldn't yell out for help.

Andreus fell to one knee with a look of terror in his eyes. I pulled my sword out of his throat, and with one swoop, I removed his head. I stood there watching while his head fell to one side, and his body fell forward. It all happened in slow motion. Before his body hit the ground, off in the distance, I could hear Satan screaming, "Nooooo!" I stood there utterly surprised. I couldn't believe my own eyes. Michael grabbed my shoulder and said, *"We need to go, now!"* We ran again for a few minutes. The next thing I knew we were back in my hotel room. I saw my body sitting in the chair. I slowly lowered myself back into my body and opened my eyes.

Michael was standing right in front of me. I said, *"Did that really just happen?"* He said, *"Yes, well done."* I said, *"It seemed too easy."* Michael said, *"Remember; you have the strength of ten angels. Enjoy the rest of your vacation. We will talk when you get back to Chicago."* He turned and left. I sat there dazed, reliving the whole experience. I was exhausted, feeling sicker than ever before in my life. My chest was on fire; if I would breathe in too deep, I would start coughing. It felt as if someone was cutting my lungs with flaming razor blades. Pretty graphic, but I want you to get the picture.

I decided to lie down for a few hours and sleep until Lana called to see how I was doing. I told her what had happened. She said, "Is Andreus really gone?" I said, "Yes. He won't be bothering either of us anymore." She asked me if I still felt strong enough to go see the movie. I told her, "Yes. I'll be fine."

I met Lana at her work and said hello to all of her coworkers. When I lived out west, I would come in all the time with my brother and have lunch or dinner. So, the people she worked with knew me pretty well. Well, kind of; they didn't know all of the special stuff going on with me.

It's not as if I can say, "Yes, I'll have the soup, diet Coke, and I see dead people. Oh, yes, by the way, I just killed the demon that controlled the whole western part of the United States. No, Pepsi is fine too."

As Lana and I ate, she kept asking me if I felt okay. I kept reassuring her that I was. Really I was thinking, *"Just kill me now!"* But I kept on telling her I was fine. She told me what time the movie was and off we went. As we walked up the stairs to the theater, Lana stopped. I looked at her and asked why we were stopping here in the mall. She said, "Surprise! Honey, I paid for both of us to have massages." I groaned which caused her to start crying. Now, I truly felt like crap, and I didn't want to be touched by anyone. She said, "That's why I kept asking you if you felt ok." She had already prepaid for the massages, and they were not refundable. I told her I was sorry. This was very sweet of her, and in we went.

Here's another reason why I didn't want to have a massage. I had such terrible gas. Not a little gas. I swear I had enough gas to pilot the space shuttle to Saturn and back. My biggest fear was that if I became too relaxed, people might die from a toxic cloud! I'm okay with killing rogue demon angels, but not people. As I lay on the table, I prayed quietly to myself, *"Dear Lord, please grant me strength."* As the masseuse ran her hands over me, I was ever conscious of my situation. Fortunately, for her, I was able to control myself and no life was lost. By that evening, I finally figured out why I was so gassy. The cough syrup I was drinking, by the gallons, was loaded with sugar. Remember, I'm a diabetic. We don't do very well with sugar. I decided to change brands, and all would be well. At least that was what I was hoping for.

As Lana and I walked around the store, trying to find any over-the-counter drugs that would make me feel better, my body decided to start shutting down. I became extremely weak and even a little lightheaded. We made a mad dash to the checkout line. By the time, we got back to the hotel I could barely move. I became as cold as ice and was shivering. Lana covered me with everything we could find in the room. I was burning up with a fever. We were planning on going out that evening to meet a friend of Lana's who worked at a really nice restaurant. I guess that wouldn't be happening now. As I relaxed, I found myself passing out. Two hours later, I woke up still feeling like crap. So, we ordered in Chinese.

As the weekend passed I found myself resting a lot; it was quite a downer for Lana, who had made a lot of plans for us. Saturday evening we had dinner with Shelly and Lannie. I felt a little better; although, every time I coughed I had to shove my lung back down my throat. I could deal with that. It was that whole gassy thing that I didn't ever want to go through again.

It was nice catching up with Shelly and Lannie in person. We talked about everything from work to church. As I listened to Lannie telling me about Tyler, I started to get extremely warm. Then I started to get hot. I asked the waiter if they were making it hot enough to breed sheep in here. Lana said that it was warm, but not hot. The next thing I knew, I was sweating like a horse after running a race. Not simply perspiring, but beads of sweat were running down my forehead. Sweat was also running down my back. I was drenched. Yes, my fever broke *again*. I was soaking wet now, but I was a trooper. We stayed for another hour or so. I couldn't wait to get back to the room and take a shower, which is exactly what I did.

Sunday, March 18, was my birthday Yay! But I was still sick. Shoot! I spent the whole day in bed. Lana went to church and then came over later. Later that evening, I mustered enough strength to let Lana take me out for dinner. It was very enjoyable. I was exhausted when we got back to the room. You know, I'm so glad I work out five days a week, take vitamins, try to watch what I eat, and get enough sleep, or else this thing may have killed me! I'm just so lucky!

The next day Lana came by early to pick me up, and take me to the airport. We sat and held hands for two hours as I was waiting for my plane. I hated to leave her again. No, we didn't talk at all about her moving to Chicago. Are you crazy? Why on Earth would we want to talk about that? I'm taking a deep breath now. I'm letting it go. No. No, I'm OK now. I kissed Lana for the last time and got on the plane. It was beyond a sad moment for the two of us. All the way home, I kept thinking, *"When, if at all, is she going to make up her mind and move here?"*

The next day when I got back to work, my department threw me a surprise fortieth birthday party. They had my cubicle draped with black streamers and balloons. It was very sweet of them to go to all of that trouble for me. We had a potluck lunch. I went home early. Yes, I was still sicker than a dog. I waited one more week before I went to the doctor because I'm an idiot! By now I was sure I had bronchitis. Once again, I'm glad I work out.

It was now April, Easter Sunday. I celebrated with my family. Once again, I was alone for another holiday. No Lana, which ticked me off. I am sure that you celebrate this high and holy day just like I do! I had an enormous fight with Lana. I have never in my life gotten to the point where I just wanted to hang up on someone, but here I was. With every question, I asked, I got remarkably little in return. I was frustrated and angry. For almost two and a half years, I felt that she had been leading me on. Wow! Once again, I sound like a woman. I don't care what you guys might think about this situation. The ladies know what I'm talking about. So there!

Guys. Have you ever loved a woman so much that your heart ached? That the more time you were apart, it caused you to feel even more heartache? The only person you think about during the day is her? Yes, ladies, I am that sensitive. Lana and I fought for over an hour. Through it all, I kept asking her to set a date, and commit to me in some way. She just kept asking why that was so important to me. Yes, I know she was only twenty years old. We finally decided to stop talking, because we were both pissing each other off. I had company over, so it was hard for me to go back to the table and be my humorous self.

Peter noticed immediately that something was wrong. He mouthed the words, "Are you okay?" I responded by mouthing the words, "It's Lana." He rolled his eyes at me. Later that evening, we sat down and talked. Peter said, "Jim, I know you love her. This is what I have feared for years; that she would be the one that hurts you. She is so young, Jim. I know love is blind, but that can't change or even cover who Lana is. She doesn't want to leave her family for you. She just doesn't have the courage to tell you. I think you have known in your heart for a while now that you two need to break up and go your separate ways." I said, "Peter, you are right about everything. My problem is that Michael told me that she could be the one." Peter said, "Michael said, she *could* be the one. It is pretty obvious to me that she has decided *not* to be the one. I know how hard this is going to be for you. Haven't you tried your best to make her happy? Each time you sacrifice for her, what do you get in return? You get very little, Brau.

Someone said to me once, a long time ago when I was with my second wife, and we were having our problems.

'Peter. I've known you your whole life, and you are an exceptionally smart guy. Your problem is that you and your wife are not equally yoked. You are pulling in one direction, and she is pulling in the other. A relationship can't last very long if the two of you are not pulling in the same direction."

Peter continued to say, "Do you understand what I'm trying to tell you, Jim?" I told him yes, I did.

The next day, Monday, during my lunch break, I sat in my car and prayed the whole time. I kept asking God what I should do. Should I break up with Lana, or should I just keep hoping this was all going to work out?

I took a deep breath and put my trust in God. Later that afternoon, Lana, called me at work. While we talked about Sunday, I just couldn't take it anymore. I told her that I thought it would be best if we stopped seeing each other. She was just devastated! I tried my best to tell her that if we lived closer together, things would be fine. I told her that I completely understood why she didn't want to leave her family. Family is everything to me. Nothing can take the place of our family.

My words didn't seem to help at all. She hung up the phone on me. I didn't blame her. She called back a few minutes later, and we talked for a half hour. I told her she could still call me now and then or email me. I wanted to remain friends. By the grace of God, I managed to keep myself together the whole time we talked. I said goodbye, and told Lana I would continue to pray for her. One of my coworkers walked into my cubicle to drop something off. He looked at me and could tell something was wrong. I told him I just broke up with Lana, and then I began to cry. He told me how sorry,; he was for me.

I walked into my boss' office with tears in my eyes and asked if I could go home. I told her I had just broken up with Lana, and I was all caught up for the day. She said by all means; take the rest of the day off. She also told me how sorry,; she felt for me too. I composed myself and went to my car. Once the door was closed, and I was on the road, I lost it. I was crying so hard I could barely see. My heart felt as if it was going to explode right out of my chest. I asked God why He would let this happen to me. I pleaded with Him to help Lana and me get through this. Most of the evening I spent crying myself to sleep.

Once again, men, I don't care what you think of me. If you were to tell me that only wimps cry, I would look you right in the eye and tell you that only strong men cry. You have got to be pretty insecure with yourself if you can't admit that you cry now and then. I am not insecure by any means. Crying is beneficial for the soul. You release more energy by crying than you would by doing anything else. Crying cleans the soul. It opens your heart up and allows your heart to start healing.

Wimps don't cry because they are too afraid of what someone else might think. You should know me by now. I don't care what anybody thinks about me, except God.

Lana and I spoke on the phone over the next few days. We tried to console each other and to find some closure. On a few occasions, we opened up and said things to each other that ended up hurting one another. But, all of these things had to be said. I told Lana that she was very young, and I hoped that what she did to me, she wouldn't do to the next guy. I told her she was a great girl and had a lot to offer. She just needed to live life a little more. I told her it would be hard for me to move on with my life. She expressed the same thing. We'd spent almost two and a half years together, and not once did either of us cheat on the other one. For over a year, we dated long-distance. I think that speaks volumes about someone's character. There was never a time when I didn't feel I couldn't trust Lana. We expressed how much we still loved each other, and then said our goodbyes.

Later that week Michael paid me a visit. He said, *"Jim. The Lord knows how hard this is for you. Lana has decided not to be the one. She has her own free will and choice. In time, the Lord will reveal more things to you. Be patient, Jim. Trust in the Lord. He is always with you."*

As the months went by, things did seem to get a little better. In June, I started to flirt with all of the ladies on the other end of the phone while I was working. I didn't care if they were married or not. I always went out of my way to make them laugh, or I tried to lighten their day with humor. Yes, ladies, I know that one of the biggest things you look for in a man is his sense of humor. I think I have a pretty good one.

One day, I had to run up to the corporate offices to leave something for one of the secretaries. When I got up there, I realized that it was still very early, and she wasn't in yet. I looked all over her desk for something to write a note on, but I couldn't find anything. I stood there for a minute until I saw a young woman sitting in a little office. I walked in, and asked her if I could borrow a post-it-note. She had the most stunning eyes. The first things I notice about a woman are her eyes. The next thing my eyes do is kind of trail down from there. Hey, I'm just being honest!

I couldn't help but think that she was so cute as she fumbled around looking for something I could write on. Yes, I was checking her out when she looked away. As she handed me a note, I said, "Hi. My name is Jim. I'm from purchasing." She said, "Hi. My name is Maci." She was freaking hot, as far as I was concerned. I thanked her for her help and ran back to my office. I walked right into my boss' office and said, "Hey, I just met some girl named Maci, up in the corporate offices. Do you know anything about her?" My boss said, "Yes, she is the assistant to the CEO. She's been here for almost a year." I said, "A year! Why is this the first time I heard about her?" My boss started to laugh as she said, "Well, Jim, for almost all of this past year, you were in a relationship with Lana." I said, "Lana who?" No, I didn't actually say that. I started laughing too.

My boss gave me very little information about her. I asked if she knew if Maci was single. She didn't know. I had to run over to our accounting department to talk to someone about an invoice problem. We had a high-school student there doing temp work for us. He and I had built a pretty good friendship over the past few months. He asked me why I was in such a good mood. I started to tell him all about this hot girl I met in the corporate office. All of a sudden Maci walked in. As she walked past me, she looked over her shoulder and said a drawn out, "Hi!" The high-school kid said, "She's not that hot!" As I pointed in the direction where Maci was standing, I said, "Are you blind? Look at her. She's smokin' hot! Look at those eyes. Look at her face. Can't you see her legs?" As I said that, Maci turned and looked at me and saw me pointing at her. The next thing I thought to myself was, *"Aw, crap!"*

She smiled and looked away. Now, I knew she didn't hear what I said, because she was all the way on the other side of the office. I wasn't talking that loud. The high-school kid told me that I was blind and crazy. I pointed back toward Maci and said it again, "Moron; she's beautiful. Look at her." Yep, you guessed correctly. She turned back and saw me pointing again. To which, I said, in my mind, "Damn it!" I finished with my invoice problem and went back to my office.

I called my friend Torry and shared everything with her. I talked about pointing at Maci and getting caught. Then I said, "Okay. I have never seen this girl before. I am all over this hospital and now twice in one day I see her. She looked back at me twice. Now, being that I am just a big dumb animal when it comes to women, am I reading into this correctly? Is she interested in me?" Torry started to laugh and said, "Yes. She's interested. If you had told me she looked back at you only once, I wouldn't have thought that she was…but twice? Yep. She's interested. Do you know if she's single?" I said, "Nope. I will be sending my spies out shortly."

By the end of the day, my spies informed me that she was single. Yeah! Uh, oh. Now I was going to have to muster up the courage to ask her out. Here's what you don't know about me. When it comes to women, I'm actually a very shy guy. No, really, I am. I can't walk up to a beautiful woman in a bar and strike up a conversation. Okay, maybe I am a little insecure when it comes to how I look. All of my female friends tell me I'm very handsome. Some have even used the word *hot* to describe me. I laugh every time they tell me this. I don't think of myself that way at all.

As the week went by, I tried to figure out how I was going to ask her out. See, ladies, some guys put a lot of thought and effort into asking you out, and in one fatal moment, you can shoot us down in a second. I formulated a plan. I mustered up the gumption, and off I went to the corporate office. The whole time, I felt as if I was going to explode. I had to pass three other secretaries before I got to Maci's office. As I rounded the corner towards the third secretary, she started to have a conversation with me. I screamed in my head, *"No!"* But, being the nice guy that I am, I stopped and talked to her for a minute. The whole time I looked to see if Maci were in her office. Nope. She wasn't there. Crap! Now I'm going to have to go through all of that again.

As I walked back into my office, all of my coworkers stuck their heads out of their cubicles and asked what had happened. I shared my little story, and all of my friends and my coworkers laughed. I waited a few hours and tried again. Nope! She wasn't there, again. It was driving me nuts. I don't normally obsess or become compulsive over things, but apparently I was with Maci. The day was over, and as I drove home I thought about her. Do you people recall when I told you about a young, beautiful brunette I saw standing on a hill with my two would-be sons and me? Maci looks just like this woman. Now, does it make sense why I'm obsessing?

The next day wasn't any better. Give me a break. Is she always in meetings? Is she never in her office? After my third attempt, I was at the point where I was telling God He needed to give me a hand. Finally that afternoon, a Wednesday, I grabbed a blank post-it-note and headed for Maci's office. While I was walking, a salesman I do business with was walking with me. He asked me what I was doing. I shared my painful tale with him. As we walked up the stairs together…wouldn't you know it… Maci was walking down the stairs and passed us. She did say hi as she passed by.

When I got to the top of the stairs, I just stood there. The salesman stopped and asked me what I was doing. I said, "You know that girl I was just telling you about? That was her!" He said, "Oh, man! She is hot! She was totally checking me out as she passed by us." I said, "You must be smoking crack. She didn't even see you!" The funny thing about this is this salesman is in his late sixties. We laughed for about a second. I started to walk back down the stairs when he said, "Jim, where are you going now?" I said, "Back to my office, so I can kill myself!" He said, "You're nuts!" I said, "Yes, very. See you later!"

As I walked down the hallway, whom do you think I saw? Yes. It was Maci. I gathered as much courage as I could and as she smiled and passed by me I said, "Hey, Maci. I was coming to see you." She said, "Really, why?" I said, "The other day I asked you if I could borrow a post-it-note; I just wanted to return a new one to you." I then handed her the blank post-it-note. She smiled. I said, "I was wondering if you would like to have dinner with me sometime?" She said, "Um, sure." Yay, she didn't say,

"No, you big loser. Get away from me before I call security!"

I said, "Do you have any plans this weekend?" Maci said, "Yes, I do. I'm going downtown to Chicago with a bunch of my friends, but I don't have plans next weekend. Why don't you call me at my extension!" I looked at her and said, "Now I'm going to need that post-it-note back." She gave me her extension, and I wrote it down, and walked back to my office. As I walked past my fellow coworkers I proudly displayed my post-it note. A cheer rang through the office.

So there I was, sitting at my desk, trying to figure out what the rules were for dating. It's been a while for me. Now, do I wait two seconds or is it two minutes? Maybe it's two days before I call her! I hate rules. I am big on breaking rules.

After I had consulted with my dating board, which is composed of my sister Ann and my friends Torry and Giselle, they told me to wait until Monday and then call.

Who is Giselle? Giselle is another married friend of mine who worked in the histology/cytology lab. She has four kids. She's a very cute, thin redhead who thinks she's fat. I keep telling her that if she loses any more weight, she's going to become transparent! I, of course, joke around with her about her weight all the time. The other day I asked her if she had to run around in the shower to get wet. She laughed. Over the past few months, Giselle and I would have in-depth conversations about our faith. Yes, she knows all about my gift. I only tell my closest friends. She told me that after talking with me, I helped her see God in a whole new light. She says that her faith is even stronger now. I always tell her to thank God. I will never take credit for something like that. I think it is a huge privilege when someone shares their faith me.

Okay, Monday rolled around after a weekend of thinking only about Maci. Yes, I know you think I'm crazy. I'm pretty sure you've been reading this book. The proof is right in front of you. I made the call; she was not there. Crap! Now I'm going to have to leave a voice mail.

I said, "Maci, its Jim. I have to confess that I was nervous when I asked you out. The whole time I was talking to you I was pretty sure that the words coming out of my mouth sounded like this, 'Blah, blah, blah'. Anyway, I was hoping that maybe we could have dinner this Saturday night. Give me a call when you have a minute. Talk to you soon." And, so I waited. Monday came and went. Tuesday came and went. Nothing! I spoke to my dating consultants, who tell me that when a guy calls you, you need to wait two days before you call him back; that way you won't appear desperate. I told my dating consultants that that was the dumbest thing I had ever heard! What is wrong with you women? Men kill themselves trying to ask you out, and then you play games with us? I'm telling God!

Wednesday came and went. I'll be honest that I was getting a little mad. Thursday, nothing! I checked with the corporate office to see if Maci was in this week; through my spies, of course. Yes, she's in. What the heck? Friday morning, I sent her an email saying:

Maci,

I'm not sure if you got my voicemail from the other day. I was wondering if you would have dinner with me, Saturday night. If the answer is yes, please call me. If you are not interested in going out with me, then reply to this email and tell me, and I will leave you alone.

Sincerely,

Jim

I shared this info with my dating consultants. They all thought it was to the point. No reply. Nothing! Now, the ladies I worked with liked to live vicariously through me. They asked me what was going on. I told them I had no idea. She never responded back to my voice mail or email. They wanted to hurt her. They told me that no one hurts their Jim. I convinced all of them that a hanging would be inappropriate. Good thing we didn't have any spare rope lying around. Once again, I had tried to date someone too young. She, as far as I know, was around twenty-five or twenty-six years old; my mistake. The ladies told me they thought it was terribly rude of her not to reply back, even when I left her an out. Yes, I agreed. Oh well, life goes on. Funny thing is, to this day, I see Maci all the time. I go out of my way to say hi to her. She still hasn't told me why she didn't want to go out with me. Good thing I'm not the stalking type.

Chapter 16
Here We Go Again…

Okay, so Maci will not go out with me. No problem. I'm moving on. It was the end of June, 2007. At work, I did a lot of ordering for a number of departments, one of which was the ICU (intensive care unit). Over the past year, I had developed a good friendship with the manager, Reegan, and her assistant, Jewel. One day, while I was talking with Reegan, out of the blue, she starts talking to me about Jewel. She was asking me if I thought she was cute and whether I would ever consider going out with her. I sat there stunned for a moment. You see, folks, Jewel is a twenty-six-year-old single mother, of a four-year-old boy. I don't have a problem dating a single mother. My problem was I always looked at Jewel as if she was my little sister.

I explained this to Reegan. She said, "Jim, you and Jewel are really great people. What's the problem with two friends going out and having a good time? I think the two of you need to go out and have fun." Just then, in walked Jewel. Now, maybe, it was the way the light was hitting her, or maybe, it was the amount of coffee I had drunk that morning and the buzz I felt while I was riding high off the caffeine. Whatever it was, Jewel looked incredibly hot that morning. She turned, smiled at me, then said hi, and walked out. Reegan said, "I saw the way you looked at her. She's a very pretty young woman, and I think you should ask her out."

I told Reegan that I would think about it. I shared this info with my friend Torry, who asked me so nicely if I was an idiot, and what was I waiting for? Yes, it's always good to have close friends who are not afraid to proverbially bitch-slap you when the time is right. I also tried to explain to Torry that I didn't have any feelings for Jewel. I considered her to be a friend. Oh, I know what all of you women are going to say. Friendship is always a good place to start before you get into a relationship. Some of you will even tell me that you married your best friend. Right? Yes, I know. So, I thought about it and said to myself, "What the heck, why not!"

The next day, Jewel called me because she had a problem with a copier. The coworker who normally handled that problem was on vacation at the time, and I was covering for her. As we both tried to figure out why the copier had a problem, I said, "Can I ask you a question?" Jewel said, "Sure, okay." I said, "If a guy likes a girl, why can't he just tell her? Does there always have to be some kind of a game involved? Why can't a guy just tell a girl he likes her, and ask her if she would like to go out?" Jewel said, "I don't see why that would be a problem. I don't like games." I said, "Great. Jewel, I like you. Would you have dinner with me sometime?" Did you see what I did, people? Before I could finish my question, she said yes. I said, "Great, how about this Saturday?" She said, "Sounds good to me." See! No games. No goofy timelines, just up-front invitations, and acceptance of the invitation. Dating, I have no idea why it is so hard.

Now, because the copier coworker does more than just that, and had taken two weeks off, my boss told me I was going to be doing her work too. You know, folks, I have always tried to walk that thin line between working hard enough to get a raise and just incompetent enough not to get any more responsibility but I have failed miserably. While my coworker was off, I started ordering from a company that I didn't do business with. I struck up a conversation with a girl named Tabitha, who was twenty-eight,. See, they're getting older now.

Apparently, it was a fluke that she answered the phone that day. She normally works with contracts, but they were a little shorthanded, so she was lending a hand. We had talked for almost thirty minutes before I gave her my order. We had such a good time talking that she gave me her extension and work email address. Over the next two weeks, I placed orders with this company. Almost every time I called the 800 number, I would get Tabitha. A few times she asked if I were dialing her directly. I told her no; it must be an omen of the good kind.

Okay, wait a second. We have to switch gears back to Jewel and our soon-to-be date. As the week progressed, I called Jewel on Thursday to confirm our date for Saturday. Wouldn't you know it; she told me she might have to move that weekend. Yes, folks, I was a little dumbfounded too. Move? Don't you usually make plans way in advance? Apparently, she lived on her own with her son. Her parents were moving away, because her dad got a new job out of state. Jewel decided that she was going to move back into their house. All of this had to happen this weekend. Hmmm, okay! I told her to let me know if the following weekend would work and get back to me. She told me she would let me know. I thought to myself, "I should have listened to my gut and never asked her out!" Okay, to be continued.

Now, let's get back to Tabitha. When we came to the end of the two-week period, I told Tabitha that I probably wouldn't be talking with her anymore. She asked if she could email me, which we had been doing on and off during the past two weeks anyway. I told her that would be fine. Over the next few months, I found out that Tabitha had a boyfriend…kind of. He didn't want to commit to her because of his last relationship. He wasn't over his old girlfriend yet. Okay ladies, pop quiz:

1. Why do women stay with guys who don't give them what they are looking for in a relationship?

2. Why do women stay with guys who treat them like crap?

If any of you women ever meet me, please tell me why! Part of me thinks you put up with this because you may feel that something is better than nothing. Am I right? I can tell you this; the only way truly to find what you are looking for, in a relationship or life, happens when you are alone. It is also the only time when you will truly find yourself. Something is not always better than nothing! Besides, there are hundreds of nice guys out there who are waiting to treat you the way you deserve to be treated, but we are not going to step in while you are seeing someone else. Hello!

Okay, back to Jewel. A few weeks went by, so I called Jewel. I asked if she would like to go out that coming weekend. She said, "Sounds good." Once again, as the weekend approached I called her and left her a few messages. After two days, she called me back. Once more, she had to move again. No, no, the first move never happened. They had to reschedule it to this coming weekend at the last minute. I said, "Okay, I understand." I give up!

So now we are back to Tabitha. We emailed each other back and forth for a while. During that time, we developed a pretty good friendship. One day, out of the blue, Tabitha called me at work. She asked me for my personal cell phone number. Yep, I gave it to her.

As I drove home that evening, after working out at the health club, my cell phone rang. I didn't know the number, but somehow I knew it was Tabitha. We talked all the way home. It took forty-five minutes to get home. We talked for another hour and a half until she said she needed to make another phone call, but she would call me back. While we talked, we both spoke about very intimate and private parts of our lives, which, I thought was a little unusual. Yes, people. I still find some things unusual. While I waited for her to call me back, I pondered over our conversations of the past few weeks and months. She fascinated me, and I didn't know why.

Okay, I hope this doesn't come out wrong. I have a very quick wit, with a good sense of humor, and a dash of sarcasm. If a woman can keep up with my wit, I find that to be a very attractive quality. If the woman can banter back and forth, and dish it out right back at me, well, I find that incredibly sexy. Tabitha had those two qualities about her. Also, there was never a lull in the conversation. I love it when a woman can challenge me in a conversation and keep me guessing. If you haven't figured me out yet, I am attracted to smart, confident, intelligent women. Yes, looks count too. There has to be some attraction.

Now, here's what I haven't told you, yet. I still didn't know what Tabitha looked like. Over this time frame, I sent her a picture of me, but she hadn't sent me one of her yet. I really didn't care at this point…well, kind of. My only problem was, as I tried to explain it to her, that she had a boyfriend. I would never get involved with someone who was in a relationship. When she called me back later that evening, she informed me that she had just broken up with her boyfriend. I told her that I hoped she didn't do it because of me. She informed me that it wasn't entirely because of me.

I asked her what that meant. Tabitha said, "Jim, over the past few weeks, I have realized that I have more of a relationship with you, whom I have never met in person, than with the guy that I've been seeing for months now. Something is terribly wrong with that. After talking with you, I have decided that I deserve better. I want someone who is sensitive, funny, and isn't afraid to express his own feelings. I would love to meet you sometime in person. I think we really have a connection. I know that talking with someone over the phone and meeting someone face to face are two entirely different things.

I've been planning on breaking up with him for a while now. Talking with you just happened to convince me that now is the right time."

I wasn't surprised by what she was saying to me. Wow. That just sounded quite conceited, didn't it? That's not what I meant. I mean I felt the same way about her. I felt we had a connection to. Part of me was always wondering what she looked like. I said, "Tabitha, I don't have any plans for this weekend. If you have time, I would be willing to drive over and see you." Okay, by the way, Tabitha lived in another state, four and half hours away from me. I said, "If you don't mind, I would appreciate a picture so I know whom I should look for. Can you tell me the name of a good hotel that's close by you, and I'll make a reservation?"

Tabitha said, "Really. You're coming to see me? I can't believe this! You don't need to make a reservation. You can just stay with me. The only picture I have isn't that current, but I look the same. I will email it to you tomorrow." Okay, so now all I had to do was ask my boss if I could get off work two hours early so I could get a head start on rush-hour traffic. We talked till one o'clock in the morning. I packed my bag, and tried to get some sleep. I was just too excited.

The next day I talked to my boss and explained everything to him. Even though I had been working for this company for over a year, my current boss had only been with the company for two months. See, he didn't know me that well. He said, "Let me get this straight. You are driving four and a half hours to spend the weekend with a girl you have never met or have never seen a picture of? You sure don't waste any time, do you? No problem. Have a good time. I hope it works out for the two of you. If not, you will have an interesting story."

I finally received an email from Tabitha with a picture attached. I opened it and stared at her. She was cute. The picture seemed to be a little outdated. I remember her saying that it wasn't a current picture, but she looked the same. No problem. In her email, she told me that it was ten years old, but assured me that she hadn't changed that much. I shared all of this with my two friends from the lab, Torry and Giselle. They both seemed a little uncomfortable and overprotective of me with the whole thing, but I told them I would be fine. Torry insisted that I call her sometime during the weekend and tell her how it went, which would also prove to her that I was still alive. I assured her that I would call.

I grabbed my things and off I went. During the drive, Tabitha would call me when she had a spare moment. When we talked, we both became even more excited about meeting each other face to face. I have to be honest, when I tell you that I had this sinking feeling in my stomach that something wasn't right. I couldn't put my finger on it, but I did my best to ignore it. Yes, I know that goes against everything I have been telling you.

I was stuck in construction traffic, but I pushed on. As I got closer, to where she lived, the excitement grew. Soon I was only ten minutes away, so I called Tabitha and had her guide me to her apartment. Turn right on this street. Turn left at this light. Look for the entrance on your right. Keep going straight when you see this landmark. Finally, I was at her complex. She told me she was standing on her balcony; as I pulled up and parked my car, I saw her.

From this point forward, I'm pretty sure that all of you ladies, who thought I was a nice guy, will think I'm a big jerk, but please hold your opinion of me, and give me a chance to explain. Please?

There she was. She was a very large girl. Now, I know you are thinking that I'm a big jerk. I grabbed my things and walked to her second floor apartment. The whole time my stomach was killing me. For some reason, I just knew that the picture she sent me was more than very outdated. I was mad. Not because she was a heavy girl, but because she wasn't honest with me. Ladies, why do some women think that this is okay to do? How are you going to be anything else than what you are? Then, when the guy reacts in a negative way, you think it's the guy's fault and not the girl's fault, because she blatantly lied to the guy and withheld the truth from him!

As I walked into her apartment, I pulled away as she tried to kiss me. I thought that was a little presumptuous of her. Now, you're going to think I'm a shallow jerk. She had no makeup on; her hair was a mess, and she didn't even get dressed up. Even her apartment was messy. I asked her where the bathroom was and stepped inside. I stood there looking at the mirror incredibly ticked off. I just drove four and half hours to realize that there was no magic and no attraction at all. What was I going to do?

I didn't want to hurt her. She was a very sweet girl, but I wasn't attracted to her at all. I took a deep breath, and said a quiet prayer asking God to help me by giving me the right words to say to her. There was no way I could stay the whole weekend. That just wouldn't be right, and I didn't want to lead her on in any way.

We sat on the couch and talked a little. I tried my best to find something in her that was attractive to me. I know ladies; I suck, but remember, she lied to me or just wasn't upfront with the truth. She didn't look like that picture she sent to me, at all. I was even more ticked off now. You would have never been able to tell though.

She could tell that I was very uncomfortable as we talked. Finally, she asked me what was wrong. I took a deep breath and said, "I don't want to hurt you." She said, "All you need to be is honest with me. I think that's one of your best qualities. You have always been honest with me." Now, you ladies are going to think I'm a big jerk.

I said, "Tabitha, I'm sorry. I am not attracted to you in any way. You are the last person I would want to hurt." She looked at me and said, "Wow! Okay. Well, we took a chance. I'll be fine. Wow! What are we going to do now?" I said, "I think it would be best if I just left." She said, "You just drove over four hours to get here." I said, "I'll be fine. Don't worry about me. I am more worried if you are going to be okay!" She said, "Sure, no problem. I'll be just fine." I knew I hurt her. She said, "Jim. It's okay. We took a chance, and it didn't work out. Nothing ventured; nothing gained. Right?"

With that, I stood up and grabbed my bag. She said, "Let me walk you to your car." It felt like a slow death march as we walked down the stairs. I didn't know what to say, so I said nothing. I gave her a hug, climbed into my car, and drove off. I could see that she started to cry and walked into her friend's apartment that lived below her. I felt like crap!

As I got back onto the interstate, I called my sister Ellen. As we spoke, I could hear Fred and my brother Peter laughing in the background. I told Ellen, "So help me God! If they say anything to me about this, I will beat the crap out of both of them!" Ellen tried to calm me down and asked if I were going to be okay. I told her I was too mad right now even to think straight. She said she would pray for me, and felt really bad. I could here Fred and Peter laughing in the background even louder now. I yelled, "Ellen, so help me!" She yelled at the two of them, and they stopped.

As I drove, I relived this whole thing over and over in my mind. It just made me even angrier. I called Torry. She was surprised to hear from me and asked what happened. I said as I yelled, "I'm such a moron! I always give everyone the benefit of the doubt. My gut kept telling me that something was wrong but no! I go anyways, hoping it would be fine! She lied to me! Why do women think that it's okay to lead a guy on, and hide behind the truth? WHY? Now I'm the jerk? I thought we really had a great connection. I feel bad that there was no attraction. Am I wrong for feeling that way? There has to be some physical attraction. Right? I am so tired of this whole dating thing! It shouldn't be this hard to find someone. What the hell?

As I ranted on for over ten minutes, Torry said nothing until I was finished. Then she said, "Jim. You are a good person. You are not a moron. Very few people today give anyone the benefit of the doubt. Most just jump to the wrong conclusion right away without giving that person a chance. You took a huge chance. I know you are disappointed, and I feel bad for you. I tried to warn you. I tried to tell you not to get your hopes up too high. I had that same gut feeling that you had. I was hoping this would work out for you." As Torry spoke, I looked down at my speedometer and realized I was going over eighty-five miles per hour. I slowed down. She continued, "You didn't do anything wrong. Jim, she misled you. She may not have thought that she was lying to you, but she didn't tell the whole truth about her appearance. She was wrong for thinking that was okay. You are correct. There has to be some kind of attraction. You are not a shallow person. I know that about you. I can feel how disappointed you are. Please don't beat yourself up over this. You took a huge chance, and it wasn't as you thought it would be. I know God has someone for you. He showed her to you in a vision. Didn't He? I think you just need to take a break from dating and just give this some time."

I took a big deep breath and said, "Funny you should say that, because before I called you, I screamed at the top of my lungs at God." I said, "I am fed up with this whole dating thing! I am done! If You want me to go out with a woman, then You will have to pick her, and have her ask me out!" I continued, "I am so done, Torry. I can't do this anymore. Each time has been such a disappointment. I know that meeting someone is never a waste of time. I just don't want to feel like this anymore."

Torry said, "I think that is the best thing for you right now. I know you don't want to hear this, but you just need to be patient, and it will all work out in the end. I am so sorry for you Jim! Are you going to be okay?" I said, "Yes. I'll be fine. I've been through worse." Torry said, "I'm praying for you. Try to have a good weekend. I'll see you on Monday." I thanked her for listening and hung up.

As I drove home, I reiterated to God once more, out loud what I said, and added, "I am making a vow to You! I will not ask out another woman for the rest of this year. You can have them ask me out! I am done!" Yes, folk, the words "ticked off" don't even come close to the anger I was mustering inside. As I continued my trek home, I began to fall asleep behind the wheel. So, I decided that I hadn't spent *enough* money on this anger-ridden journey of mine. So, I had better spend more money and get a hotel for the night. So I did. The minute my head hit the pillow I was out.

I got up early in the morning because I didn't exactly know how far I was from home. Once I saw the sign for Chicago I knew how far it was from that point. I could have killed myself. I was only ninety minutes away from home. I could have saved myself $90! At least, that's what I told myself. When I got home, Fred started in right away with making jokes. I glared at him, and he shut up pretty quick. Ellen smacked him and told him to leave me alone. I talked with my sister for a while. She said pretty much the same thing that Torry said to me. It didn't make me feel any better. I guess all I needed was time; that, I had a lot of.

I also forgot to tell you that, during this whole incredible adventure of dating, I met someone else that I worked with. Once again, one of my fellow coworkers was on vacation, and I was covering for her (a girl named Wendy, who worked in the plant-ops department),. Over that period of time, we built a pretty good friendship. Don't get too excited, folks. She's married. Over those few weeks, I found out that she would go to the movies by herself. Her husband just didn't like the whole theater experience. I told her that maybe she should come with Peter and me some time. We went all the time.

I invited Wendy to come with us on Friday. We were planning to see

Ocean's 13, and then we were going to get something to eat afterwards. She accepted. I sent an email to my brother informing him of my plans. Wouldn't you know it!! He tells me he's made other plans for that Friday night and wouldn't be joining us. Great! Now I'm dating a married woman. I told her it would be just the two of us, and if that was too weird for her, we could reschedule. She said she was OK with just hanging with me.

After the movie, we went to a restaurant, and spent the next two and a half hours talking to each other about our lives. Yep, the whole "I see dead people" came up in our conversation. I have no idea why. As I shared my experience about the soul in Shelly's house and my two daughters, she listened intently.

At one point, I stopped myself and said, "I really have no idea why I'm telling you all of this. You probably think I'm crazy, and that I'm making it all up!" Wendy said, "I don't think you could make this up. I can tell by the sincerity in your eyes that you are telling me the truth. Have you ever thought of writing a book?"

I laughed, and said, "Who would want to read a book about my life? Everyone will think I'm crazy. I think most people do when I share this with them." She said, "I honestly think people will be very interested in what you have lived through." I said, "You may be right, but I really don't think I can do that. Sometimes, I think I'm losing my mind, but my sister confirms things for me before I even say anything to her. So, I know I'm not crazy, yet!" Wendy said, "I find all of this truly interesting, and I think most people will too. You hear about things like this in the Bible, but you wouldn't think it could happen in our time."

I said, "That's why I hesitate so much about writing a book. No angel has ever told me to write a book about this, so I have never really thought about it." Wendy said, "Please think about it. I think it would really do well. And once Oprah finds out about it, you will be on the best-seller list." I laughed and said, "Oprah! That will be the day." Wendy said, "No, really. She is very spiritual. I think she would be very interested in this." I said, "Okay, Wendy. I will think about it, but I make no promises. I don't even know where to start. I have never written anything, and grammar was never my strong point. Let alone, I suck as a typist." She said, "Just think about it."

As I drove home, I started to get that feeling of 'Oh crap, you shouldn't have spoken about this to her'. But Anthony…remember, my lead angel…told me to tell her these things. Folks, I am extremely cautious about what I share, and how much I share. I usually check with him before

I open my mouth. He gave me the nodded head sign, so I proceeded. As I looked up at my phone, I felt Wendy was going to call me. Sure enough, she did. She said, "I just wanted to say thank you for sharing what you did with me. I have been going through a tough time, and questioning things. Now that I've talked with you, I have some clarity, and a better understanding of my own situation. So, thanks again, and write the book! Okay?"

I said, "Wendy, it was my pleasure to share these things with you. I will think about the whole book thing, and let you know." As I hung up the phone, I looked at Anthony. He just nodded his head and said nothing. He's always like that; all business.

On Monday, Wendy stopped by to see me and said, "Okay. Don't kill me. I was talking to a friend this weekend and…" I cut her off in mid-sentence and said, "You told her I have a gift?" She cringed and said, "Well, maybe I did." I said, "Wendy, I don't want people that I work with to think that I'm some kind of a nutcase." She said, "She won't. I told her very little about what we talked about…kinda. I just have a question that maybe you or someone you know can help her with. Okay?" I said, "What?"

Wendy said, "My friend is from England. When she moved here, she lost touch with a very close friend of hers whom she thinks has died now. She has been to many mediums and clairvoyant people, but no one seems to have the answer for her as to what happened to her friend. She has also lost contact with her friend's family. Can you help her?" I said, "Wendy, my gift works in the here and now, not the past. I do know of someone that might be able to help her, my sister Ann. She has had her gift since the age of twelve. I make no promises. I will call her and let you know. So, who is this friend?"

Wendy said, "Her name is Diana. She works here in the spa. She's beautiful, brunette, has blue eyes and a British accent, and she's gorgeous!" So I said, "And why is this the first time that I'm hearing about her?" Wendy said, "She's married, Jim, and has a newborn child." I said, "Nice. Thanks for building the suspense and dropping me on my head. When can I meet her?" Wendy said, "Oh, no way! She will fall for you and then the next thing I know you are breaking up a happy family." I said, "Wow! Thanks for giving me that much credit." Wendy said, "I just know her. There is no way I will ever let the two of you meet." I said, "Well, then I'm not sure if I can help Diana." Wendy said, "Oh, knock it off! Please, help her." I said, "Fine! Let me call Ann. I'll get back to you."

Wendy had her friend Diana email me a recent picture of her friend and I forwarded it to Ann. Then I called Ann and explained the situation. As the two of us talked and looked at the picture, my heart started to hurt. Folks, what is that a sign of? No, I'm not having a heart attack. When my heart hurts that means something evil is around, or it has something to do with the situation. Remember? Ann said, "My chest is hurting, is yours?" I said, "Yes. I think she died in a very terrible way. What do you think?"

Ann said, "I get that same impression, but I can't see the situation very clearly yet. I need to talk to her, and then I can read her space and see her friend more clearly." I said, "Okay, but before you do that, I will have a talk with her and explain to her how this whole thing works. I don't want to mislead her in any way. Is it okay if I give her your cell phone number?" Ann told me that would be fine, and to have Diana call her after 6 pm when she gets out of work.

I called Wendy and told her what Ann and I talked about. She fought with me for a while about my wanting to meet Diana, but finally she relented. I just don't get her sometimes. Later that afternoon, Wendy, arranged for me to meet with Diana. We met outside because I didn't want anyone to hear our conversation. Can you blame me?

As I met Diana, I could feel her trying to get into my space. It was the strangest feeling. Clairvoyantly, to protect myself, I pulled out my sword and shield. As we talked, I looked deep into her eyes. She truly was quite beautiful, but I could see that there was something in her space and that she too had a gift of some sort. Well, back to business. I explained to Diana how my gift works, and how Ann's gift works. I told her, Ann, and I compared the feelings we had, as we spoke about her friend. We could not draw any conclusions at that time.

I also explained to her that in some cases, our friends and relatives that have passed on before us don't want to be bothered or found. I said that I could make no promises. She understood. I gave her Ann's information and said, "I hope you get the answer you were looking for."

All I wanted to do was get away from her. I realized as we talked that it wasn't Diana who was trying to get into my space, but the thing she had in her space. It was trying exceptionally hard. As we talked, clairvoyantly I pointed my sword toward this thing and warned it to stay back, or I would destroy it. It moved away and waited for me to leave. Later that afternoon, Wendy, called me and said, "Well, you left a huge impression on Diana." I said, "Okay, share." She told me she didn't want to because it might give me a big head. I told her to give me a break and just tell me. She said, "She thinks you are very handsome, and that you have the most amazing eyes. Diana noticed that your eyes twinkled while the two of you spoke. I think I'm going to throw up!" I laughed out loud. She continued, "She also wanted me to ask you why you cut your conversation short. She said she felt like you were a little uncomfortable talking with her." I asked Wendy if Diana was aware that she had a gift too. Wendy said, "Oh, great! You mean she really does have a gift?" I said, "What does that mean?" Wendy said, "For as long as I have known Diana, she would walk up to us and out of the blue she would say things like, *'Um, you really shouldn't be thinking about changing your mind on that situation. Or, do you really want to know what I think is going on with you?'* You mean she really has a gift? Oh, crap! Jim, please don't say anything to her. She will play this out to the point that she will drive me and Heidi nuts!" I said, "I won't say anything. Who is Heidi?" Wendy said, "She's my other beautiful friend. You should meet her some time ." I said, "Okay. Why haven't I heard about Heidi till now?" She said, "Heidi is in a longtime relationship. I don't really care for the guy she's with. I think she can do much better." I said, "Well, have Diana call me tomorrow after she talks with Ann. I would like to hear what she has to say."

The next day, after I had spoken with Ann about her conversation with Diana, Diana called me. She said, "I spoke with your sister. She told me that my friend was killed in a horrible car accident. She was killed immediately, but her body was burned in the crash. I have always thought she died in a horrible way, and now I know that to be true." See folks, that's why our hearts were hurting so much when Ann and I looked at her picture; she died a horrible death.

Diana continued, "Ann said that she gets the impression that my friend is in a pretty good place. What do you think?" I said, "I have that same impression. She just wants you to let her be in peace and now you can. I'm glad Ann was able to help you." Diana said, "You have no idea how long I have been waiting for an answer. Thanks to you and your sister I finally too, have peace." I said, "I didn't do anything. I will tell Ann how much you appreciated her help, and I wish you all the best. I'm pretty sure I will see you around." Diana thanked me again, and I called Wendy to let her know that Ann answered Diana's question.

As we finished our conversation, Wendy asked if we could have coffee sometime so that we could talk about Diana. I informed her that my sister and I treat our conversations about this kind of stuff just like Vegas. What happens in our conversations stays within the conversation.

Wendy said, "No, I don't want to know about the details, I just want to know how to deal with Diana and her gift." So, we made our plans to meet after work that day. As I was leaving work, Wendy called to ask if it were okay if Heidi joined us. I asked, "Why?" Wendy said, "Well after Heidi talked to Diana she told her that she needed to meet you so she could she how amazing your eyes were too. Now I know I'm going to throw up." I said, "The more the merrier and I'll bring you a bag to hurl into."

The three of us sat and talked. I stared at Heidi. I had to stop myself from peering too deep into her space. If you remember, I don't like doing this because I feel as if I am violating someone else's space. Heidi was incredibly beautiful with long brunette hair down to the middle of her back, and the prettiest big brown eyes I have ever seen. Her skin was perfect, and her smile would melt the ice off any glacier. She was amazing. My problem was that she looked just like the woman of my dreams that I had been looking at in the center of my mind for almost four years. I was quite smitten with her. After about forty-five minutes, Heidi told us that she didn't want to leave, but she had to meet her boyfriend and his mom for dinner. She seemed extremely disappointed.

After Heidi had left, I looked at Wendy and glared at her. She said, "What?" I said, "You know you are a lot like God and the tree in the middle of the garden. Isn't this tree pretty? But no, don't touch it. You have me meet two of your friends who are both in relationships. They are both drop-dead gorgeous. Please stop doing me any favors. You are driving me nuts!" She laughed and said, "I wish they weren't in relationships, because I think you would treat them the way they should be treated. Their men take them both for granted." I said, "Well, there is nothing I can do for them. I don't get involved with women who are taken." Of course, maybe I should rethink that! Hmmm…No! I'm not like that.

As I drove home, I couldn't get Heidi out of my mind or space. There she was, just standing there. So I decided to write her a letter and then burn it. I wrote the date, July 2, 2007, and poured out my heart into the letter. I explained how I felt just meeting her and how attracted I was to her. But my attraction went beyond flesh. After about forty-five minutes of writing, I texted Wendy and asked her to call me. I informed her that I wrote Heidi a letter and that I was going to burn it.

One hour later, Wendy called and said, "You better not have burned that letter before you read it to me!" I said calmly, "No, I've been waiting for you to call." As I read the two-page letter, I could hear Wendy crying. When I finished, I asked her what her problem was. She said, "Jim, holy cow! I have never heard anything that beautiful before in my life. You are very romantic."

I said, "I just opened up my heart, and that's what came out." Wendy said, "And you don't want to write a book? You are crazy. That letter is awesome. You have to save a copy just so you have it for the future." I said, "Nope. I was burning it while you were talking to me. It's gone." Wendy said, "Well, I guess time will tell. I'm sorry I have caused you so much frustration." I told her she didn't and that I was OK.

The next day wasn't any better for me. Heidi was in my space, again. No matter how much I asked her to leave, she wouldn't. I'll be honest with you; I liked her in my space. After I arrived home that night, I composed another letter. I kept a copy of this one. I don't know why I did. Well, here's what I wrote her:

July 3, 2007

I understand that Wendy told you how I felt about you today. I hope that didn't embarrass you, too much.

It is difficult to write this letter, because I don't truly know how you truly feel. Well, that's not entirely true. You see you have been in my space all day long.   Not that I mind. You're very cute. Someday, I might explain that to you, but for now, I'll just say what I said and leave it at that.

I made the mistake of listening to a group called Shedaisy today. They sing a song called "Rush." The beginning lyrics start off by saying, "To be the first in someone's life, to set the sun, and raise the moon in someone else's eyes. To see heaven, just for a day. To hold a moment in your arms and never let it slip away." This would sum up, once again, how I feel about you. I know this is just so psychotic. I spent one hour with you, looked in your eyes and almost lost myself, and here I am almost unable to function.

Today at work, I found myself staring at my computer screen thinking about you, and forgetting what the heck I was supposed to be doing. I'll have you know that I don't normally have this kind of problem. Ever!

A sales rep came in today and asked me how my dating life was. I just sat there. She said, "Give!" So I started to tell her all about you. She said, "Wow. So what are you waiting for?" So I said, "She's in an eight-year relationship." The sales rep said, "Never a dull moment for you, Jim!" I said, "No. Life would just be too easy. I just might be happy with the way things went for me. The next thing you know, I would just start taking everything for granted in my life. No, really, I   would."

I have been talking to Wendy about you and this "drug-related" situation. She's been quite a support and cheerleader on your behalf. Well, as you know, she started all of this. No, no, I forgive her. It's all good. See Heidi, my life has never been, nor shall I say, uncomplicated. My dad always told me, "If you want something in life you have to work for it." I am willing to do whatever it will take until I have you in my arms; to gaze into your eyes, and hold you; to see a smile grow across your face as you realize that maybe, for the first time in your life, you can also have what you have always wanted. What might that be, you ask? It's the same thing I have always wanted. It is to receive back just as much as you have given out. To be appreciated because of the small stuff. To know that the eyes of the one you are staring into expects nothing more of you than your entire heart. To not be afraid to share your feelings with that person, no matter what it is. To know you can trust them. To know they will always be there for you, no matter what. To have times of laughter where you think you may pass out, because you're laughing so hard you can't breathe. Just to sit and snuggle on the couch while listening to some music or watching a movie. To look into each others eyes, say no words at all, but know exactly what we are trying to say to each other. And dare I say, to know that they love you with their whole heart. I don't know what you think, but this is what I've been looking for my whole life.

When I think of you, I find that I have this goofy little grin on my face. One of my coworkers asked why I was so quiet today. I said, "I'm just contemplating life." She looked at me with a puzzled look. So, I told her all about you and your situation. She smiled and said, "Jim. If it's meant to be, it will happen."

I am a very simple man. I don't have many possessions, wealth, or even my own place to live right now. All I'm asking for is a chance to change your life for the better and win your heart.

Yes, I know just how crazy that sounds. I know deep down inside of you there are questions that you keep asking yourself as you look at your current relationship.

1. Is this the best *I* can have?
2. Is it wrong for me to want more?
3. Should I just settle for what I have?
4. And maybe you ask yourself this question.

Why am I talking to myself? (Sorry. I just thought I'd interject a little humor.)

I can honestly say that I have never been smitten, enthralled, or even captivated as I am with you. I just wanted to let you know how I felt so I can let go of this, and stop driving myself crazy.

I know this may seem a bit overwhelming to you, and perhaps not even real. But it is. I would like to get to know you as a friend, and then see where it might go. If you are interested, here is my cell phone number. You can call me at any time. I'm hoping your answer is yes, because I know I would really like to get to know you. I will not pressure you into anything. I just hope you know just how very sweet, incredibly sexy, and intelligent I think you are, and if I may, answer one of your questions, please?

You can have whatever your heart desires!!!!!

Once again, happily lost in the wake of your beauty,

Jim

I read this letter to Wendy. She was sobbing as I finished it. She said, "When you told me you were writing her another letter, I assumed it would be just like the first one. But, this letter is completely different. Once again, it is the most romantic thing I have ever heard. You have to write a book, Jim." I said, "What do you think would happen if I emailed it to her?" Wendy said, "You would blow her away. I don't think she could handle it. Why don't you call your sister Ann and see what she says." So, I called Ann. She said the same thing that I would blow her away. But, if she were the woman of my dreams, it would all work out.

Yep! You guessed it. I sent it. Two hours later Wendy called me to tell me that Heidi was completely blown away and that her boyfriend was home when she opened it even though Wendy told her not to because she knew how open I was when I wrote. Heidi was crying so hard that she ran into the garage to hide from her boyfriend so he wouldn't ask why she was crying. Wendy told me that Heidi had never read such beautiful words directed towards her. She also wanted to know how I knew, and what I knew about her, when I asked her those questions. Heidi asked Wendy if I was reading her mind. Wendy, in true fashion, told her that she was giving me too much credit and that I couldn't read minds.

Wendy told Heidi that, with the way I chose those questions, any woman would have felt they could relate and feel something about them. She explained to her how open I am when I express my feelings. She was completely overwhelmed. Wendy told me not to contact Heidi. She would try to feel her out and let me know.

As the days went by, I heard very little about my letter. As a matter of fact, I heard nothing. I was so sure that Heidi was the one; she looked like the woman in the center of my mind. As the weeks went by, I realized that

Heidi was *not* the one. I felt like an idiot for pouring out my heart. But, folks, all I can be is me. Live and learn.

After thinking about it for a month, or so, I decided to write my book. I thought to myself, *"I have never written anything in my life. I hated grammar and English in school but what the heck. I will give it a try and see what happens."* I called Wendy and shared with her that I had decided to write my book. She was ecstatic about it. Then she said that she would expect to read each chapter as I wrote them. I told her that I would think about it and let her know. She didn't like that answer very much.

Chapter 17
The Book...New Experiences

On Wednesday, July 18, 2007, as I was driving to and from work, I tried to come up with titles for my book. I wanted something that would grab the attention of the reader and then leave them wondering.

Here are a few of the titles I came up with:

The Battle, The Crusade, Heaven's War, Blind Belief, A Quiet Struggle, The Tasks, Phases, First Love, Tested Faith, A Test of Faith, One Faith, Won Faith, More Than You Know..., A Surrendered Will, The Journey to Find your Heart, A Strong Conviction, A Measure of Grace & Love, Through the Fire of Love, The Protected, Tested in Fire, My Crusade, One Final Stand, Freed Will, Free Will, A Test of Love, A Sacred Pledge, and my favorite, *The Tickling Uncle*. My five-year-old niece, Sydney, came up with that title. I could not argue with her logic, though. She said, "Well, Uncle Jim, you do tickle me, you know."

As I was getting ready to go to church that evening, I prayed and asked God to help me find the right title. As soon as I stopped praying a new title swept over my heart.

One Wish...
Won Battle!

I paused for a moment and said that title to myself a few times. I ran to my bedroom and wrote it down. It just felt right.

The next day, I went straight home from work, without working out. I was anxious to get started. I was surprised at how page after page just flowed out of my mind. I'm certainly not that great of a typist. The "hunt and peck" method seems to work for me. I can type almost thirty or thirty-five words a minute. Hey, I'm trying my best, people.

As I wrote, I felt a quiet calm sweep over me. Then I heard a voice say, *"Jim. Because you have decided to write this book, the Lord will grant you the woman of your dreams next year in June 2008. I will help you recall important aspects of your life that the Lord would like you to write in your book."*

As I sat there, I tried my best to figure out who was talking to me. I had heard his voice one time before, when he had told me how our offerings affected those in the realms of the departed. I said, *"Who is talking to me, please."* The voice said, *"I am the Holy Spirit. God has sent me to guide you through this process. He loves you very much Jim. In time, He will reveal to you more of the plan He has for you. Because of your faith, He will grant you the woman of your dreams, one year from now. In the meantime, be patient."* I was completely caught off guard and overwhelmed. As He spoke to me, an incredible feeling of peace washed over me, and then He appeared right in front of me.

He appeared to me as an apparition. He has no lower body and looks like a cloud. He has an upper body with a head, torso, and arms. He wore what looked like a large white coat. He wore no armor and had no shield. But He did have a sword attached to a belt He wore around Himself. Below Him was a flowing garment that swayed as He floated in front of me. He spoke very calmly and gently. He appeared to be made out of a light blue energy, transparent, but with form. He had big hair; He wore it similar to the way Liberace did. Yes, I know how crazy that sounds. Just work with me. He had soft blue eyes and gentle facial features.

He told me that every time before I start to write, I should pray that the Lord sends Him to help me. He told me not to worry about the content of the book, because He would lead and guide me. He told me not to worry about how I was going to remember everything, verbatim. He said that He would help me recall in detail every conversation and experience. He reassured me that I was not alone. He said that the Lord and His Son were both with me, as they have been throughout my life. He finished by telling me just to have faith and trust the Lord.

Within the first few days, I had a couple of chapters done. I printed off one copy and let Torry, Giselle, and Wendy read it. That was a big mistake. Now, they were constantly beating me up every day asking me when the next chapters would be finished. When I had completed the fourth chapter, I decided at that point that the first four chapters would be all I was going to let anyone read until it was published. They were not too happy when I told them that, but they tried to understand.

The following week, Wendy seemed to be acting a little strange to me. She was obsessed with my book. Not a little obsessed but a lot obsessed. It was all she would talk about. It was creeping me out. Every time we talked, or when she would stop by to see me in person, she would ask about my book. My heart was hurting while this was going on. I knew something wasn't right, but I didn't know what it was.

The following Friday, one of our managers was retiring, so they threw him a party. I sat there listening to all the people talk about their past experiences with this manager. Wendy stopped by to say goodbye to him. She had worked with him for a while.

As she sat down, at a table about twenty feet from me, I noticed out of the corner of my eye that something stepped out of her space. It was standing in front of her facing me. It was a demon.

He was clad in full red and black armor, and he was surrounded by ten of his little minion soldiers. His face was hideous; he had a lizard's head with snake's eyes. His complexion was dark. His hands looked like lobster claws. Clairvoyantly, I sprang to my feet. Anthony grabbed my shoulder and said, *"Jim, stand your ground."* In other words, do nothing. As I stood there, this demon spoke. As he spoke, it was almost as if he was hissing like a snake.

He said, *"My name is Tiberius. I control the central part of the United States. I just wanted to come and introduce myself to the great Supplanter! If I had the chance, I would destroy you right now. I've been toying with your friend Wendy. She has been completely oblivious of my presence in her space."* I cut him off mid-sentence and said, *"I don't care who you are, but I will warn you to leave my friends and family alone. If, I see you again, so help me God your fate will be the same as Andreus!"* As I spoke, Anthony put his hand on my shoulder and pulled me towards himself and said quietly in my ear, *"The Lord God is not provoked."* Tiberius laughed out loud, turned, and as he left he said, *"We will see each other again, Supplanter. Be careful!"* I sat there fuming in my anger. Anthony told me again to control myself. So, I took a big deep breath and let it go. Later that afternoon, Wendy called me to ask what had happened at the party. She had noticed that I looked at her for a while. I told her it was no big deal and to forget about it. But she insisted I tell her. So I did. When I finished telling her everything, I asked her if she were happy now. She said, "The next time I insist on you telling me something, from your "special world," would you please tell me no!"

The next evening, as I was driving home from my parents' house, the reality of everything started to crash in all around me. I started thinking about my life on the west coast and how I was persecuted. I thought about all of my experiences with my demon possession, and all of the conversations I had with Michael. I started to doubt and ask if all of this were real. I felt as though I was being crushed with every negative emotion I had. I broke down. I began to cry as I yelled to God to please help me! I asked God why? Why would you pick me for all of this? I can't do this. I feel as if I'm losing my mind.

I kept driving around. The whole time I was crying like a three-year-old. I thought to myself, once my book comes out I will be the laughingstock of the world. Who is going to believe me? Why would they believe me? I am nobody. To my surprise I heard a quiet, calm voice say,

"I chose you because of your heart, Jim. Because you believe in Me and gave Me your free will. I love you more than you will ever know. And in times when you feel you are alone, I am with you, as I am with you right now. The task I have given you is not an easy one to carry, but I have also blessed you with strength and wisdom so that you can carry this plan out for Me. I would like to thank you for your faith and for what you are doing for Me." I screamed out loud, *"Please don't thank me! I don't deserve any thanks! I feel so lost Father! Please just take me, now! I can't do this anymore! Please?"*

The Lord said, *"My dear Jim. There is no one else that can do this for Me. I know you feel overwhelmed by all of this, and I want you to know that I will now renew My covenant with you. I am always with you. You are never alone. My Son is also with you. I give you peace to fill your troubled heart. Trust in Me and I will see you through all of this. In difficult times, I will always be there with you. When you feel weak, I will give you strength. When you feel lost, I will guide you. When you feel fear, I will give you courage.*

Because you do all of this for Me, I will restore to you tenfold what I have taken away from you. I will not take you now, because I need you here. In time, you will see My blessings, and you will feel My love for you. Jim, you must be patient, and always know that I love you very deeply."

As I pulled into my driveway, I sat there and continued to cry. Not because I was felt overwhelmed, but because I had doubted what I have always known to be true. The Lord God loves me and is always with me. Wow. I feel like such an idiot sometimes. When God speaks to me, it is one of the most amazing things that I have ever felt. It is hard to put it into words. It is as though He is holding me in His hand while He speaks to me. Nothing can harm or touch me for those brief moments. I will always cherish these moments.

The following weekend I continued to write my book. I spent almost all of Saturday just writing. In the evening, as I wrote, I heard the Holy Spirit speak to me. I heard Him speaking behind me, so I turned my chair to face Him. He continued, *"Do you recall a conversation you had with Jesus a few short years ago, about the 30,000 lights?"* I said, *"Yes."* He said, *"Do you recall how He told you that you were the brightest light in the center of the tree?"* I said, *"Yes."* He said, *"Jesus told you that, in time, it would be revealed to you as to how this would be. The book you are writing will be the catalyst that will bring in the 30,000 lights into the church."*

Yep, you guessed it! I started to cry, again. The Holy Spirit reached down and put His hand on my head and said, *"Receive the blessing of God."* As I sat there crying, a warm energy came from the top of my head and filled my whole body. I began to get goose pimples as the warmth filled me. Then I felt a peace like I had never felt in a long time. The Holy Spirit said, *"The Lord God, His Son, and I are always with you. You have no reason to fear anything. Continue writing. The Lord would like you to complete your book by the end of this year, December, 2007."* I wiped my eyes, blew my nose, and kept writing. Too much information? Sorry!

Okay, so the following weekend, August 18, I did something that you may think is totally out of the ordinary for a guy like me. I got a tattoo. Yes, I know how crazy that may sound to a lot of you folks. For the past three years, I had been talking about it and finally I did it. So, now you're asking yourself what did I get, and where did I put it? Hmmm!

I had my church's emblem put on the center of my right arm between my bicep and triceps; it's five inches in size. The outline is in black. The center is filled with bronze, and the rays are accented with gold. You may be saying to yourself, but Jim, we don't know what your churches emblem looks like. You can go to this Web site www.nak.org and take a look for yourself. Copyright laws protect the church emblem so I changed the colors of my tattoo so they would not look like the one on the Web site. Besides, a blue and white tattoo wouldn't look right on my skin tone.

Oh, yes, it hurt like crazy. I told all of my friends that getting a tattoo is a lot like taking a flaming hot razor blade and cutting your skin with it. Is that graphic enough for you? No, I didn't cry or pass out. The only thing I was nervous about was how my parents and family would react. After I had finished spending forty-five minutes in the artist's chair, I climbed into my car and started to drive home. I went to a place out of state because a woman I worked with, Daisy, recommended her tattoo guy. I was afraid of getting something nasty if the needles were dirty. She assured me that this guy was extremely professional and clean, and he was.

As I drove home, I thought of what my family would say to me. All of a sudden my grandma showed up in my passenger's side seat. She said, *"Jimmy. You don't have anything to worry about."* I said, "Grams, Mom is going to kill me!" Grandma said, *"No, she isn't. She is going to love it. Do you have any idea how many people you will give testimony to because of this tattoo? It's very pretty, Jimmy. I like it. In time, people will know who you are because of this tattoo. Don't worry about it. You will be fine. Tell your Mom I say hi and I love her."* Then Grams left. I sent a text to my brother Peter to tell him that I got a tattoo. He didn't believe me until I pulled the bandage off and took a picture of it and then texted it to him. He couldn't believe that I did it. I couldn't believe that I did it, either!

By the time I got home, Ellen and Fred knew about it. Ellen was mad at me for getting it. She asked me if I were smoking crack and if I had lost my mind. I explained to her that because of everything I lived through as Supplanter, I viewed this tattoo as a medal of honor. I earned it. I still wasn't done with the task at hand for the Lord; much more was coming. Ellen didn't talk to me for days.

The next day, Sunday, after church, the entire family went out to dinner to our favorite restaurant. I ended up sitting at the end of the table with both of my parents, which never happens. I sat there trying to figure out when it would be an opportune time to spill the beans. There wasn't a good time. So, out of the blue, I said, "Hey, Mom. I saw grandma yesterday." Mom asked why I saw her. I said, "Oh, she just stopped by to tell me that she liked my tattoo." I waited. I cringed as I waited for my parents' response. My parents both stopped eating and said, "What tattoo? What did you get?" I rolled up my sleeve. Wow, did that hurt! I showed both of them the tattoo. I almost fell off of my chair because of what they both said. Mom said, "Wow, Jimmy. That's very pretty, I like it." Dad said, "Son, that's very nice." Peter yelled across the table, "I'm going to get one too, on my left arm." Hey, what can I say? My tattoo looks pretty cool.

After a few days, Ellen began to talk to me again. I was happy about that. She asked if I was going through some midlife crisis. I told her she would be the first to know if I pulled up in her driveway with some tiny sports car. We both laughed.

As the weeks went by, I kept writing. I was near the end of the eighth chapter. On September 8, Michael showed up and told me to kneel in front of him. As I knelt down, he put his hand on my head and said, *"Receive the blessing from God. (Clairvoyantly), you now have the strength of twenty angels. He grants you wisdom and clearer vision to see into the future. With these gifts, you will be able to see into people's spaces, to understand their hearts."* As I stood up, he continued to talk to me. Michael said, *"Jim. Do not provoke Satan! There are times when you make comments about him, and it enrages him. That is why the Lord will now give you six angels to watch over you. Please watch what you say, and remember you are a representative of the Lord. You are also not to speak to the leaders of your church about your book; they will not understand. I will tell you when you can approach them. Also, the Lord gave you the strength to overcome your flesh and to stop swearing."*

Yes, folks, I'm human. I have many faults. I am trying to overcome myself just like everyone else, and sometimes I fail miserably at it, but no excuses. I actually hate myself when I swear. Most of all, I seriously hate the "F" word. I don't use it that much, but on occasion, it does slip out. So, from that day forward, I made a conscious effort not to swear.

The following Monday, September 10, while on my way to work, I was praying. Oh, I pray to the Lord every morning while I'm driving to work. I have a hard time rolling out of bed in the morning and praying right away. I have found that, on occasion, I would fall back asleep. Since the angels carry our prayers to the throne of God, I wouldn't want an angel hanging around with a pad of paper waiting for me to regain consciousness. They have better things to do.

Okay, so as I'm driving, I said, "Dear Father, I wanted to tell You how excited I am to meet the woman of my dreams. She's incredibly hot and sexy; nice job! Now, I can't make You any promises, but I am going to try my best not to know her biblically until we are married. I know the three of you don't like that." I paused, and looked up at the sky with a little smirk on my face and said, "Come on now, that was funny. You have to admit that was pretty funny." I finished my prayer and kept driving. Once I was at work, I went about my day. Nothing really exciting happened today. It was actually a normal day.

As I drove home, from work, I prayed and thanked God for all of the difficult times He had put me through. Once again, I was reliving everything that had happened to me when I lived on the west coast. Don't ask me why, I just was. At one point, I prayed out loud and said, "Father, I just wanted to let You know that if I had to live through all of that again, I would gladly go through it and not change one thing."

A split second later, I heard Jesus' voice say, *"You have reached a new level of faith Jim. Because of your faith my Father will grant you the woman of your dreams sooner than you think, sometime before March of next year. You will do nothing; she will approach you. I am very proud of you, Jim. You have come a long way from where you used to be, and it has not been easy for you. Along the way, we have told you to be patient. You are not doing well with this word, or with what it means. I have a new word for you. It is called long-suffering. Try working on that for awhile."* As I drove, I sat mesmerized by every word He said.

Jesus continued, *"Your prayer this morning made my Father smile. Open your heart and pray more like that."* I began to cry. Jesus reached down, and with His thumbs, he wiped my tears away from both of my eyes. He leaned down and kissed me on the forehead and said, *"In time, my Father will restore everything to you tenfold; fear nothing. We are with you. I now renew My promise to you that I am always near you. Satan is mad and afraid of you. You are My warrior, and the power of My Father that you currently hold will destroy all of them. My Father's will will be served. I am with you."*

Okay, folks, when I got home, I looked up the definition of long-suffering. Let's see what Dictionary.com says:

Long-suf·fer·ing

1. **Enduring injury, trouble, or provocation long and patiently.**
2. **Long and patient endurance of injury, trouble, or provocation: years of long-suffering and illness.**
   Adj. Patiently enduring wrongs or difficulties.

I'll be honest with you, after I read this; my first impression was, *Oh, crap!* I called Marty front and center and asked him what all of this meant. He said, *"Jim, you have already gone through most of this. The Lord is not going to put you through anything you can't handle. He was just trying to give you another word than patience to work with."* If this were a movie, I would be staring at you people from the screen right now with a look on my face of, really? Did you notice how Marty said most of this? Hmmm! Okay!

Two days later, as I was on my way to work, Jesus appeared in front of my eyes while I was still driving. He said, *"Jim. My Father's plan will move forward. Before time began He picked you. You have surpassed our expectations with your faith. My Father and I love you very much. He will always test you, but you will not fail us. I know all of this has been very overwhelming for you, and you still question these things. Take my hands."* Jesus held up His hands. I could see the holes in them. Folks, I was still driving, but clairvoyantly I reached up and held His hands. He said, *"Can you feel My hands?"* I said, *"Yes, Lord."* Then He said, *"Touch My face."* I reached up and put both of my hands on each side of His face. He said, *"Can you feel My face?"* I said, "Yes, Lord." *He said, "Then you can definitely feel the love I have for you in my heart."* I began to cry. Jesus continued, *"All of this is real. Every soul that has ever walked on the face of the earth will know who you are. My Father's will, will be done, and you are very much a part of this. I need you to do something for Me.*

I need you to be nice to Wendy. She looks to you for guidance. Do the same things you have always done for her. Listen to her, and do not give her answers to her problems. My Father has given you many gifts, and in time He will unlock them. These gifts will be used for His plan only. You will see into the future. You are not a soothsayer or a prophet. I remove all doubt and fear from you. You are My Warrior. Be strong, and keep that wonderful sense of humor. I love you, and I am always with you." As Jesus left, I reached up crying and grabbed His garment. As He stopped, His power flowed into me. He turned, looked back at me, and with a smile, said nothing.

The next day, in the afternoon, I sent an email to Wendy asking how she was. She told me that things were not going well for her. I responded with telling her, *"JC talked to me yesterday about you."* Hey, I was sending an email across our company network. I don't want someone reading my email and thinking I'm crazier than I actually am. She responded back with, "What did He say?" I said, "He told me that I needed to be nice to you." Folks, if you forgot, I had always told Wendy that she was the sister that I never wanted. As a joke, I would tell her that. So as I typed this out, it wasn't easy for me to tell her. Please, don't get me wrong; I love Wendy as a friend. I have always told her that. I waited for almost ten minutes for her to respond, and she did by saying, "No way!" I called her on the phone and told her the extent of my conversation about her with Him. She got very quiet and said, "I can't believe it." I asked what she couldn't believe. She said, "It's just too embarrassing to tell you."

I told her to give me a break. She had told me things in the past that were probably more embarrassing than this thing could have been. She refused to tell me, so I told her I understood. I finished by saying, "If you ever wondered if they knew who you were; I guess you can now see that they do." A few hours later, I got an email from Wendy explaining what had happened. You see folks; Wendy is a little overweight. Not a lot, but she has big hips. She's going to kill me when she reads all of this. Can all of you who read this do me a favor: please pray for me, so she doesn't kill me! Thanks, I really appreciate it!

She said, "Yesterday was such a bad day. All of the people that I have known for years kept making comments about my weight. Even the people I have considered being my friends made negative comments. They hurt me so much that the moment it was time for me to leave, I ran to my car trying to get in it before anyone saw that I was crying. I was so upset that I prayed to God. I said, *"Why do people have to be so mean to me? Did I ask for this? Why can't people just be nice to me? It's not like I'm asking for a miracle, like Peter and Jim to be nice to me."* I started to laugh a little and said, *"Well Wendy, how is that for a confirmation of your faith?"* Wendy told me that she couldn't believe it. Over the next few weeks, every time I made a joke about her, she would throw in my face, "Um, didn't someone tell you that you needed to be nice to me?" It was killing me!

I should probably back up a few weeks prior to this all happening and give you a little history as to why Wendy felt this way about Peter and me. I asked Wendy if she would like to come to a Wednesday night church service with us, and she did. After service Peter, Wendy, and I went out to get something to eat.

During that time, Peter made a comment to Wendy that her butt was big enough to cross over two state lines. Peter said that to her because she was making fun of him because he had been married three times. People do not think that Wendy is this little defenseless young woman. Oh, she is just as sarcastic as I am, and can make comments that go straight to the bone. All is fair in love and humor I always say.

A few days later, Wendy called me because she had a problem with how she felt about herself. She was talking about how her whole life she was never the pretty one. I was of course multitasking while she was talking to me. I was cutting a purchase order and confirming purchase orders. I also was quickly replying to an email and was working on invoicing issues the whole time she was talking. Sometimes Wendy goes on and on. Now, she is going to kill me for saying this! Anyway, I was half listening to her when she made the following statement. She said, "Give me a break; it's not as if I'm ugly or anything." Please remember that I was half-listening when I said, "Oh Wendy. You're not *that* ugly." There was dead silence. Then I could hear her gasping for air as she began to yell at me. Her voice kept getting higher and higher. I swear dogs were the only ones that could actually hear her at this point. As she continued to yell at me, she said, "Well, I see how it is! I have to go now! Thanks for being my friend!" I said, "Wendy, calm down. I was multitasking and didn't hear everything you said." She hung up on me. Can you believe that? I sent her an email right away apologizing. She ended up forgiving me a few days later. So, now can you see why she prayed the way she did when she told God that she wasn't looking for a miracle? Everything is OK now.

It was Friday as I drove home from work. Are you starting to see a pattern here? I'm just telling you how it is. Apparently, some of my best conversations happen while I'm in the car driving to and from work. Personally, I like it very much, because, in the morning, it takes me forty-five minutes to get to work, and over an hour to get home. So, as I'm driving can you guess what I'm thinking about? If you guessed that I was thinking about the woman of my dreams, then you get 100 points! Points are not redeemable at any time. Ha, ha!

Yes, I was thinking about her, when I heard the Holy Spirit's voice say, *"Jesus told you that you will meet her sooner than you think; be patient. I am here to tell you that she will ask you out, and you are to do nothing but wait."* I rolled my eyes. HS appeared right in front of me, and came very close to my face as He said, *"Just so I am clear on this. You don't think that the Creator of the Universe can provide to you a woman with enough courage to ask you out?"* I said, *"That's not what I meant."* HS said, *"Oh, that is exactly what you meant!"* I said, *"Well, when You put it like that, I sound like an idiot."* HS said, *"Jim, everything will happen in the Lord's time, not yours. He is not slack in keeping His promises to you; be patient. I am also here to tell you that the Lord is considering whether He will allow you to go into the realm that your girls work in; the realm of the unredeemed."*

I cringed inside myself. HS continued, *"Do you recall who those souls are?"* I said, *"Yes, all those who persecuted a Christian."* He said, *"Yes, that is correct. In a few days, your girls will come to you, and let you know what the Lord has decided. I can feel the fear in your heart, Jim. You have no reason to fear anything. The Lord will protect you. Wait and watch."*

Okay before you get mad at me and think I'm being disrespectful when I am referring to the Holy Spirit as HS, I asked Him if that would be all right. He said, *"Because you and I are spending so much time together I do not have a problem with that, I know your heart. If it were anyone else, I would take it as being disrespectful. Okay?"*

On Sunday, as I sat in the bench before service, my girls told me that the Lord had decided to let me go to the realm where they worked; the realm of the unredeemed. My girls were extremely excited. I, on the other hand, was not, and they could tell by the look in my eyes. Amanda said, *"Papa, you don't have any reason to be afraid. Anthony will be there to protect you."* I said, *"I'm not afraid because I feel I will be in any danger. I am a little concerned about what I will see, and if I can handle it, that's all."* Carrie-Ann said, *"Oh, Papa. You will be fine,"* as she put her small hand on my face and patted my cheek.

Almost one week later, on Friday, as I drove home from work, yep, you guessed it, HS appeared to me and said, *"The Lord would like you to go to the realm with your daughters tomorrow. You will have Marty and Amanda give you a healing before you go. In the center of your mind is a treasure chest that the Lord placed there when you had your very first conversation with Michael. Marty will know what to do. I will come to you after your healing and instruct you. I know you are feeling a little uneasy about all of this. Fear nothing, Jim. The Lord is with you."*

Saturday afternoon, I called upon Marty and Amanda to give me a healing. As I sat in the chair, the two of them reassured me that everything would be fine. Halfway through my healing, Michael showed up. I could see him off in the distance. He nodded his head as he had done many times to tell me that he is supporting me. I will be fine. I motioned to him and said thanks. As I received my healing, the two of them picked up on my concern. Marty said, *"Jim, what are you worried about? You are clad in armor. The Lord is with you, and nothing can harm you."* I said, *"I am just a little on edge about what I am going to see that's all."*

As Marty and Amanda got to my sixth chakra, which is my third eye, they paused. I could see Marty, Amanda, and myself standing in the center of my mind where between us was a large wooden chest with a big lock on it.

HS appeared right in front of me, and said, *"Do you see the key Marty is holding in his hand? That is the key that will unlock the chest that is in the center of your mind. Within this chest, is the blessing from the Lord, which has been lying dormant until now. Once this chest is unlocked, the gift of deeper understanding and comprehension will be yours, so that you will understand what you see. Anthony will guide you. Stay behind him, and listen to what your girls tell you. You will observe what you see and share everything with your family and friends. God needs you and your family to pray specifically for this realm. When you get to the entrance of this realm, you will meet some of your ancestors before you go in. Anthony will introduce them to you. Relax, Jim. The Lord is with you."*

Marty held up the key and said, *"Okay, Jim. I am going to unlock the chest; I will only open it up just a little. There is a lot of energy inside the chest. I don't want to overwhelm your body, so we will take this very slow. Take a deep breath, here it comes."* I took a deep breath as I watched Marty crack open the lid of the chest. Immediately, a bright light filled my mind and blinded me in an instant. I screamed in my mind, *"I'm blind! I can't see anything!"* Marty said, *"Take a deep breath, Jim. Calm down. Your eyes will acclimate to the energy. You are just not used to it."* I kept breathing deep and gradually I could see the two of them again. Marty said, *"Okay, I'm going to open up the chest all the way; brace yourself."* He flipped open the lid, and I was blinded, once again. Only this time, I kept inhaling and inhaling. It was so intense I couldn't breathe. I started to panic a little as I heard Marty yelling, *"Breathe, Jim! Breathe! You have to exhale, or you are going to start hyperventilating! Breathe!"*

I could feel the energy filling my mind, and on the top of my head, it was tingling. It was the weirdest feeling. Marty and Amanda kept saying, *"Keep breathing. Take a deep breath. Relax. You can do this. You are fine; we are here with you. You are doing great. Breathe. Breathe."* In an instant, I could see the two of them as clear as day. Then I saw my two girls walking into my bedroom, where I was sitting while all of this was happening. Marty and Amanda finished my healing, and my two girls walked up to me. They both took one of my hands as I stood up. I could feel my spirit leaving my body as I stood up. I looked back and saw my body still sitting in the chair in my bedroom.

Anthony drew his sword and shield and said, *"Stay close to me, and keep moving."* The next thing I knew, the four of us were walking together through several dark tunnels. The tunnels went back and forth, up and down. We walked for a while. The whole time, Amanda and Carrie-Ann tried to reassure me that all would be well. We walked for what seemed like an hour. No matter where I looked it was total darkness. We reached the top of a hill. As I looked down, it was again completely dark. I could barely make out what was in the distance. There was no end to the size of this place. All I heard was screaming and crying and people in pain. I held onto both my daughters' hands and squeezed them hard. Anthony turned to me and said, *"Follow me down this path. When we get to the bottom, I will introduce you to some of your distant family members that work here in this realm."*

When we reached the bottom of the hill, little Shamus ran up to me and said, *"Jim, I am so happy to see you. I work here with Amanda and Carrie-Ann."* I bent down on one knee and gave him a huge hug. He sat on my knee, put his hand on my face, and said, *"Jim, you're going to be all right."* He could tell by the look on my face that I was a little on edge. I said, *"I know, Buddy. This is all kind of new to me; it's great to see you too."*

The five of us walked up to the main entrance of the realm. It looked like a prison block where they had processed everyone before they brought them in. As we walked up, I could see people standing in a line off to the side waiting for us. Anthony said, *"Jim, these are some of your ancestors from the Kondrachik side of your family; you already know*

Tom." I stuck my hand out and shook Tom's hand. You know I don't think I told you about a soul I met in my sister Ann's house. His name is Tom.

Fine I'll tell you the story about Tom. My siblings and I got together at Ann's home one Sunday evening to talk about the things that I had experienced. I got up from the kitchen table because we had been talking for hours. I needed to go to the bathroom.

As I walked into the family room towards the bathroom, something, or should I say someone caught my eye. My older niece, Nicole, was sitting on the couch watching TV, and sitting next to her was a soul. She had no idea he was there. As I stood there, I said, *"Who are you?"* He said, *"My name is Tom. I am your distant uncle on the Kondrachik side of your father's family."* I said, *"I don't mean to be rude, but I need to go to the bathroom really bad. Can you wait a minute and we can talk?"* He said, *"Sure.."*

As I stood in the bathroom, I thought to myself how could he be a distant uncle? He looks so young, around twenty years old. He did resemble my Dad, but usually when a soul passes away they look just as they did when they left this earth. Shouldn't he be older? I walked back into the living room, and Tom was still sitting there. He stood up and walked towards me. I said, *"Can you answer this question for me? If you are my uncle why do you look so young?"* Tom said, *"I died from cholera when I was twenty years old."* I thought to myself, *"Okay that makes sense."* Tom said, *"For months now you have been praying for your ancestors. I was given the privilege to come and thank you on behalf of all your ancestors."* He stuck out his hand, and we shook hands.

All of a sudden Ann walked out of the kitchen into the family room and said, *"Who is that?"* I said, "Ann, meet our distant Uncle Tom, from the Kondrachik side of our family." She smiled and waved at him. As Tom left he turned and smiled at us and said, *"Please don't forget us. You have no idea how much your prayers are helping."* I said, *"I won't. Please tell our family I love them all and will continue to pray for them."* And then he disappeared. Ann turned to me as I explained everything to her. Yes, we truly are a strange family!

Okay, back to the original story! Tom said, *"Jim, it's so great to see you again. Thanks for all of your prayers. They have made a huge difference in many lives."* I said, *"Tom, it's great to see you again too!"* Anthony continued, *"Jim, this is your Aunt Claudia."* I stepped in front of my aunt. She had tears in her eyes, as she grabbed my face with both of her hands, and pulled me towards her. She said, *"It is a privilege for us to be in your family bloodline."* As I cried, I had a smile on my face. I said, *"Auntie, I think you have that backwards; it is a privilege for me to be in your family bloodline."* I hugged her for a few moments.

Anthony continued to introduce my other family members by name, *"These are your cousins Rose and Maggie. This is your cousin Steven and Aunt Beth."* One by one we shook hands and hugged each other with tears in all of our eyes. Never would I have ever thought that I would have the honor to meet some of my distant family in eternity. I just can't find the words to express it!

Anthony spoke up and said, *"Jim, we must keep moving. Stay close, and follow me."* I waved goodbye to my family and grabbed my girls' hands. We walked through the gate into the realm of the unredeemed. It was dark. I could hear wailing, crying, and screaming as we walked past the different realms. Each opening we walked past had steel bars in front of it. Inside, I could see different souls.

The first realm we came to, I stopped and peered in. There were men chained across large stones. Next to each one of them, was a spirit holding a whip that looked like a scourge. One of the spirits noticed I was standing there. It turned to me and said, *"Supplanter. You have no authority here!"* With a devilish grin on his face, he pulled back the arm holding the whip and hit one of the men chained on the rock. I could see the man's flesh being ripped away from him with each lash from the whip. The man cried out in agony. Over, and over again, this spirit whipped every soul in that realm. I stood there horrified as I watched the flesh being torn off all of these men. I could feel their pain.

I fell to my knees crying and looked at my girls. Amanda said, *"Papa, these are the Roman guards that beat Jesus. You need to pray for them."* I said, *"Why don't they just ask for forgiveness and leave this place?"* Amanda said, *"They are just too stubborn to admit that what they did was wrong. Pray that they stop being so stubborn. That is why the Lord has asked you to come here. He needs you to understand these souls so you can pray for all of them."* I said, *"How can you come here every day and see this?"* Carrie-Ann put her small hand on my face and said, *"Papa, we are not as we appear to you. We are not little girls. Your mind could not comprehend what we really look like. We appear to you this way so that you know it is us you're speaking with."* Anthony said, *"Jim, keep moving."*

We kept walking. We walked past realms where I watched souls being boiled in oil. Some were tied to tables and tortured. Others were dismembered. The screaming was almost too much for me to handle. Once outside of the cell holding areas, I turned to my right as we came to a large field. I stood there in agony as I watched as far as my eyes could see souls being drawn and quartered. Spirits would take these souls and place them on the ground. Then they would take a large wooden stake and drive it through the center of the souls' bodies. They would then tie a horse to each one of their limbs and smack the horses on their rear ends. Each horse would run in a different direction. I screamed out loud as I watched these souls' limbs being torn from their bodies. The minute the soul lay there lifeless it was as if someone would rewind a movie. It would happen over and over again. It was like this in every realm. Anthony put his hand on my shoulder and said, *"Jim, please keep moving."*

We continued to walk. This time, I turned to my left. As far as my eyes could see, I saw hundreds of thousands of souls being crucified. Some were tied to the cross, and others were nailed just like Jesus was. I looked up at one of the souls hanging on a cross. He cried and softly said, *"Please. Pray for me…"* I could barely hear him. I said, with tears in my eyes, *"I give you my word that I will pray for you and not forget you."* We kept walking.

We came to a large area that looked like the Coliseum in Rome. I stood and watched as souls were thrown into the center of the arena. In a short moment, the gates flew up, and animals came running out and tore these souls to pieces. The moment there was no sign of life; everything would rewind, and it would happen over and over again. I fell to my knees crying, as I pulled my daughters close to me.

Amanda said, *"Papa. What you have been seeing is actually worse than what your mind could ever comprehend. The Lord opened your understanding so that you can go back and share this with our family. It is very important that you tell everyone what you have seen so that you can all pray very hard for all of these souls. I know how hard this has been for you, Papa. I don't think you completely understand what affect you had on this realm. As you walked through, there was a light that shone from you and lit up every realm. Everyone knows who you are. You gave all of these souls hope."* Anthony spoke up and said, *"Come. Jim, we have to keep moving."*

I held my girls for a minute, and both of them wiped my tears away. As I stood up, I took both of their hands, and we kept walking. A few seconds later, we found ourselves walking again through tunnels, back and forth and up and down, until we came to the top of a cavern. As we walked into this cavern, there was such a bright light coming from it. We all stood on the edge of the cliff that overlooked this area. As I stood there with my mouth open, I surveyed the entire place. It was very bright, but there was no sun, just light. There were beautiful waterfalls, trees, bushes, and flowers everywhere. It had green meadows, and it smelled incredible, just like a warm spring day. It was just so tranquil and peaceful. I turned to Anthony and said, *"Where are we?"* Anthony said, *"We are in the realm of Paradise."* I couldn't believe what I was hearing or seeing. Anthony said, *"Come! Hurry! Follow me down to the bottom; everyone is waiting for you."*

We ran down the pathway to the bottom of the hill. As I walked up a small hill, and reached the top, I stopped to see hundreds and thousands of people standing off in the distance. My dad's sister, my aunt Stephanie, came running up to me and gave me a huge hug. As I walked down the hill, my mom's parents greeted me. Grandma Mueller pulled me towards her and said, *"Jimmy, we are so proud of you."* My dad's parents ran up to me, and both of them gave me great big hugs. My little niece Emily, Peter's daughter, hugged me, and asked me to tell her dad that she said hi. All of my Kondrachik ancestors were there too. Even though I had never met some of these people when they were alive, I just knew in my heart that we were related. I saw all of my Mom's siblings that were killed in World War II.

There was such excitement. I kept hugging people. All of us were crying. I looked around and noticed that some of my former priests, whom I had served with and who had passed away, were there too: Priest Teichman and his wife Donna, along with Priest Guderian. We waved to each other.

All of a sudden, everyone started to quiet down. It got very quiet. One by one, everyone started to kneel down and stopped talking. I could see an image off in the distance, walking on the path to where all of us were standing; it was Jesus! As I knelt down, Amanda leaned into me and said, *"Papa, He hasn't been here since He brought the malefactor on the cross. And this is the malefactor."* A very skinny man stuck out his hand and said, *"It's nice to meet you."* I shook his hand and said, *"It's nice to meet you too."* All of us knelt down on one knee with our heads bowed.

Jesus walked up and stood in front of me. He put His hand on my shoulder and said, *"Jim, please stand."* I stood up and looked up at the Lord Jesus as He put both of His hands on my shoulders. He said, *"I hope you can now understand the love My Father has for you. No human alive on this earth has ever been allowed to see the Realm of Paradise. Now, while you are here I think it is only fitting for you to meet a few people."*

Jesus took me by the arm and led me over to the side where a number of people were standing. He said, *"This is David."* I thought to myself, *"No way! King David?"* Out stepped this little five-foot-tall man who stuck out his hand. As he smiled at me, he said, *"Supplanter. You have quite a reputation. It's a pleasure to meet you."* As I shook his hand, I was smiling too. I said, "*Little man, you have an enormous reputation. The pleasure is all mine."*

Jesus said, *"And this is Moses."* Out stepped an old man with white hair and a beard. No, he doesn't look like Charlton Heston. As he extended his hand to me, I shook it. He then pulled me toward himself and in a very quiet voice said, *"You've got the wrong guy!"* I immediately broke out laughing. Moses was laughing; Jesus was laughing, and everyone around us was laughing. I was crying, and laughing so hard at the same time. Now, perhaps you're asking yourself why that statement was very funny. Folks, Moses argued with God, just like I argued with Michael, telling Him, *"You've got the wrong guy for this job!"* That's why that was humorous. Moses said, *"It's nice to meet you, Jim."* I said, *"It's nice to meet you too."* I have to tell you that, for the past twenty years, I have always wanted to meet David and Moses. Sometimes when I would pray, I would ask God that when I get to Heaven, and we are at the Marriage Feast if possible, I would like to sit by these two great men of God and have a chat. For me, this was a dream come true.

Jesus took me by the arm and brought me in front of a group of men. He said, *"And this is Abraham. This is Isaac, and this is Jacob."* One by one, each one of these great patriarchs of old extended their hand to me. We shook and told each other how much of a pleasure it was to meet. It was all so humbling for me to meet these amazing men who had such a tremendous faith in God. Jesus took me by the arm and said, *"And this is Potiphar's wife."* You're asking yourself why He introduced me to her. That week, I had been reading all about Joseph, and how Potiphar's wife lied and Joseph was put in prison.

I had thought and wondered, while I was reading, what she looked like. I can tell you this much; she was incredibly beautiful. As I shook her hand, she looked me in the eye and then looked down at the ground. She said nothing to me, but just smiled. I thought to myself that even after millenniums have passed, she still felt guilty about what she had done to Joseph. But she must have found grace or she wouldn't have been in the Realm of Paradise.

Then, Jesus said, *"And this is Joseph."* We shook hands and exchanged greetings. Jesus turned me around, stood behind me and with

His hands on my shoulders said, *"And you already know all seven of the chief apostles who have served me faithfully."* The crowd parted, and there all seven chief apostles stood. Each one held up his hand and waved to me. Jesus then turned me around so that I was facing Him and said, *"Please kneel. I have a blessing for you."*

As I knelt down in front of Him, He put His hands on my head and said, *"I now activate all the gifts from My Father. You will now be able to see into the future and understand the task at hand. He grants you wisdom beyond any human being. I remove from you all of your infirmities and grant you a deeper understanding of the Mysteries of Heaven. I restore to you tenfold riches here on Earth and more in Heaven. I reserve a place for you in My Kingdom. Satan will now fear you, because of the power you hold in your hand from My Father. You are now the second in command of My Father's Army. Michael and you will destroy Satan's forces on that appointed day. This terrible period of time will come to an end, and the Kingdom My Father has always-wanted will be established. You have no reason to fear anything. Spirits will be destroyed by you. I grant you peace from My heart."*

I felt Jesus take His hands off my head. As I looked up at Him, He pulled out a sword. He then said, *"I knight you, sir Supplanter. I give you all of this on your new birthday."* Then He took His sword and tapped me on each shoulder with it. He then said, *"Please stand."*

As I stood up, I was crying. Jesus once again placed His hands on my shoulders and said, *"Jim, I need you to do three things for Me. I need you to be kind to everyone, be less sarcastic, and be more positive."* I broke down crying even more. He gave me a big hug and whispered in my ear, *"I am always with you."* I stood there and watched as He walked back up the path to where He came from. Part of the way up, He paused and turned back to me and said, *"One more thing, please finish the book. My Father is waiting."* I smiled and said, *"I will."*

As Jesus left, everyone sprang to their feet and surrounded me. We were all crying and hugging. They all started chanting my name, *"Supplanter, Supplanter."* I put my hand up and stopped all of them. I told them not to do that, that I am no one special and don't deserve that. Anthony reached in through the crowd and grabbed my shoulder and said, *"We have to leave."* I said, *"I don't want to leave."* Anthony said, *"That is why we have to leave, now. Come!"* I said all of my goodbyes very fast. As we reached the top of the hill, we stood there waving to everyone.

I knelt down and asked Carrie-Ann how it would work for us to get home. She said, *"Concentrate on your bedroom."* So I did. The next thing

I knew, I saw my body sitting right where I left it. My girls helped me sit back down in my body. We all hugged each other and said our goodbyes.

On Sunday, my brother and I went over to our parents' home. I shared with all of them what had happened. My dad sat very quietly the whole time. He said nothing till I finished. Then my mom asked him what he thought. He took a deep breath and said, "Well, Hilda, I guess we now know what Mary and Joseph felt like. Son, I am not in any way comparing you to the Son of God. I am merely pointing out that Mary and Joseph knew that their son was part of God's plan. They didn't always understand what He told them. I may not always understand everything you tell me, Jim, but I now can see that you will play a big role in God's plan, too. The only thing that I can do for you is to pray even harder." I sat in awe of what my father had said. He got up and left. My mom came over and gave me a hug as I cried. She said, "Wow. I would have never thought that would have come out of your dad's mouth, but I think he believes you now."

On Monday, I spoke with Torry, Giselle, and Wendy. I had coffee with Torry and Giselle that week, separately, at a restaurant. Giselle and I spoke in her office. All three of them asked me why I was telling them all of this. I told them I had no idea. Maybe they should ask God and see what He said. One thing was for sure; they all told me that their faith in God was a lot stronger after I shared this with them. They told me that they would pray for me. I told them that I prayed for all of them by name every day.

On Tuesday, I called Ellen and shared everything with her. The following Sunday, I went to Ann's house and sat down with her whole family and shared everything with them. While we were talking, Satan showed up outside of her window. He stood off in the distance from where we were sitting.

I paid him no attention as he made comments threatening me. I motioned over to Anthony and asked him to escort Satan off the property. Anthony and Jonathan drew their swords and asked him to leave. Satan didn't leave quietly. He verbalized how quickly my end was at hand. I thought to myself, *"Whatever."* As the evening went on, and it was getting late, I said goodbye to my family and left. As I walked out the front door to my car, I could see Satan standing on the corner. I got in my car and drove down the street. Suddenly Satan turned into a huge red fire breathing dragon. As I turned the corner where he was standing, I looked up at him and said out loud, "Oh grow-up!" and just kept driving. Yep, never a dull moment in my life, right folks?

Chapter 18
Won Battle!

Okay, so maybe you'll remember that while I was in the Realm of Paradise, Jesus gave me a blessing. He had made the comment that He removed from me my infirmities. After about two weeks from when this had happened, I asked myself what Jesus had meant by that statement. The Holy Spirit showed up out of the blue while I was driving to work and said, "Why don't you look up the definition and see what it means." And then He was gone. When I was at work, I pulled up the definition from Dictionary.com.

Infirmity

1. **A physical weakness or ailment: the infirmities of age.**
2. **Quality or state of being infirm, lack of strength.**
3. **A moral weakness or failing.**

As I sat and read this, I thought to myself, *"No way. I'm not sick anymore? I don't need any of the medications I'm on? I'm not diabetic? I don't have circulation problems, thyroid problems, high-blood pressure, cholesterol problems, and allergies?"* Yes, folks, I'm a mess! I blame my family. Lousy genes! Suddenly HS appeared in front of me. He said, *"Yes, this is true. Slowly start taking yourself off of the medications you are on. It will take some time for your body to acclimate, but in time, you will be healthy again. You will find that you will not get sick that often anymore. He has also removed from you your shortcomings, as well. Stay the course, and be strong, Jim. In time, all will be revealed to you."* I couldn't believe my ears. The very next day, I started taking half the doses of medicine that I would normally take. I monitored my blood sugar very closely. Of course, working out every day has its benefits too.

On October 5, 2007, as I was driving home from work, HS appeared and said, *"You will meet the woman of your dreams within the next two weeks."* I said, *"Wait a minute! Jesus said sometime before March of next year."* HS said nothing and just disappeared. Now here's the ironic part of this experience. My ex-wife's birthday was today. Okay then. I'm going to meet the woman of my dreams within the next two weeks.

As I neared the end of the two weeks, I didn't give it a second thought.

Yeah, right. Of course, I was thinking about the woman of my dreams! On Monday, October 15, yes, please do the math, there were only four days left till the two-week deadline. A sales rep named Brad, whom I had bought supplies from for the hospital, struck up a conversation with me about dating. Brad told me some of his dating stories, and ended the conversation by saying that he met his wife at a health club. I, of course, shared my dating horror stories with him too. Most of the time, Brad was laughing, but apologized every time. I couldn't blame him. Sometimes I am an idiot. As I finished telling him my latest dating story, he asked if I would be willing to meet a friend of his wife's. Folks, once again if this were a movie you could see me staring right at you. I asked my standard question: what did she look like? He said, "She's cute."

I said, "Brad, you would be surprised how often I hear that, and well that's just not the case. I don't mean to be rude, but please don't tell me she has a big heart and sweet personality." Brad laughed and said, "She's very slender, Jim. She's a runner." I said, "Sweet, continue." He said she was forty-one years old and had never been married. "She works with my wife, Sheila. They have been friends for years." I said, "Please forgive me for asking, but I am going to have to see a picture, with a time and date stamped on it. Okay, maybe just a current picture then?" Brad said, "Let me check with Sheila, and see if her friend Lena is interested in meeting you." I'll be honest with you people; I wasn't going to hold my breath.

The next day, to my surprise, Brad called to tell me that Lena wanted to meet me. I said, "Do you have a picture?" Brad said, "Sheila said we were going to have to do this the old-fashioned way. You will just have to meet her in person, first." I said, "Brad? Did you share my dating stories with Sheila? Did you tell her how traumatized I am about dating?" He said, "Yep, she doesn't care about the past. We thought that maybe the four of us could meet this Thursday, after work, around 5:00 PM at a martini bar. And we'll just see what happens. This way you won't be so uncomfortable, okay?" I said, "Okay, but you know if this works out I can't ask her out, right?" Brad said, "Yes, I understand. Let's just see what happens."

I sent an email to my dating consultants to see what they had to say. Who are they again, you ask? I had five consultants now: Torry, Giselle, Wendy, Jewel, and my sister Ann. All of them knew I was to meet the woman of my dreams within the two-week period. I think they were more excited than I was. No, they weren't. I told them what the plans were. The next thing I knew, they were all planning what outfit I was to wear. I pointed out the fact that guys do not wear outfits. They didn't care. They asked me what I was planning on wearing. I told them, and they shot me down. The next thing I knew, the girls were conspiring behind my back telling Jewel that she had to take me shopping. I said, "No way!" Well, you guessed it; we made plans to go shopping on Thursday. I am so whipped.

It was Wednesday evening. While I was sitting in the service, before the choir started to sing, clairvoyantly I surveyed the congregation. I noticed that my girls were sitting with a man who was dressed in rags who were also wearing chains. Clairvoyantly, I stood up and walked over to them. As I did, this man stood up. I immediately recognized him. It was the guy who was hanging on the cross who asked me to pray for him. As I stuck out my hand to greet him, this man threw himself around my waist and gave me a big hug. He held onto me for a minute, and then let go. With tears in his eyes, he said, *"My name is Joshua. Thank you for remembering me."* With tears in my eyes, I said, *"Welcome to grace, my friend."* We shook hands again and hugged one more time before I went back to my seat. There were a few others from the realm of the unredeemed. All were dressed in rags and were wearing chains. It was a wonderful service. As they left I waved to all of them, and promised them that we would all continue to pray for them.

It was my personal D-day; Thursday, October 18, 2007, the day for my date with Lena. I sent an email to Brad asking him to at least describe Lena to me. I told him we could keep it between ourselves so that he wouldn't get in trouble with his wife. He responded back with, Lena is very slender. She has long black shoulder-length hair and brown eyes. She's about five foot six inches in height, and she loves animals. I thanked him for taking such a great risk in divulging this information to me, and I promised him that I would take it to my grave.

All morning long, my consultants kept calling and emailing me. Wendy called me and told me to take a picture of Lena so she could see what she looked like. Then she said, "No, wait. That would be kind of creepy." I said, "You're right that would be creepy for me to ask Lena if I could take a picture of her. I can tell her it is because I keep a scrapbook with all of the pictures of the woman I date. I could continue by asking her if she wouldn't mind giving me a lock of her hair, so at night when I go to sleep I can rub it against my face so I can fall asleep thinking of her." Yep, I won. No pictures of Lena would be taken. Wendy thought that was incredibly creepy.

At lunchtime, Jewel and I ran to the store. All the women told me to buy a pair of jeans. Folks, I hate jeans. All my life I was always fat. Jeans always presented a problem to me with all of the rubbing, pinching, and binding in places. I never liked wearing them. Jewel pointed out the fact that I wasn't fat anymore and that I should be OK. So, just to be safe, we went to a store that I knew never had my size for pants. Wouldn't you know it, Jewel found two pairs of jeans that were my size. Aw crap! I reluctantly went to the dressing room, pouting like an eight-year-old kid. I put them on, and the shirt that I picked out for myself, and presented myself to Jewel. She checked me out and then exclaimed, "You look great! I think we found your dating outfit!" I said, "Well, these jeans really aren't that bad. They aren't even pinching or binding. One more thing that I need to remind you of; dudes don't wear outfits!" She just laughed. Then I told her how it was all part of my fiendish plan to bring her here knowing they never had my size. She didn't think that was very funny.

When we got back to the office, everyone had to hear about my "outfit." I managed to finish my work, and then drove over to the martini bar. I was a little nervous about wearing the long-sleeved shirt that my consultants had talked me into wearing. My fear was that I would start sweating like a cow, since I get hot very easily. I was hoping that the bar would have the air-conditioner on high because it was seventy-eight degrees outside. But I had listened to my consultants; I've already told you that I was very whipped, right?

I got there early and got us all a table. Brad showed up, and we spoke for a while. I didn't really know Brad that well. We just did a little business together. We never actually talked on a personal level. After talking with him for a while, I found him to be a genuinely funny guy. Sheila arrived and informed me that Lena was running a little late. Ladies, guys know you want to show up to a date late to leave us wanting and expecting you.

Yep, we know that. I was okay with Lena being late. It gave me a chance to talk to Brad and Sheila for a few minutes. I found Sheila to be very funny also, and very beautiful. Next thing I knew, in walked Lena. I stood up and shook her hand; she looked just like Brad had described her. We talked to one another, laughing our butts off, and had a good time. I started off our conversation by telling Sheila that I thought Brad's eyes were just dreamy. I continued to say that every time he came into the office to talk to me; I would just lose myself in the conversation because of his dreamy eyes. Sheila, of course, knew I was just joking. Brad, on the other hand, said that I was making him feel very uncomfortable, and then started to laugh. I found out a lot about Lena and her life. She was a very quiet person, so I was glad the other two were there.

We had something to drink and eat. Two hours later the two ladies got up from the table to go powder their noses. Brad and I decided to compare notes. He asked me what I thought of Lena. I told him that she was nice and that if she wanted to go out again, I wouldn't mind. The only thing is, she would have to ask me out. Brad told me that she was probably just too shy, and that wouldn't happen. I told him then it just wasn't meant to be. I couldn't break my promise to God about not asking a woman out. He told me just to ask her out. I said, "No way! I have broken so many promises to God. There is no way I was going to break this one. Besides, the next thing you know, I'm walking down the hallway in the hospital, going to my office, and my heart decides to explode out of my chest, spewing it against the walls. Now, how would I explain that?" He just laughed and said, "Let's just see what she says."

The ladies came back to the table, so I excused myself so I could go "powder my nose". This was all part of my plan to see if the three of them would talk about me while I was gone. When I came back to the table, the check was there, and Brad already had paid. I told him there was no way I was going to let him pay for the whole thing. I told him that I would then feel obligated to buy a hundred cases of hand sanitizer from him. He laughed and told me that wouldn't be necessary. I relented, and let him pay. I, of course, thanked him. We then said our goodbyes. I asked Brad if Lena said anything about me. He told me he had no feedback as of yet, but he would call me in the morning. I said, "You have got to be kidding me?"

As I drove home, I relived the evening. There was something about Lena that made me feel as if I knew her. I just couldn't put my finger on it. I was disappointed in my heart and confused. There was no magic. No excitement when I met her. I felt nothing for this woman. What the heck! I called my sister Ann and shared the evening. She told me that maybe our love for each other would grow very slowly. I was just to wait and see what happened, but to not write Lena out of the picture. I was to do nothing and just let it happen, if it was right. I didn't know what to say, except that I was a little confused about this whole thing.

The next day, all the women wanted to hear about my date. Not just the consultants, but also the five women I worked with in my department. I told everyone how I felt. I made a comment about how she looked her age. I could feel the flesh melting off my face.

But, hey, understand my point. All the women were more disappointed than I was. It was just so weird.

On Saturday, I decided to meditate to put this situation behind me. As

I began to meditate, Michael appeared in front of me. I said, *"Can you explain to me how this woman can be the woman of my dreams? I'm not even attracted to her. She's nothing like the woman I've been looking at, for the past few years."* Michael said, *"The Lord will present you with many options and you will have to choose."*

I said, *"Options? I will have to choose? I don't want to pick her. I had asked God to pick her for me. This sounds as if He's playing games with me."* Michael stepped closer to me and said, *"The Lord does not play games, Jim. In time, you will understand. All of these women still have their own free will. The Lord will not interfere with that."* I said, *"I am beyond confused here. First, I'm told I'll meet the woman of my dreams next year around July. Then, I'm told sooner than I think; sometime before March of next year. I don't even know what to believe or think anymore. How am I supposed to function like this?"* Michael said, *"You must search your heart and trust in the Lord. He has your best interests in mind. He is not playing a game with you, but He is testing you. You will always be tested, Jim. Stay strong, and keep the task at hand in the forefront of your life. All else will be added to you. Always remember that He is with you."* As Michael left, I continued to meditate. I tried to wrap my head around all of this. I'll be honest with you; I didn't know what to think.

The next day was Sunday. After the service, my family got together for lunch. As I was sitting across from my mom talking with her, it suddenly hit me why Lena seemed so familiar to me: she had eyes like my mother's! Well that kind of freaked me out a little. I now knew that for sure, I could never date Lena.

As the weeks went by, every day I would pray for the realm of the unredeemed. I would remember Joshua and Lannie's friend Tyler by name. I would pray for all of the groups, and individuals that I had been praying for over the past four years. Sometimes, I would even break down and cry, as I remembered how I felt as I walked through the different realms. I would remember how I had experienced their pain firsthand. I could feel their agony and I would plead on their behalf that the Lord would be kind to them and help them move to a better place.

One evening after work, my nephew James said to me so nonchalantly, "Uncle Jim. Can I talk to you for a minute?" I said, "Sure buddy, what's up?" James said, "I was walking past your bedroom this afternoon, and I saw that there was a guy sitting in your chair." I said, "A live person, or a soul?" James said, "No, I think he was a soul." I said, "Were you scared of him?" James said, "No. He was just hanging out in your chair." I asked,

"How was he dressed?" James said, "He was wearing clothes that were ripped. Do you know this guy, Uncle Jim?" I said, "I think he's from the realm of the unredeemed. His name is Thumyus. Don't ask me how I know that, I just do. Well at least that's the impression I'm getting. We both need to pray for Thumyus, ok, buddy?" James said, "Okay Uncle Jim, I will." Every day I prayed for Thumyus too.

Now, I would like to pause for a moment from the storyline. I wanted to point out a great achievement that my nephew James and my niece Sydney have accomplished. They both received an A+ in physical education. Now, no one has ever in the history of our family ever gotten an A+. So, you can now see why I am praising them. Nice job kids!

Okay, back to the story. As I drove home from work in the afternoon on November 2, I heard a voice say, *"Glad tidings of great Joy I bring you from the Lord God. Rejoice in the Lord, Supplanter, for it is my good pleasure to bring you news for the task at hand."* As I was listening, I was trying to figure out who this was that was talking to me. His voice was so upbeat and friendly. He didn't sound like anyone I had ever spoken to in the past. Clairvoyantly, I leaned forward so that I could see who it was. I could barely make out a figure. I spoke up and interrupted him when I said, *"Please, forgive me for interrupting you, but who is speaking to me?"* The voice said, *"I am the Archangel Gabriel. I am God's messenger, and it is my good fortune to bring you the glad tidings of the Lord God. In the past, you have received your information from Michael. From this day forward, you shall also receive your information from me too. The Lord knows that you have been struggling with many things. He has asked me to come and share some of His plan with you."*

As Gabriel spoke, I tried to get a better look at him, but he was just out of my sight. Gabriel spoke up and said, *"Jim, you are trying to get a better look at me, are you not? I am sure you would like to describe me to your friends and family. Take a deep breath, and I will step towards you."* I did as he asked. I could see him step closer to me until he was about four feet away from me. Gabriel said, *"Is that better? Can you see me now?"* I said, *"Yes. I can see you now."* He looked exactly like all of the pictures that I have seen. You have also seen how he looks; you just had no idea at the time that you were looking at him. Gabriel looked just like the pictures depicting what Jesus looked like. He had long brown hair pulled back behind his ears, light brown eyes, a neatly trimmed beard and mustache. He was dressed in a large white coat with a gold breastplate over it. He had a sword and shield just like all of the other angels that I have seen; except on the belt that he wore around his waist, he had a number of scrolls hanging off of it. He wore the same beige pants tucked into a pair of boots.

Gabriel said, *"Now that you know what I look like, you can share all of this with your family and friends. I would like to share with you some information pertaining to the woman of your dreams. But first, the Lord would like you to stop referring to yourself as the dateless wonder. He knows you say these things in jest, but you already know He has already picked someone special for you. She is unlike any woman you will ever meet. She will have an exceptionally strong faith just like yours Jim. In the future, when your book comes out, you will be persecuted. It will not be only by others, but also by the leaders in your church. She will stand by your side and defend you. You will not tell any of the leaders in your church that you are writing this book. They will not understand. You will not approach any of them. Your apostle will come and seek you out with a problem, and you will help him. The love that you and her share will not be like any love two people has ever shared. When others look at the two of you, they will marvel over the love the two of you have. They will know this simply by watching the two of you interact with each other. In time, you will have two sons. They will do even greater works than you and your wife will do. This is the Lord God's gift to you. But Jim, you must be patient."* I began to cry as I listened to him speak.

Gabriel continued, *"You must understand, Jim, that this woman will have her own free will to. The Lord is testing her and strengthening her as we speak. She has to be an unusually strong person to be with you. You are not like most men. She will be unlike anyone you have ever met. She will ask you out. You will also know her because she will work with you. The Lord will grant her a dream about you. All of this will come to pass. You must not date anyone during this time. If you are in a relationship with another woman, then how will you be able to date her? The Lord knows you are lonely, but you must be patient. The Lord would like me also to remind you to not provoke Satan. He is terribly angry, and will stop at nothing to destroy you. If some spirit is foolish enough to step near you, then you have permission to destroy it. The Lord has given six angels to protect you. You have been well trained by Michael and fully understand how to use the weapons that you currently hold. You also currently hold in your hand the Staff of God. It is not your place to run around destroying what you would like. There will be times when you will need just to stand your ground and listen to what Anthony tells you. You must also realize by now, that your sister Ann and your brother Peter play an extremely significant role in all of this too. Please stop making fun of your brother. Even in jest, you hurt him deeper than you know. He looks up to you, Jim, and respects you completely. Be kind to him also. Your brother's role will be just like Aaron's role was for his brother Moses. He will not speak on your behalf, but he will stand up for you and defend you in times when it is needed. Your sister believes that all of the information she receives is from God; it is not always from God. In some cases, it is Satan trying to mislead you and her. Be wise when you hear her counsel, and discern for yourself where this information is coming from. Ann's role will be to confirm for you things that only you know to be true. She will have visions and dreams, just as she has in the past. She will also stand up for you in certain times as well. I know how hard it is for you to stand by and watch as you see the demons that are in your family's spaces. You will not interfere. The Lord is testing them to. If they attack, you have permission to destroy them. Be strong, Supplanter. For the Lord God is with you. He will defend and protect you from all evil. In time, He will reveal more to you. Sunday is a very special service. Many from the Realm of the Unredeemed will be there. Keep your eyes open, and sharp. Pay particularly close attention to what takes place. I do not believe that you will truly understand the power of your prayers, and that of your family's prayers, on this realm until you witness it on Sunday. I will see you again, very soon. We will talk again. Till then, receive the blessing of the Lord God, and peace from His Son Jesus."* And then he bowed in front of me and left. Yes, I know that was a lot to digest; can you guess how I felt?

Sunday was here. What a joyous occasion. Clairvoyantly, I looked around the congregation. I could see a lot of my family, and ancestors there. But, what surprised me the most was seeing my Kondrachik family sitting with souls from the Realm of the Unredeemed. There were thousands of them surrounding the church building; inside and out, hundreds of thousands of souls from all walks of life. As I stood up to sing the opening hymn, all of a sudden, I felt an overwhelming joy fill my heart. Within seconds, I felt an indescribable amount of sadness. I had never felt this kind of emotion before in this way. I realized that I felt what all of these souls felt. I had to stop singing as tears rolled down my face. I closed my eyes, trying to contain the emotions I felt, but I couldn't stop crying. I finally figured out why I was felt these emotions.

All of these souls were overjoyed, because they were allowed to leave their realms and come to the service. But the reality was that once the service ended they would have to go back to their realms. It was a bittersweet experience for all of us. From that day forward, I promised myself that I would pray even harder for them. I pulled myself together by the time the opening prayer was finished. As I sat down, I waved to Joshua and Thumyus. As I looked around, I saw many children filling the aisles of the church; all of the side aisles and even the center aisle, too. As I looked to my right, I saw a little girl about five years of age. She stepped towards me and said, *"My name is Clara; can I sit with you?"* I said, *"Sure honey. You can sit on my lap."* She sat on my left leg; Carrie-Ann was sitting on my right leg, and Amanda my oldest was sitting next to me on my left side. Clara looked up at me with her big blue eyes and said, *"My mom aborted me, but I have forgiven her. That's why I'm here, please remember me."* I held her head close to my chest and said, *"Honey, I will."*

    As the service continued, I closed my eyes to get a better look at how many souls were actually attending our service. Clairvoyantly, it was as if I was seeing everyone from a bird's eye view; as if it was a satellite taking a picture of the church building. I looked down from the sky. I could see for miles all around the church: souls, listening intently. As I pulled up towards the sky, even farther away from the church, I could see our other congregation that was fifteen miles away from us. I could see all of the souls that were listening to that service. As I pulled up farther, past the clouds, I was given a satellite view of the United States. From where I was looking, I could see a bright little light representing every soul that was listening to our services across the United States. I began to cry as I realized there was no way I could count the millions of lights that I saw.

    As the service was coming to an end, we celebrated Holy Communion. I physically walked back to my seat and sat down. Clairvoyantly, I noticed a Roman Centurion Guard dressed in his full uniform walking towards me. He stopped in front of me and stuck out his hand and said, *"My name is Barabus. I am one of the souls from the realm you have been praying for."* I stuck out my hand and grasped his forearm as he grasped mine. We greeted each other as they did in his time. With tears in his eyes, he bowed his head and said, *"You don't know me, but I know you, Supplanter. Would you please pray for me by name? I have done many horrible things, and I am seeking grace."* I said, *"Barabus, it would be my pleasure to remember you by name."* I bowed my head to him, and he took his place.

    I also noticed that my Uncle Bill was there too. He is not actually my blood uncle. His son Ken and I were best friends in my childhood, until I was about sixteen years old. They used to live next door to us. One year, they moved away to Mentor, Ohio. Uncle Bill's job transferred him there.

Every summer, my dad would pack all six of us in the car, and we would spend two weeks at Uncle Bill's house. They had a huge in-ground pool. Uncle Bill had come to me months earlier and asked my family and me to pray for him; which we were all doing. He told me with a big smile on his face that he was going to be baptized today. I was overjoyed.

I saw my Uncle George, who was sitting with my Aunt Stephanie. If you remember, my Aunt Stephanie was the first person to hug me when I walked into the Realm of Paradise. Uncle George smiled at me and told me that he was going to be sealed today. I once again was overjoyed. At the end of the service, the priest prayed that the Lord would guide the souls with angel's protection to the apostle's altar so that they could receive the sacraments. As he prayed, a bright light shone out from the altar, and a doorway was opened. One by one, those souls who were ready to receive the sacraments walked toward this doorway and disappeared. The other souls, who were not ready, turned and walked the other way. I continued to watch as these souls left my presence. I noticed two other Roman Centurion guards dressed in full armor. They introduced themselves to me. One told me his name was Antious, and his friend's name was Dracous. They also asked me to remember them too.

Once the service ended, and all of the souls had left, I noticed that my sister Ann was comforting my nephew Scott; he was crying. I walked over to them. Ann told me that, during the service, Scott had noticed that there were hundreds of small children everywhere. As our relatives were leaving, one by one, they leaned in and kissed my dad on his cheek. Scott had never witnessed anything like this before in his life. I smiled at him and said, "Welcome to the family of freaks! The force runs strong in our family." Scott just smiled at me. Ann said, "I noticed that during the service that you had a little girl on your lap. Who is she?" I shared with Ann everything Clara told me. Then Ann said, "Did you see the two Roman guards?" I said, "Yes." She said, "Can you explain to me what they were doing as they left you?" I said, "What are you talking about?" She said, "Before they walked away from you, they bowed their heads, made a fist with their right hand, and then held their arms diagonal across their chests until their hand was resting just below their left shoulder. Then they dropped their arms and walked away from you. What does that mean?" I said, "They were saluting a superior officer. They must know that I am the second in command of God's army, and out of respect for my commission, they were paying me their respects." For me, that was a very humbling experience.

The next day, I got an email from Karen, a friend of my sister Ellen.

She goes to the same church we go to. In her email, she told me that she has been having problems with getting her girls to sleep in the bedroom of the new apartment they had just moved into. She told me that her girls refused to sleep in the room because they would always have nightmares.

When she would put her newborn in that room, he wouldn't sleep at all either. She explained to me that the kids were always with her and her husband in their bed, and they couldn't get any sleep. They prayed all the time, but nothing seemed to be helping. She asked me if I would be willing to come to dinner one night and see if I could determine if there were a spirit behind all of this. I told her that Tuesday would work for me. She responded back telling me that would be fine.

When I got to work, the next morning, Karen had left me a voice mail telling me that they had to reschedule dinner because something came up. I sent her an email telling her to let me know when a better time would work for her. As I drove home, I thought about all of this. I got the impression that it was a demon, and this demon was attached to some children's book tucked away deep in the closet of this room. Marty showed up, and we began to discuss all of this. He told me that my impression was correct. I thought, *well maybe I can grab the book and bring it back to my sister's house and burn it.* The only problem with that plan was that this demon would then come into my sister's house. Marty agreed. He told me that I should wait for HS to talk to me about this situation.

Two seconds later, HS appeared in front of me and said, *"The Lord has given you permission to dispatch this demon. You cannot physically go to the apartment, because the minute you step into their place, this demon will leave. Clairvoyantly you will have just to show up and dispatch him. On Saturday, you will meditate. Anthony will lead you to this room; you will project yourself there. When you arrive, you will not hesitate or speak with this demon, you will act quickly and destroy him. Do you understand?"* I spoke up and said, *"HS, I was under the impression that I am not supposed to interfere with my family or friends' tests?"* HS said, *"You have been given permission, by God, to step in and take care of this problem for one of His children. It will be a confirmation of your faith, but it will also be a confirmation of Karen's faith too. The Lord is with you."*

On Wednesday, I had to go to one of the immediate care centers. I was responsible for training one of the nurses on how to use our new software package. I had decided to grab some lunch before I went. I pulled my car into the parking lot of the shopping center just down the road from where I had to go and started to eat my lunch. As always, Anthony stood by my driver's side door, and the other angels completely surrounded my car. There is no greater sense of security than seeing that.

As I ate my lunch, all of a sudden, I heard a voice coming off from a distance. As the voice began to get louder, my chest started to hurt. My angels drew their swords and shields and stood waiting. I looked off to my left and noticed something was walking toward me. It was a demon. He was dressed in full black armor wearing a long black coat. His skin complexion and hair were completely white. His eyes were red like blood. He was very tall and thin. When he was about twenty feet away from me, he stopped and said, *"Ah, the mighty Supplanter! I wanted to pay my respects to. My name is Silas. As you may have already figured out, I am one of the fallen ones that now serve Lucifer. I am in charge of the eastern part of the United States. I thought I would stop by and introduce myself."* As he spoke, I continued to eat my lunch. I didn't even look at him as I could have cared less about what he had to say to me. Silas spoke up and said, *"You know; it is awfully rude of you to ignore me when I am addressing you. You should not be so arrogant, Supplanter. There will be a day when I face you on the battlefield, and you may fall. If I were given the chance, right now, I would teach you some manners myself!"* I stopped eating and said, *"Silas, you already know in your heart that it will be you who will fall on that day. I am not arrogant. I am confident that you and all your little friends will all be destroyed on that appointed day. And, I will take great pleasure in destroying you myself. I have no respect for anyone who feels that they know better than the Lord God! If anyone is arrogant, and oh let me also add ignorant, it would be you, Silas!"* Anthony turned to me and said, *"Jim, stand your ground. The Lord is not provoked."* I acknowledged what Anthony said to me, and stopped myself. Silas spoke up laughing and said, *"Very good, Supplanter. You fight for what you think will really happen. In the meantime, there is nothing that you can do to me. Oh, by the way, there has been a new general appointed to take Andreus' place on the west coast. His name is Andronius. He also would like to extend his respects to you as well. Soon Supplanter, watch yourself, we will meet again!"* I watched as Silas left. I looked at Anthony and said, *"Andronius? Come on give me a break! People are going to think that I made that name up by merging Andreus and his brother's name Antonius together. Andronius!"* Anthony said, *"That is his name."*

My lunchtime was over. It was time for me to go to the immediate care center. I walked in the building and a nurse asked me how my lunch was. I smiled and said, "Good." I then thought to myself, *"Just your regular standard lunch: sandwich, soda, light conversation with a homicidal demon who was threatening my life. Yes, just another boring lunch."* Life is good.

After I had finished training the nurse, I drove back to the office. As I parked my car and started walking into the building, I heard Satan talking in a very quiet, condescending voice. He said, *"Make way for the mighty Supplanter; destroyer of evil, prince of Heaven. No, no, get out of his way, make way, for here comes the chosen one of God."* There he was, fifty feet away from me walking backward, as though he were throwing flowers in front of me as I walked. He was motioning with his arms for everyone to part the way for me to walk through. Anthony spoke up, *"Jim, stand your ground."* I just kept walking towards the building trying to ignore him. Suddenly, off to my right on the top of a small hill, Tiberius with a hundred demons appeared. Anthony repeated himself, *"Stand your ground."*

I kept walking as I listened to Tiberius trying to provoke me; I ignored him too. Satan continued with his ramblings, *"Make way, step aside, and let the mighty Supplanter, God's newest general, pass. Let us all fear him, for he will destroy all of us!"* Then all of a sudden, Satan stopped walking backward and addressed me. He put up his arms and motioned all around himself as he said, *"Mighty Supplanter, do you see all of this around me?"* As I looked around, I noticed very pretty women walking through the parking lot; there were many expensive cars too. He continued, *"I have the power to give you all of this and whatever your heart would desire. All you have to do is switch to my side. Is there anything I can do for the Mighty Supplanter?"*

I paused for a moment and then I said, *"Yes! Can you do me a favor? Will you let Michael bind you now, and cast you into the Lake of Fire? Then I can pass by and watch you suffer for all eternity for everything you have done to all of mankind!"* Satan became outraged and screamed at me, *"You arrogant fool! I will be seeing you soon again, very soon!"*

I continued to walk right past him as two angels grabbed him by both of his arms and held him in place. He was still yelling at me, but I ignored him, and continued to walk into the building. Anthony said, *"Jim, you still need to respect the power he holds. You provoked him. Please control yourself in the future."* I apologized to the Lord for my actions and got back to work. As I sat at my desk, I couldn't believe that he would even try that. Tempt me with worldly things? All I honestly would like to do is leave this planet and just go home.

On Saturday, I meditated. I was trying to ready myself to dispatch the demon at Karen's home. Once I was in the center of my mind Anthony said, *"Follow me!"* Within seconds, I found myself standing in a bedroom I had never seen before. I looked all around. I saw a crib and beds. I looked by the closet door, and there he was; big, brown, hairy, and a very nasty-looking demon. He was surprised. Before he could draw his sword, I lunged at him with my sword and removed his arm. As he turned to pull his sword out with his other arm, I removed his head. I stood there as I watched his body hit the ground. In an instant, he disappeared. I looked into the closet and saw the book that he was connected to; buried all the way in the back. Anthony told me we had to leave. Within a moment, I was back in my own bedroom.

The next day, I asked my sister Ellen if she were going to see Karen. She told me yes, she was planning on seeing her. I decided to share with Ellen what had happened yesterday. Later that evening, Karen, came over. I pulled her aside and asked her if Ellen had talked to her. She told me that Ellen hadn't said anything to her. I sat Karen down and took her through the whole process; when I finished she shook her head. I said, "What's the matter?" She smiled and said, "Well that would explain it. Last night we were so tired that I told my kids they had to sleep in their *own* room. So they did. They had no nightmares. They actually slept through the whole night. Thanks, Jim, for your help." I said, "You're welcome, but the Lord is the one who you should be thanking." The following week, when I saw Karen, she told me they found the really old book that was in the kid's closet. They ended up throwing it out.

A few days later on Wednesday, I had a conversation with HS. He informed me that with the authority given to me, by Christ, I no longer needed to invoke Christ's name to remove Satan or any of his minions. He reminded me that I was the second in command of God's army. He reminded me to be patient, and all would be revealed to me in time.

That evening, in church, I stood up to sing the opening hymn, "A Mighty Fortress is our God." All of a sudden, I started hearing souls screaming. As I turned to look across the aisle, I saw souls running to the back of the church. I then heard a voice that was all too familiar to me.

He was singing the opening hymn with us. It was Satan, himself. He was pretending as if he were holding a hymnbook, looking pious as he sang the words out loud, looking around. Clairvoyantly, I drew my sword and walked over to where he was standing, and pointed my sword at his throat. I said, *"You can leave now!"* Satan said, *"Supplanter; you are being so rude! This is not how you should act when a guest comes into the Lord's house!"* I spoke up and said, *"NOW!"* As I said this to him, I pushed the blade of my sword even closer towards his throat. He began to walk backwards. Satan said with an angry growl, *"Watch yourself, Jim. I have free domain over all of the earth!"* I spoke up and said, *"You can domain all you want outside of the church; leave now!"* I watched as two angels escorted him outside the building. I walked back to my body, and prayed, asking the Lord to surround the church building with angels so that we wouldn't be bothered by him again. Within moments, the building was entirely surrounded by angels in full armor; swords and shields poised ready and waiting.

Then the priest read the Bible text for the service, 2 Thessalonians 3:3 (KJV), "But the Lord is faithful, who shall stablish you, and keep you from evil." I smiled to myself as I sat down waiting to hear the service. How cool is that, people? No one had a clue what had just happened, except the souls from the departed. See, the Lord's word is always so timely.

On Friday, November 16, as I was at work sitting at my desk, I felt that all-too-familiar pain in my chest, telling me that evil was near. I closed my eyes and surveyed my space. Standing just behind me were three demons. They were ready to attack me. Yes, I know how crazy that sounds, but there they were. Without even thinking, I raised my right hand. As I did, a light blue energy shot out of my hand and destroyed all three of them in a second. They were incinerated. I didn't even have to draw my sword. I stopped in awe of myself and then realized that the power had come from the staff I was holding, The Staff of God. I cringed a little, because I had been warned not to use this power as I saw fit. I stood silently, waiting for HS to appear and enlighten me as to how I just abused this power. But nothing happened. So I focused my attention back to my job and continued working. Yes, I have to tell you, I thought that the whole experience was very cool.

The following week, on Wednesday, as I drove home, Gabriel appeared to me and said, *"Supplanter, rejoice in the Lord, for I bring you more news about the task at hand. The Lord God is very proud of you for how you have been handling yourself. He has asked me to tell you more about the Staff of God that you currently hold in your hand. With this power, you will completely destroy all of Satan's forces. I need you to remove the orb from the top of the staff and hold it in your hand."* I did as Gabriel instructed me to. Then he said, *"Now, take this orb and place it in your heart."* I must have had a goofy look on my face, because he stepped closer to me and repeated what he said, but very slowly this time, *"Take the orb and place it in your heart."* I looked at him again very puzzled. He said, *"Reach around your armor, and place the orb over your heart. It will slowly sink into your chest. Take a deep breath as you do this."* So I reached through my armor and placed the orb over my heart. Sure enough, it sunk into my chest. I could feel it entering my heart, so I started to take very deep breaths.

I had never felt this kind of energy before in my life. It was so intense! Within a few moments, all of the hair on my entire body started to stand straight up. Suddenly, the color of my armor changed. It turned into the color of the power I now had inside of me. My entire suit of armor changed to a light blue-silver color. My armor shone brighter than it had ever before. It now looked like snake scales. In the center of my chest was an emblem that has the letters A and O, which stands for alpha and omega and between the two letters is a rising sun. I was now wearing black pants tucked into boots that resembled my armor. My helmet was the same color; it covered almost all of my face. I had a crimson cloak, and my shield is still poised on my back.

Gabriel then said, *"You are now in the final stages of becoming the man the Lord has always known you could be. This is the final suit of armor that you will wear. When your sister Ann had her vision of the final battle, this is the armor she saw you in. Continue to follow the Lord and He will bless you. Now, you have been experimenting with this power. The other day you destroyed three demons. This was a test from God to see how you would react. You did very well, Jim. The power you hold in your hand, no man has ever had before. With one thought Jim, you will now have the ability to direct this energy to destroy whatever comes before you. I will caution you to be extremely careful with this power. You may use this power at times when you feel it is necessary. In all other cases, you are instructed to defend yourself using your sword and shield. Do you understand?"* I said, *"Yes."*

I pulled up in front of my house, and parked my car as Gabriel continued, *"The Lord is aware of how overwhelming this may be to you. He would like me to show you something. Close your eyes, and take a deep breath."* Suddenly, I found myself standing next to Gabriel. We were standing in the center of a realm, on a cliff that overlooked as far as the eye could see. All around us were angels clad in full armor. Gabriel said, *"All of these angels are yours to command. They support you and will follow your orders on that appointed day. You may think that is amazing, but what should be more amazing to you, Jim, is that they support you."* As Gabriel finished talking, he turned and pointed up towards the sky. Just off in the distance I could see someone in the center sitting on a throne. I could not see His face, but I knew in my heart it was God. To His right, Jesus stood, and on God's left side stood the Holy Spirit. Jesus smiled and waved to me. HS nodded His head.

All I could do was to stare in awe at everything I saw. Gabriel continued, *"Jim, Satan will stop at nothing to harm you. You must be on your guard at all times from this day forward. Anthony and the others will watch you very closely. Please do not provoke him anymore; it only outrages him more. The Lord is with you."* I focused my attention back to myself and found myself sitting in my car. I prayed a short prayer thanking the Lord for always being there for me, and for helping me through this process.

On Monday, November 26, I decided to hold my first meditation class for six of my close friends that I worked with. They had been nagging me for over a year to teach them what I knew. So, I relented, and developed a condensed version of what I was taught. I made all of them commit to four classes, lasting two hours each. I would hold the class on Monday evening, after work, for the next four consecutive Mondays.

Everyone did a great job of practicing. It was a lot of fun for me too, as I watched everyone move energy in his or her spaces and move forward in their lives. If this worked out, I was planning on opening it up to the entire hospital. My plan was to hold one class on a Monday night and a separate class on a Saturday morning, for four consecutive weeks. I felt that I could handle twenty people per class. Time would tell.

The next day, I got up and checked my blood sugar. Remember, I was healed from all of my infirmities. So, over the past few weeks, I had not been taking all of my medications. When the reading came up as 165, I got angry. I got dressed and went to work. As I drove to work, I became even angrier. See, I had stopped taking the medication for my circulation problem, so my feet were killing me too. Then I just lost it. I started yelling at the top of my lungs. I was furious! I said, *"Lord! What is going on? Why am I being lied to? Are you just playing a game with me? This sure feels like a game! Oh, let's just see how Jim reacts to this! You know what, Lord, I'm fed up with everything! I gave you my heart and this is how I get treated? What am I suppose to think? I have never asked you for anything! Oh wait. Yes, I did. I asked you if it would be possible for me to live in my own apartment like a big boy! But that's too much to ask! Do you have any idea how demoralizing it is to be forty years old and have to live with my sister? If you are trying to humble me, I don't think I can humble myself any more than that! For the past five years, I have had to live with someone else in their house! And then there's the woman of my dreams. First, I'm told I will meet her next year. No wait now you're going to meet her sometime before March. Oh but wait, there's more. You'll meet her sooner than you think! Oh, but then it turns into you'll meet her within the next two weeks! Boy that worked out just great. What do You want from me? Am I just a big joke to You? I tell people, friends, and families about all the things that have happened to me. What amazes me the most is they all believe me! I personally think that I should be heavily medicated and put into a padded room. That way I can wear a coat that forces me to hug myself. I sure could use the time off from all of this! This has not been easy for me. I tell you what... You can keep the woman of my dreams, and my boys, and just take me, now! How about that? I am sorry that I'm yelling at You, Lord, but I think I have reached my breaking point; yes I have! See, Jim is cracking up!! He can't take much more! I am just a human being! I am not like Your son. I am this close to telling You that I can't do this anymore! It's been five years! You know what would be really sweet, Lord? Now, maybe I'm asking for too much, but if for one day, just one whole day, I would like to be left alone! I don't want to see anything, or hear anything! Can I be a normal human being for only one day? Oh, and Satan, God help you if I see any of your little jerkweeds running around! I swear to you if God would let me, I would come and hunt you down myself and inflict on you the pain you've been inflicting on all of mankind! How dare you defy God! Who the hell do you think you are, you big prick! Why are you angry, Satan? Is it because God has set the playing field even for the first time in history? Are you mad because, for the first time, a human being can strike back at you and hurt you and your merry group of little bastards? You had better warn your little minions that they should steer clear of Jim because he's not happy right now, and his ability to control himself is nil!*

When I finally finished ranting and raving, Marty appeared in front of me. Before he could say a word I said, *"I don't want to hear a word out of you!"* Marty said, *"Okay, I'll talk to you tomorrow."* Yep, I was ticked off with a capital "T"! I parked my car and started to walk into the building. Who should show up outside my door but Tiberius! Before he could even say a word, I drew my sword and yelled, *"I will kill you where you are standing!"* And then poof, he was gone. I guess he could tell I wasn't in a good mood! You think?

I was angry all day. In the morning, I had to talk to Torry about a work problem. I walked into her office and tried my best to pretend that I was OK. She looked up at me and said, "What's the matter with you? I have never seen you like this. Are you okay?" I told her I was fine. She said,

"Jim, I've known you a long time. What's going on?" I told her a little about what I had said in the car. She insisted that we go for coffee after work. I kept telling her I was fine, but she wouldn't let up, so I said, "Fine, let's have coffee."

I stopped off to use the bathroom before I went back to my desk. We had those paper towel dispensers with the electric eye, the ones that you wave your hand in front of and it spits out a piece of paper towel. As I stood there, the paper towel dispenser went off all by itself. I looked over at it, and there was some little dweeb spirit laughing at me. Without even thinking, I drew my sword, and as I watched his head hit the ground I said, *"I warned all of you. Whose next?"*

I managed to make it through the rest of the day without killing any of my coworkers. They could all tell I wasn't happy. You see, folks, I'm always an upbeat kind of guy. When I'm down, everyone around me is down. I have never been able to figure that out.

I met Torry at the coffee shop across the street from the hospital, and we talked. Torry said, "You're kind of making me a little nervous. I have never seen you this angry before." I said, "I just don't get it, Torry. I have always gone with the flow. But this time, nothing I've been told is happening, and I'm ticked! I don't know what He wants from me. I feel like all of this is just a game. All I know, is I feel in my heart that I am letting Him down, big time. I know I hurt Him this morning, and I have disappointed Him, but I just can't shake this feeling. Usually, I'm mad for an hour, if that. Then I bounce back, and I'm fine. This time, I'm still just as mad as I was this morning, and I don't know what to do. I even told Him how everyone believes me when I tell them what I've seen. All of you should think that I am completely nuts! Oh and today, even while I was in this mood, I talked with someone who was down. You know what I did, I told her that the Lord loves her and that it would all work out. Even when I'm ticked off, I still talk about Him in a good way. I know I still love Him."

Torry just sat there and let me vent. I continued, "I feel as if I'm losing my mind sometimes. How can all of this be real? Maybe I'm just making this all up because I want to make a name for myself? I feel so lost Torry. I don't know what to do anymore. All I know is I hate being like this. This is not who I am, but I don't want to stop being mad. I have never been this angry!" Torry said, "Can I ask you one question? Did you give up your free will again?" I sat for a minute and thought. I then said, *"Oh my gosh, I completely forgot. Yes, I did on Sunday after Holy Communion. I prayed and told the Lord I was giving Him my free will again. Only this time* when I prayed I cringed inside because I didn't want to be put through anything again."* I broke down a little, and started to cry. Yes, folks, it's always fun to cry in a public place in front of perfect strangers. I managed to contain myself, and pull myself together.

Torry said, *"Jim, I think the Lord understands why you feel this way. I don't believe He would think for a minute that you meant to hurt Him in any way, or even that you let Him down. C'mon Jim, you have the strongest faith I know. You even said you're only human. I think He's testing you, and you will be fine in the end. I know for a fact that you are not lying to me. I'll be honest, when you told me all of this at the beginning; I thought you were crazy. I have watched you continually change into the person you are right now. And so many times, you have helped me to understand my own faith. You couldn't make this stuff up, even if you tried. I will pray that God gives you the strength to handle this. I know you can still do this."*

As I drove home, I broke down a little, and asked the Lord to forgive me for the way I had been acting. I pleaded with Him to help me understand why I was still ill, and why I felt I should still be taking my medicines. I asked Him to open my understanding for all of this, and I finished by telling Him whatever He wanted to do with me was fine. As I finished my prayer HS showed up and said, *"Jim, your body is having a hard time believing that it is not sick. For over ten years, you have had these illnesses. Your body needs time to acclimate to this process. Be patient. Talk to your body, and help him understand. If you don't truly believe in your heart that Jesus healed you, then how can your body believe?"* I said, *"HS, I know in my heart that all of this is true. Look into my heart and you will see, I believe. I will talk to my body and tell him. Thank you."*

Okay, now. Usually after I pour my heart out to the Lord, and I have a conversation with HS I feel better, but not this time. I was still very angry, and that really concerned me. I had never felt that angry for so long.

As I drove into work the next morning, I continued to plead with God for help. I was still very angry. I don't know why folks, I just was. That scared me a little because it wasn't just anger; it was rage. I managed to get through the day. I spoke with Giselle about this too. All she could tell me was that she was praying for me.

Marty showed up at the end of my work day, and said, *"Jim, Amanda and I can give you a healing as you drive home. I know you are tired, so we felt this would be a good time to do this."* I agreed. As I drove home, I took a few deep breaths. I could feel Marty and Amanda running energy through me.

At one point, the thought crossed my mind not to go to church that evening. Marty stopped what he was doing and pointed his finger at me and said, *"Oh yes you are. You're going to church tonight, but you don't have to sing in the choir. You are going to service."* I said, *"Okay, mother!"* He smiled and went back to my healing. When they both got to my heart chakra, I braced myself. Usually there is a lot of energy there that I needed to get rid of. Nothing happened; nothing! I thought that was really odd. They continued working. As they got to my sixth chakra, my third eye, the center of my mind, I concentrated. I saw myself sitting in the middle of my Alpine ski lodge with the two of them walking around me giving me my healing. Suddenly, I heard a voice that said, *"Jim, you have greatly disappointed me. How dare you dictate to me when and how I should dispense my grace! Stand up, for it is the Lord God that speaks to you!"*

As I stood up in the center of my mind, I thought to myself, *"Stand up? I don't stand up when I'm in the presence of the Lord, I kneel."* Something didn't feel right. The voice kind of sounded like God's but the tone was all wrong. I stood up and bowed my head. He continued speaking. *"Time and again I have told you to be patient, but you will not listen. My patience with you is becoming strained! It is not your decision whom I will be gracious to!"* As I stood and listened I felt a slight pain in my heart. It wasn't as intense as it had been when I knew evil was near. He continued, *"You continually disappoint me, Jim."*

I looked up, and just almost outside of my sight I could see a figure of a man standing there. I became enraged. In an instant, I had my hands around his throat. It was Satan! I picked him up and slammed him to the ground. He fought trying to break free of me, but he couldn't. The look on his face was of sheer terror and surprise. I tightened my grip around his throat and began to squeeze. I leaned in toward him and whispered very quietly into his ear, *"Do you feel the power of God?"* He fought even harder trying to get me off of himself, but I possessed the strength of twenty angels. For the first time in my life, I knew that to be true. I grabbed his throat even harder and pulled his face toward mine. I stared right into his black eyes and whispered once again, very quietly, *"Do you feel His wrath?"* With my left hand still clenched around his throat, I grabbed his thigh with my right hand and picked him up off of the ground. With one motion, I threw him out of my space. He stood up completely shocked and then disappeared.

I walked back to the chair in the center of my mind and sat down.

Marty and Amanda walked back toward me. As they did, Marty said, *"Well, that was different. You passed the test."* I said, *"I passed the test, what test?"* Marty said, *"You controlled yourself."* I said, *"I controlled myself? I had my hands around Satan's throat choking the crap out of him. You call that controlled?"* Marty said, *"Yes. You didn't kill him, and you could have! Well done Jim."* I said, *"I really don't understand all of this. I am tired of being played with by him. He had better stay away from me."* Marty said, *"Up until now, he didn't really believe that you were The One. He didn't believe that you had it in you physically to stand up to him and challenge him. I'm pretty sure you changed his mind and removed any doubt that he may have had about you being Supplanter."* I said, *"This is all so psychotic, Marty."*

Marty said, *"It was a test, and you passed it. Now Satan knows that he should fear you. We will finish your healing now, and you need to go to church tonight."*

I went to church that night. I had arrived ten minutes before the service started. I sat in the back. My two girls sat with me. They didn't say one word. They both hugged and kissed me. Then they sat on either side of me; each was holding one of my hands. I was still very angry. The service was about how God is always there for us through all of the tough times we may find ourselves in. We are never alone. I sat there listening. Yes, I had a bad attitude. I kept saying, really Lord, because I sure could use some help right now. No, no, really; right now would be an excellent time to offer me some help.

I'm sorry folks, but I am human. It's not every day I wrestle with Satan. I'll be honest with you. It did feel pretty awesome pinning him to the ground, and seeing the fear he had in his eyes. I think he realized for the first time in his existence that we as lowly human beings are not going to take his crap anymore. And the only reason I was able to subdue him was because the Lord God gave me these gifts and the strength to show him that his days are now numbered. I have never been afraid of Satan. I have never paid him any attention. I decided from that day forward that I would refer to him as "the little one." Why, because he's so insignificant to me. I'm pretty sure he's going to be ticked off at me, but I don't care. Yeah, I know I'm not supposed to provoke him.

After the service, my sister Ann, who was sitting behind me, looked at me and said, "Jim what is the matter with you? I can feel how angry you are." I quietly explained to her and my brother-in-law what had happened over the past few days, and the whole wrestling with Satan thing. When my friend the evangelist walked up to say hi, he could tell I wasn't doing well. I tried to fake that I was okay, so I shook his hand and just walked away so I could go home.

My sister Ann called me in my car. She felt bad that we couldn't finish our conversation. I told her I was fine, but she didn't believe me. I told her how angry I was, and that I felt I had let the Lord down. She tried to comfort me by saying, "Jim, I don't get the impression that He is mad or disappointed with you. I feel you are exactly where He wants you to be. He has put you through things, and as you pass these tests you grow more and more into the person He needs you to be. You are like fine gold that is being tried in the fire. He knows what you can handle and has given you the strength to endure. You have an amazing faith. You trust Him on everything that is spiritual. You can easily believe everything you are told by angels. You have never doubted what you have seen. You have destroyed spirits, demons, and even Andreus with your sword. You know in your heart that you are clad in full armor, and you have a shield. You can tell in a moment who is speaking to you. You know if they are friend or foe. You know all of this to be true." As Ann spoke, I began to cry. She continued, "What you have a hard time believing in, is all of the material things. Like the woman of your dreams, getting an apartment, living on your own, and having the ability to support yourself. I feel in my heart that the Lord would like you to trust Him with everything, spiritual and natural, Jim. Once you do, I know things will start moving forward for you. He is waiting for you just to trust Him on everything."

I said, "But I am so angry! I am never like this." Ann said, "Are you sure that there isn't anything in your space?" I said, "I have looked all around, and I don't see anything. My chest has been killing me for days. I assumed it was because Satan was so close."

Ann said, "I have a very uneasy feeling in my chest too. Are you sure?" As Ann was talking, clairvoyantly I decided to check immediately behind myself by turning around as fast as I could. As I did, I saw a huge black demon standing right behind me. As I drew my sword, I cut him across his chest. When he reached for his sword, I hacked into his shoulder and removed his arm. I swung around and cut off his right leg just below the knee. As he began to fall, I spun back around and removed his head. Suddenly, my chest stopped hurting. The next thing I heard was Ann saying, "What just happened? My chest stopped hurting." I said, *"I just killed a huge nasty demon that was in my space. He was mirroring me. Every time I would turn and look around he stayed directly behind me, so I couldn't see him. I spun around so fast he didn't have time to react. He's dead."*

Suddenly HS appeared and said, *"Jim, when you gave the Lord your free will, He allowed this demon into your space to test you. He loves you very much and has already forgiven you for everything you said to Him. Be patient Jim. All shall be revealed to you in time. If the Lord has already forgiven you, then maybe you should forgive yourself."* I said, "It's not that easy, HS." He said, *"Yes, it is. Just let go, and forgive yourself."* And then he disappeared.

I finished talking to Ann. Wow, did I feel a lot better now. As I went to bed, I prayed and apologized to God and thanked Him for His forgiveness. I told Him I didn't deserve it. I told Him I still loved Him very much, and from this day forward, I would stop worrying about all of the physical stuff. I told Him I trust Him now, completely with everything, spiritual and natural.

It was now Wednesday, December 5, and as I sat at my desk working, my heart began to burn and ache. Not that, *oh, I shouldn't have eaten that bean burrito with onions for breakfast this morning*, kind of ache, but that all-too-familiar pain that evil was near. I closed my eyes and went into the center of my mind. As I surveyed all around me, I realized that I was completely surrounded by demons. Yes, I know how truly crazy that sounds. I yelled to Anthony and the others to help me. With swords and shields ready, they attacked us. All around me I could hear swords clanging. The moment I killed one of them, another one would step up and fight me. Back and forth, round and round we went. The whole time this was happening, I was still cutting purchase orders and answering emails. I told you I could multitask.

They just wouldn't stop coming! There seemed to be no end to it. I called in reinforcements. Ten more angels showed up, and we continued to fight them off. At one point, I had to go to the lab to talk to someone. The fighting continued. As we walked through the hall, I yelled at Anthony, *"Are you going to help me or not?"* He said, *"We are doing our best, Jim."* I grabbed him by his breastplate, and pulled him toward me and yelled, *"Your best isn't working!"* Then I shoved him away from me, and kept walking. I spoke to the person I needed to see.

You would have never known I was hacking off limbs and heads of demons just by looking at me. It really is a good thing that I don't do drugs. What do you think? Hmm!

I walked back to my desk and sat down. I was mentally exhausted. For almost two hours, this was going on. As quickly as it started, they stopped and ran away; beats me. All I know is I was thankful it was finally over. I finished my day at work. Clairvoyantly, every few minutes, I would glance around, to see if anything was coming, but it was quiet now.

I was on my way home that evening when I pulled up to a traffic light. I waited my turn to go through the intersection when suddenly my heart began to burn and ache, again. Clairvoyantly, I looked around and once again I was completely surrounded. I said to Anthony, *"Hey, I'm trying to drive here."* He said, *"You can do both."* And off we all went again; sword hitting sword, shields being shattered by our swords, limbs and heads flying everywhere. I felt as though we were going to become overpowered very soon. Suddenly, I remembered that I had the Power of God within me. I fought them off with my sword in my right hand, and then I held out my left hand. A light blue energy shot out from my fingers, and consumed everything that was in my path. I tossed my sword into my left hand and then held up my right hand and watched as this light blue energy completely destroyed all the demons that were in my way. They all started to scatter. I decided to chase after them, throwing balls of energy. As soon as they were hit with one of these balls, they would explode and disappear. Within a few minutes, the five of us stood there all by ourselves.

I was almost home by the time we were all alone. Suddenly, I heard someone clapping. He was clapping very slowly, as if in a highly condescending way. He started to speak, saying, *"Well done Supplanter. Well done!"* Without even thinking, I reached behind myself and grabbed him by the throat and pulled him right in front of me. It was Satan. Once again, I slammed him into the ground and held him there. He couldn't move. I pulled out my dagger and pointing it at his face, I said, *"You piece of crap! Can't you be a man and face me or do you always have to be a spineless weasel that sneaks up from behind? I am going to give you one last warning. I swear to God if I see you again, I will start cutting small pieces off of you."* Satan looked up at me and said, *"You don't have the nerve!"* I took my dagger and started to cut him across his right cheek and then said, *"Apparently, I do!"* Then I tossed him out of my space. He ran off.

Later that evening, HS appeared in my bedroom and said, *"There are a few things you need to understand, Jim. The Lord will always test you. He was testing you today. You would have never thought that you could defend yourself as well as you did today, but you did. Anthony was ordered to stand down and let you handle it this morning."* I motioned to Anthony to step towards me and then I said, *"I feel horrible that I grabbed you this morning and shoved you; please forgive me."* Anthony said, *"You are my General, Jim. I serve Him first and then you. There is nothing to forgive."* HS continued, *"You did very well today; you used the Power of God and defeated them. This is just a prelude as to what will take place on that appointed day. Satan will not let up, Jim. Be on your guard and watch yourself. The Lord is with you!"*

The next day, as I was walking into work, Satan showed up on the sidewalk near the entrance I use. Suddenly Michael showed up between both of us. I said nothing and just kept walking into the building. As I walked down the stairs to my office, I heard Michael say to Satan, *"It would be wise of you to leave, now. Jim has been given the authority to inflict pain on you."* I stopped walking, and as I opened the door to my office I stood there for a moment and said to myself, *"Sweet!"* In a moment Satan disappeared.

A few days later, on December 15, I went to a movie with Peter and his friend AJ. Just as the movie previews were starting, Satan appeared in the main aisle in front of me. I could see the scar I gave him on his cheek. He drew his sword. Then Tiberius, Silas, and Andronius appeared on each side of Satan. All of them had their swords drawn. Clairvoyantly, I stood up and said, *"Not today."* Then I sat back down and ignored all of them. I heard Anthony say, *"Well done, Supplanter, the Lord God is not provoked."* I have no idea when they all left. All I know is I looked up halfway through the movie and they were already gone.

Folks, there is one thing that I know in my heart to be a fact. On that appointed day when the line is drawn on the battlefield, and Satan's forces will be on one side and God's armies on the other, once the order is given for us to attack, it will truly be a WON BATTLE.

GOD BLESS ALL OF YOU!!!!

To be continued...

www.ingramcontent.com/pod-product-compliance
Lightning Source LLC
Chambersburg PA
CBHW071901290426
44110CB00013B/1228